Before Zion

An Account
of the
7th Handcart Company

Before Zion

An Account
of the
7th Handcart Company

by

Allen C. Christensen

COUNCIL PRESS

Springville, Utah

ISBN: 1-55517-749-2
e. 2

Published by Council Press
an imprint of Cedar Fort Inc.
www.cedarfort.com

Distributed by:

Cover design by Nicole Shaffer
Cover design © 2004 by Lyle Mortimer

Printed in the United States of America
10 9 8 7 6 5 4 3 2 1

Printed on acid-free paper

To Niels Christensen and the pioneers
of the 7th Mormon Handcart Company.

Handcart Pioneers

A bugle sounds as the morning dawns
'Tis a call to duty each must meet
Another night with earth for a bed
to face a day with so little to eat.

For one tiny girl the journey is o'er
With sobbing hearts, their tears brushed away
only freshly dug prairie to mark the place
Fatigue and hunger have shortened her stay.

In streams, cholera and quicksand lurk
The trail's also dogged by dust and by heat
Yet while they are beyond the scoffer's smirk
There's precious little but flour to eat.

Their shoes are gone and clothes are worn
Along with the dust and sweat and grime
The sun's blazing hot this summer morn
Perhaps some wild fruit they'll be blessed to find.

Along the Platte road they push and pull
sand and thirst their will doth not break
From the lead cart flies the banner of faith
'Tis their trek of love for the Gospel's sake.

    Allen C. Christensen

ACKNOWLEDGMENTS

No one ever produces a historical work alone. Many people have helped make this book, including those pioneers now long since gone who wrote or passed on through others the story of their challenging pioneering experience. Without such first-hand accounts, there would be much conjecture and little intimate detail. I am grateful also to many long-time fellow students of the Mormon migration. One such individual is Dr. Don H. Smith, a Pullman, Washington orthodontist, who for over 30 years has made an intense study of the handcart migration. Another is Jackson K. Sauvarin of Auckland, New Zealand, who taught me much about the history of sailing ships. The Mormon Immigration Index of The Church of Jesus Christ of Latter-day Saints, edited and compiled by Fred Woods, provided much information that was essential in the writing of this history.

Many individuals, including Cecil Ray Hansen, J. Dewey Nelson, Dale Zabriskie, Robert H. Garff, Gertrude Ryberg Garff, Eileen C. Cooke, Ruth M. Mickelson, Russell M. Nelson, Jimmie B. Parker, Val J. Anderson, John W. Welch, Marlene M. Burton, Charles Castleberry, and Karl Snow have graciously shared the intimate histories of their families. Count Ulrik Ahlefeldt-Laurvig of Denmark and the Royal Danish Consulate General of Los Angeles have answered many questions about the history of that nation. Bryan Skelton and Nicholas J. Evan have been sources of information on conditions in Great Britain during the 1850s. Peter Svanevik provided information on Norway. Phil D. Jensen and Gertrude Ryberg Garff shared much eye-witness information concerning the LDS Mission in Denmark prior to the outbreak of World War II. The staff of the

LDS Historical Department, Salt Lake City, Utah has been especially considerate of my many requests. Also helpful have been the archivists of the Community of Christ in Independence, Missouri. A special thanks is due to Jeremy Munns who prepared a number of the illustrations. Katherine B. Seibert, Susan Easton Black, Ronald T. Halverson, Quentin L. Cook, C. Max Caldwell, and Gale E. Norton have painstakingly read the manuscript at various stages of completion and have offered many helpful suggestions. I am grateful to Kathleen, my devoted spouse, who has painstakingly supported this effort. To all of you and any others whom I may have inadvertently overlooked, I can only say an inadequate thank you. Without you this book would not have been possible.

I am grateful to the Springville Museum of Art and The Church of Jesus Christ of Latter-day Saints for permitting the reproduction of paintings which are a part of their extensive art collections.

In the final analysis, I bear the sole responsibility for the interpretation of events as I have faithfully attempted to accurately piece together the history of this relatively unknown company of courageous Scandinavian pioneers. They were a part of the most daring experiment in America's westward migration.

Allen C. Christensen

CONTENTS

PART I

SCANDINAVIAN BEGINNINGS

<u>Chapter 1</u>

INTRODUCTION

This is an account of the 7th Handcart Company, the 1857 experience of recent Scandinavian converts to The Church of Jesus Christ of Latter-day Saints. It is a remarkable story, albeit not so well known as the accounts of the Willie and Martin companies. Part of that lies in the fact that there is a paucity of written documentation on their journey, at least documentation readily available in the public domain. Where accounts of their conversion, ocean passage, and handcart journey were written in detail, it initially was done, in all likelihood, in a Scandinavian language. Neither was there the dramatic rescue in present-day Wyoming. Yet their journey was unique in many ways, including the fact that for a time their trek paralleled and was in sight of elements of the western march of the army of Colonel Albert Sidney Johnston. They were the last handcart company to depart from Clear Creek, Iowa. The 8th, 9th, and 10th companies all began the handcart trek west from Florence, Nebraska. The 7th Company made the journey from Clear Creek, Iowa, to Salt Lake City in 93 days—the fastest trail time for any of the Iowa City handcart departures.

It is noteworthy that the 7th Company made the trans-Atlantic and plains crossing without financial assistance from the Perpetual Emigration Fund. Remarkably, the effort to take the west-bound *Westmoreland's* 544-passenger complement to America was made possible by a number of Scandinavian saints who chose to forego the opportunity to go west by ox-drawn wagons and instead elected to pull handcarts to Zion. The money in excess of that required to go west by oxen and wagons was consecrated to a general fund. Their faith and charity enabled others to go to Zion who otherwise would have had to remain in Europe.

Among those who came were a significant number who had served devotedly as missionaries and as presidents of conferences. Though young in the gospel, this pioneer company was not without significant church leadership experience. They had left their farms and shops to follow Jesus—to preach His gospel in Denmark, Norway, and Sweden. They had been beaten, jailed, and placed on diets of bread and water. They had been the target of the mob's fury. They, like Peter and John, were grateful they had been counted worthy to suffer persecution for Jesus' name. And unlike the rich young man who declined the Savior's invitation to sell all that he had, give it to the poor, and follow Him, these Scandinavian saints placed all on the altar of sacrifice in their quest for Zion. They had been through much, but the trek to Zion would stretch this group of farmers and artisans even further.

Among the challenges they faced were the matters of language and culture. The 3rd Handcart Company had come from Wales, and probably spoke Welsh as their first language. However, as Wales was a part of the United Kingdom, one might guess that a number of the Welsh saints were bilingual.[1] In contrast, the 7th Company was apparently the first handcart company composed predominantly of people whose only language was from continental Europe. Scandinavians had come in smaller numbers in earlier wagon companies; there were some 90 Scandinavians who were members of the Willie or 4th Handcart Company. What unique first-time challenges would have been faced in a company which essentially spoke only one of three Scandinavian languages?

There was also a serious dietary challenge. After late July the 7th Company subsisted largely on flour products which occasionally were enhanced with wild fruit. Why did they have such a limited diet when there were vast herds of buffalo on the plains that year? According to one account, the company sidetracked to avoid the great herds of buffalo, and a number of surviving records indicate there were no skilled hunters in the company. Was it a lack of planning? Was it an indication that hunting in Europe had become an activity largely limited to the aristocracy and landed gentry? Hunting skills seemed to have come almost naturally for Americans who descended from colonial stock. The musket, the rifle, the axe, the plow–these were principal among tools used to roll the American frontier westward. In contrast, by the mid-1850s Europeans were more occupationally specialized than were their American counterparts. Industrialization was more advanced in England than it was in either America or Scandinavia. Yet, regardless of their prior vocation, all who went west during this decade did so as first-time pioneers. The journey to Zion was a long, rugged road, a route not taken by the fainthearted. However, the overwhelming majority of these Scandinavian Saints went happily at the daunting task for they were trying to become like Jesus.

The Scandinavians were better fitted for an agrarian lifestyle than were their British counterparts. Between 1850 and 1857, some 55 percent of those from Scandinavia were farmers and their families. Included in this mix was the occasional shepherd, gardener, or other agricultural professional. Other common vocations included blacksmith, cabinet maker, carpenter, cooper, chimney sweep, fisherman, government clerk, joiner, laborer, logger or lumberman, merchant, miller, policeman, servant, ship's captain, sailor, stonemason, tailor, teacher, wagon maker, weaver, and wheelwright.[2] The gospel net gathered people from every vocation, increasing the leadership challenge to turn European emigrants into pioneering farmers and ranchers. That was a very big challenge, for raw ground had to be broken from shrub-covered land; irrigation canals and ditches had to be dug; and cattle, sheep, and horses had to be imported into the Great Basin.[3] However, within this wave of European emigrants were craftsmen with unique skills who would help construct temples and other edifices.

Arriving in the Territory of Utah, many new arrivals settled in Cache, Box Elder, Weber, Davis, Salt Lake, Utah, and Sanpete counties.[4] Sanpete County became the Utah home of a number of the members of the 7th Company.

Over the next two or three decades missionary success in Scandinavia was substantial. It resulted in large numbers of converts immigrating to Utah. It is a Sanpete County tradition that Norway provided a number of skilled craftsmen for the Manti Temple. Those craftsmen took the plans of a ship and built it upside-down for the temple's roof. Fascinatingly, the practice of using an upside-down ship construction for the roof is used in Norway today. The spectacular ice skating arena constructed at Haman for the 1994 Lillehamar Norway Winter Olympics was built like an upside-down Viking ship.[5] Some of the Manti Temple craftsmen are known to have come west with the 7th Company. For example, C. C. A. Christensen, a Dane and a company sub-captain, did interior landscape painting in the Manti Temple.[6]

Both the *Westmoreland's* passenger manifest and the 7th Handcart Company's roster are incomplete. The Journal History of the Church states that "most of the emigrants crossed the plains immediately afterward, in either Captain Matthias Cowley's wagon train or in Christian Christiansen's handcart company."[7] *The Pioneer Sesquicentennial Almanac* reported there was no roster for the Cowley company.[8] There were a few who remained in the Midwest until they had acquired the means or the health to go. Who were they? When and with whom did they go west? Intriguing questions, which probably can be answered completely only from the collective memories of their descendants. From the *Westmoreland's* passenger manifest, one can find names similar to names given for the 8th, 9th, and 10th companies, but there are no exact matches on the existing rosters. Are those indications of spelling difficulties that are magnified when coupled with a patronymic naming system?

When Scandinavia used the patronymic system, the surname changed with each succeeding generation. For example, Anders Jensen's son, Poul, was named Poul Andersen. Poul Andersen's daughter, Ellen, was named Ellen Poulsdatter (or Poulsen). It was a shorthand form of "Poul, son of Anders" which would have been akin to the Hebrew expression "ben," or the Arabic "bin or ibn," as in Poul ben Anders or Poul ibn Anders. Ellen first married Peder Christensen. Their sons were surnamed Pedersen. Patronymic naming was law. However, on the Danish isle of Bornholm there was resistance to that system. The Kofod or Koefoed or Kofoed family managed to keep that surname alive by inserting the patronymic name just before Kofod, even though such an approach was banned by law in 1828. Apparently the girls were less frequently christened using the patronymic system.

Given the reality of name similarity, the identification of individuals represents an intriguing challenge. For example, one Manti Temple craftsman, Andreas "Steamboat" Olsen, had been a Norwegian sailor before coming to the United States. As an apprentice, he had learned the sailmaker's trade. He became a master carpenter. He would invite those who climbed the temple's fabled spiral stairways to run their hands along the railing to see if they could feel the joints in the wood.[9] This is probably Andreas C. Olsen, born in 1822, who came to Utah in 1873. From Copenhagen he had gone to Hull, England aboard either the steamer *Pacific* or *Milo*. He was part of a large company of Latter-day Saints who took the steamer, *Wisconsin*, from Liverpool to New York.

If the foregoing conjecture is correct, then one might have heard the earlier arrivals teasing their fellow Scandinavian: "We're not sure you count as a pioneer, Andreas. You came by steamship and steam engine train. You had it soft. The real pioneers came by sailing ship and walked. We'd better call you 'Steamboat.'" There were other Olsens with the same or similar first name. A 4-year-old Anders Olsen sailed on the *Westmoreland*. An Andreas Olsen born in 1852 came on board the *William Tapscott* in 1860. These Olsens don't seem to fit the description of having learned the sail-making trade.

Part of my motivation for writing this account is deeply personal. As a young man growing up in a home where there was an abundance of love and hard work, but a shortage of money, I foolishly thought the only pioneers were those who had come by ox-team and wagon, of which there were many in my direct ancestral family. Furthermore, the 1947 U.S. commemorative postage stamp of the Utah Pioneer Centennial featured an ox-drawn covered wagon. As a child, I understood something of the faith and courage required to be a pioneer. However, in my youthful insensitivity, I seriously undervalued the greater faith required to undertake the arduous, perhaps herculean, task of pulling a handcart 1,300 miles to Zion. As I've grown older, I've come to recognize that handcart pioneers were heroes of remarkable proportion.

Much of late has been written of the Willie and Martin companies. My 2nd great-grandparents, John and Jane Allgood Bailey; their four sons; Langley Allgood Bailey, my great-grandfather; and his three younger brothers, John, Thomas, and David, were all a part of the Martin Company. I have made a contribution to the record of the Martin Handcart Company through an editorial transcription of the Journal of Langley Allgood Bailey. To his record, which is part journal and part reminiscence, I added considerable commentary. In the course of writing this history of the 7th Company, I learned that my great-grandfather, William Wilford Allen, who in 1855 had initially been called as a missionary to Texas, drove one of the four wagons which accompanied the Willie Company to Fort Laramie, and then went on with the Martin Company from Devil's Gate.[10] William Allen was one of seven Latter-day Saint missionaries in St. Louis, Missouri, in November 1855 assigned by John Taylor to design a handcart and determine the supplies which would be needed to make the plains crossing. One hundred carts of their design, with some modification, were fabricated by a St. Louis wagon maker. Built with iron axles and covered with canvas tops, they were used to carry the children and held up well.[11] Some of these may have been pulled back to Florence, Nebraska in 1857 by missionaries headed east to their assigned fields of labor.

From St. Louis W. W. Allen went south to Texas. He apparently assisted a Texas company of Latter-day Saints under the leadership of Jacob Croft to emigrate to Utah and additionally helped drive a herd of cattle from Kansas City to Florence.

These cattle were to supply the immigration. He returned to Florence in time to go west with the Willie Company. William's wife's widowed half-sister, Mary Ann Fenn Bird, and her sons were a part of the Willie Company, which company had among their ranks saints from Herefordshire who would have been known to him.

In an extensive Christensen family history, I wrote something of the 1857 handcart experience of my 2nd great-grandmother, Ellen Christensen, her second husband, Hans Christensen, and her sons, Paul (Poul) and Niels (Pedersen) Christensen. Niels is my great-grandfather. When the boys were very young, their father, Peder Christensen, died of injuries suffered when he was kicked in the groin by a cow. To preserve an ancestral stewardship conferred by the Danish crown for gallantry in military service upon her grandfather, Anders Jensen, it was necessary that Ellen be married. She married Hans three-and-a-half months later. Shortly thereafter, Hans was taken into the Danish Army. He fought in the bitter 1848-50 war with Germany when Denmark failed in its attempt to annex Schleswig-Holstein. Schleswig and Holstein had been the personal fiefs of the House of Oldenburg, a long line of Danish kings.

Parenthetically, early remarriage among the Danes was a cultural pattern, a practice seemingly born of economic necessity. A farmer or a cottager (a small holder) who leased land could keep it until his death. Then his widow had to find a younger man to marry her and assume the obligations of the lease, or she would lose it. Ellen's remarriage to Hans fits this pattern, for Hans was nine years her junior. A husband who lost his wife usually married shortly thereafter for he needed someone to care for his children and assume the duties of the wife which included milking the cows and churning the butter, shearing the sheep, cleaning and spinning the wool into yarn, weaving and knitting the yarn into clothing. The preparation of linen from flax, grown in Denmark, was hard, tedious work. The process was more difficult and took longer than the making of woolen goods. The wife also helped to slaughter the meat animals and then prepare and smoke sausages. Some meat was dried while some was salted in large barrels as a means of preservation. The optimal time to buy herring for drying and salting was during the harvest season, a period of peak workload for the Danish farm family. These burdens were in addition to those of cooking and serving the meals, cleaning the home, and caring for the children. The men worked hard as well—there were few machines to ease the drudgery of farm work.

While acknowledging at the outset my deep admiration for my Scandinavian ancestors who were a part of this company, this account is intended to encompass the overall experience of the 7th, or Christian Christiansen Handcart Company, and to address that experience within the sweeping panorama of Mormon immigration history as measured against the backdrop of European history and American political conditions of the 1850s. There are abbreviated reports of the 7th Handcart Company's journey in various family histories and in Hafen and Hafen's *Handcarts to Zion*. However, there does not seem to be a comprehensive account for the 7th Company which captures their conversion, sea voyage, and land trek in the larger historical setting. Nor have the participants been individually identified. Insofar as possible, I intend to address these issues and the drama of the trail within the context of their times. Where records and reports have been found in descendant family archives, and where such records and reports are collaborated by others or by generally accepted documentation, these family records have been written as fact. Where suppositions or conjectures have been made, they are identified as such.

The members of the 7th Company were common folk, who, by virtue of the process through which they passed, became remarkable people who accomplished extraordinary things. This is their story.

NOTES

1. Nicholas J. Evans, 258 Kingston Road, Willerby, Hull, England HU10 6ND, United Kingdom. Personal Communication, 23 December 2000. Evans states, "The educated Welsh would have been bilingual." Since The Book of Mormon has been the instrument of conversion historically, one could assume a reasonably high rate of English literacy among the Welsh converts. According to the *Deseret News 1997-98 Church Almanac,* pp. 401-2, the first Welsh language materials were printed in 1844 and the work progressed more rapidly afterwards.

    The first known missionary in Wales was Henry Royle. His great-grandson, Dr. Homer F. Royle, has served as a bishop and stake president in American Fork, Utah, and as president of the Spanish-American Mission. (Homer F. Royle was the author's family dentist for many years. Ed.) One of Henry Royle's converts was Arthur Smith, the 2nd great-grandfather of Merrill J. Bateman of the Seventy who served from 1 January 1996 to 1 May 2003, as the 11th president of Brigham Young University. Henry Royle married Ann Capstick in Nauvoo. The ceremony was performed by Brigham Young. Henry Royle settled in Lehi, Utah in 1850 and died two years later (Homer F. Royle, Personal Communication, 23 December 2000).

2. William Mulder, *Homeward to Zion: The Mormon Migration from Scandinavia,* University of Minnesota Press, Minneapolis & London. Published in cooperation with Brigham Young University Press, 2000, pp. 110, 113.

3. Evans, Personal Communication. p. 3 of 3. Evans concurs that the conversion of European emigrant to frontier farmer was difficult. Evans offers it as an explanation as to why more people from Wales often emigrated to Australia since sheep ranching was common to both countries; that Norwegians emigrants often moved to forested areas since they had worked in the logging industry in Norway. Evans also states that by the mid-nineteenth century irrigation systems on the scale required in the United States were something new to Europeans. However, at this point they were quite experienced in digging canals, reclaiming land from rivers, and enclosing fields and lands.

    Edward Norris Wentworth (*America's Sheep Trails,* The Iowa State College Press, 1948, Ames, Iowa, p. 230.) tells of two Welsh brothers, Samuel and John Bennion, who heard of the Mormon Church in Liverpool in 1840. (The brothers brought their father with them when they emigrated to Nauvoo. Father Bennion died after the Latter-day Saints were driven from Illinois. Ed.) They arrived in the Salt Lake Valley 6 October 1847. They became highly successful livestock men. By 1875, they had 7,000 head of sheep, 1,600 head of cattle and 100 horses. Their operation ranged from Cedar Valley on the east, across Rush Valley and out into Skull Valley. It was from two of their grandsons, Samuel O. and Glynn Bennion, that Wentworth got his information. One of those grandsons, Samuel O. Bennion, served as one of the seven Presidents of the First Council of the Seventy from 6 April 1933 to 8 March 1945. Glynn Bennion served as an assistant LDS Church historian from 1934-39.

The Bennion brothers were assisted by Brigham Young, John Taylor, and Abraham O. Smoot, who provided them with livestock to be operated on shares. Smoot's son, Reed, became a prominent United States Senator and a member of the Quorum of the Twelve Apostles. (In 1932-33, John Bennion's grandson, Glynn Bennion, homesteaded a desert land entry in Skull Valley, Tooele County, Utah, at Indian Creek, five miles south-southeast of Simpson Springs on the Pony Express Trail. Indian Creek flows from the Indian Springs up the hillside some four miles away. In the 1950s and 1960s, Glynn's son, George Bennion, homesteaded a desert land entry seven miles south of the River Bed station on the Pony Express Trail. Samuel was the grandfather of Samuel O. Bennion. George Bennion, 9 February 2001, Ed. Personal Communication.) The Madsens of Sanpete County are those of Scandinavian origin associated with Utah's sheep industry. They were influential producers of Rambouillet sheep. Many of the Scandinavian immigrants settled in Sanpete County.

4. Sanpete was the largest county in the territory at the time. Map of the Territory of Utah, Department of the Interior, General Land Office, October 2, 1866. All of Carbon, Emery, Grand and Sevier counties and parts of Duchesne and Uintah counties in present-day Utah were created from Sanpete. The names of the small towns of Elsinore and Siggurd in Sevier County have a definite Scandinavian ring.

5. Ronald T. Halverson, Personal Communication, 13 December 2000. Elder Ronald T. Halverson of the Quorum of the Seventy of The Church of Jesus Christ of Latter-day Saints was the president of the Norway Oslo Mission from 1990 to 1993. (As a young man in his twenties he served an earlier three-year mission to Norway.) Norway is his ancestral home. Prior to his call as an LDS General Authority, Elder Halverson was a prominent mechanical contractor in Utah and served 16 years as a member of Utah's Legislature.

6. *The Manti Temple*, published by the Manti Temple Centennial Committee, privately published, 1988, p. 22.

7. *Journal History of the Church*, 13 September 1857, p. 23. Hafen and Hafen in *Handcarts to Zion*, p. 149, state, "About 2,000 Latter-day Saints sailed from Europe under Church auspices in the spring of 1857. Of these, 566 planned to go west by handcart, 311 by wagon teams. The remaining 1,302 expected to stay in the eastern United States until they could earn and save sufficient to make the journey to Utah."

8. *Deseret News 1997-98 Church Almanac, Pioneer Sesquicentennial*, The Church of Jesus Christ of Latter-day Saints, 1996, p. 172. Company number 122: Matthias Cowley [2] ["Scandinavia Company"] left Iowa City, Iowa, 15 June [1857, left Florence, Nebraska 6 July] with 198 people and 31 wagons, arrived 13-15 September. No roster.

9. *The Manti Temple*, op. cit. p. 28

10. Don H. Smith, E-mail communique, 10 January 2001. Dr. Smith has researched the Willie Company and the handcart trail for 30 years. He said he learned recently that the driver he had identified as William Wilford was actually William Wilford Allen. This information was not previously known by living members of the Allen family.

11. Don H. Smith, E-mail communique, 29 April 2002.

Chapter 2

EUROPE: A RELIGIOUS AWAKENING

At the beginning of the 21st Century the world looks on Denmark as a small nation, a place of considerable charm and beauty, a country which produces some of the world's best pork and dairy products. Norway, with its North Sea oil reserves, fjords, and forests, is one of the world's most prosperous and beautiful nations. Sweden, too, has its vaunted steel industry and magnificent scenery. Yet, amid the world's contemporary power brokers, Scandinavia is not viewed as possessing great military might or worldwide political prowess, though this was not always so. Tradition has it that when William I the Conqueror invaded Britain and killed Harold II Godwineson, the last Saxon king, in the battle of Hastings 1066 AD, it was a case of two related kings engaging in a deadly quarrel for they both descended from Danish Vikings.[1] One of the knights who followed William was "Pied de Buef," the French expression for "Foot of Beef/cow." The direct translation of the Danish surname Kofod into English is "Cowfoot" or "Foot of Cow."[2]

The Danish Vikings, William the Conqueror's direct ancestors, conquered and settled in the north of France sometime in the 9th or 10th century. The Normandy name of that French region means "the land of the men of the north," hence the name "Normans." Normandy's capital, Rouen, was founded by the Danish Viking chief, Rolf Ragnvaldson, who was also known as Robert I, Duke of Normandy. One theory has it that Bornholm Vikings put their ships ashore in Burgundy, as the Latin name for Bornholm is Burgundia or Burgundiaholm and the Latin name for the French duchy of Burgogne was Burgundia.[3] While the Burgundy connection has not been proven, what seems abundantly clear is that the Vikings were a fierce, adventuresome people on the move. Among their numbers were capable and ambitious leaders.

For centuries Europe had been a scene of armed conflict. Its monarchs had territorial ambitions. In particular, Columbus' voyage of discovery whetted their appetites for increased jurisdiction in the new world. The armies and navies of Europe's kings and queens fought, bled, and died for the cause of their sovereign's empire. Nobles also began to assert themselves in the quest for power and wealth. They did not want to be left out of the new economy.

However, not all were driven by worthy ambition. There were occasions when unprincipled hearts and greedy hands sought to grasp the scepter of authority thereby creating political, social, and economic situations which frequently were painful to correct. Under such trying circumstances the common people suffered dreadfully. Yet, an irrepressible yearning for a better life was growing among the common folk. Those hopes and aspirations produced a social energy resulting in an ebb and flow which ultimately cracked the barriers erected against economic and educational mobility, thereby freeing the general populace from a subservient mentality. Heaven had not dictated that they should always be peasants. While the barricades protecting class were not easily breached, the ramparts of privilege were under siege.

There were more than economic and political changes in the air. New religious thinkers attempted to reform the Roman Catholic Church. Among the reformers were courageous idealists, some of Europe's best minds, who paid with their lives when they attempted to get the Bible into the hands of common folk. The political pendulum swung back and forth between limited freedom of religious thought and strict adherence to the doctrinal dictates of Rome. Cardinals made kings and kings made Cardinals. The doctrine of separation of church and state was still in the future. Yet, the winds of freedom blew waves of flood tide proportion. The world began breaking out of the long night of intellectual, scientific, and economic poverty known as the Dark Ages.

France, for a time, allowed the French Calvinists, the Huguenots or "covenanters," an opportunity to preach their doctrines of reformation. Then, the Huguenots decided to make of themselves a political force with whom France and all Catholicism would have to reckon; it led to their undoing. Henry II of France determined it would suit His Majesty's royal purposes to side with the Vatican. Henry moved vigorously against the dissenters. He billeted his troops in the homes of the Protestants with the instruction to make them just as miserable and unpleasant as they possibly could. He declared Protestantism to be heresy, called it a vile plague, and introduced the Inquisition. In 1557 the penalty for heresy was death; two years later, an edict specified that death should be accomplished by burning.

Within the Parliament of France was a group of moderates. Anne du Bourg, a son of a former chancellor, was one of them. (Yes, in this case Anne was a man's name.) On 10 June 1559, Henry, in company with French Cardinals and high officers of the crown, entered the parliament and commanded that the discussion of religion continue. Du Bourg courageously declared that it was "no small thing to condemn those, who amidst the flames, invoke the name of Jesus Christ." In December 1559, at the king's command, du Bourg was burned at the stake. (Even well into the 1800s, the French throne remained politically bound to the Vatican's altars.)

Religious persecution and other forms of repression did not bode well for the long-term future of the French monarchy. Ultimately, the extraordinary abuse of power by the kings of France, coupled with their utter disregard for the poverty of their people, resulted in the French Revolution. The winds of change which arose from that uprising blew the seeds of French republicanism all the way to Denmark. The irreversible forces of liberty were set in motion—forces which would profoundly affect the government of Denmark in the nineteenth century.

Faced with a choice of forced conversion or death, those who could emigrate went elsewhere. Elizabeth I, a Protestant, invited the French Huguenots to become her subjects on the

Isle of Guernsey. Not all of her new subjects followed pious pursuits though. From some of those French Huguenots sprang a hardy group of Guernsey privateers who operated on the high seas under the authority of a "Letter of Marque" granted by the English Crown. They were a plague on French and Spanish shipping. At one point on Guernsey, 600 men were employed as coopers, making 10-gallon casks to support the illicit brandy trade. Importing brandy from France and capturing it on the high seas necessitated a market. These brandy runners dropped the re-casked French brandy at secretive locations along the English coast.[4] The brandy cartel ran England's custom officials ragged chasing those "five and twenty ponies trotting through the dark." Their illegal exploits were immortalized by Rudyard Kipling in "A Smuggler's Song."

The effort to reform Catholic theology was not confined to France. One economic innovation instituted by the Catholic Church met with strenuous objections from an influential German priest. In 1517, Martin Luther issued 95 theses opposing the sale of papal indulgences which provided financial support for the rebuilding of St. Peter's Cathedral. Luther refused to recant his scathing criticism unless the validity of indulgences could be shown as approved in the Bible. It was the beginning of a complete break with the Roman Church. Leo X's papal bull directed that Luther and his followers must recant within 60 days or they would be excommunicated. Anything but contrite, Luther called it the work of the antichrist and defiantly burned the papal bull 10 December 1520.

It had been a busy year for the Augustinian monk. Among other things, he had a prolific pen. He published *To the Christian Nobility of the German Nation*, a treatise disclaiming the supremacy of ecclesiastical authority over civil government and urging the civil authorities to reform the church. He also published *The Babylonian Captivity of the Church* and *The Freedom of the Christian Man*. Called the primary works of the Reformation, they assert the primacy of the Bible as the rule of faith and practice, and developed the concept of a priesthood of all believers, or every man a priest. Leo issued a formal bull and excommunicated Martin Luther. Frederick III, by prearrangement, had Luther kidnaped and hidden away to protect him from Leo's ally, Charles V. Sequestered at Wartburg Castle and using the alias, Junker Georg, Luther began his translation of the Bible into German. Perhaps his stay at Wartburg influenced the language of his famous hymn, "A Mighty Fortress is Our God."

Taking a political page out of the church from which they had dissented, Luther's disciples created a state church of their own. That church developed a reluctance to tolerate any new expression of Christianity. The faith which arose from Luther's efforts to reform Catholicism became a powerful force in Germany and neighboring Scandinavia. Sweden, Norway, and Denmark became overwhelmingly Lutheran and remained confessional states wherein separation from the national Church was illegal. In fact, conversion from Catholicism to Lutheranism had been legislated. In August 1536, Christian III, king of Denmark, jailed the Catholic bishops and made Lutheranism the basis for the Christian church of Denmark and Norway. By the end of the 16th century, the reformation rebellion in Denmark had settled into Lutheran orthodoxy. As a result, there was not the civil conflict over religion which had occurred elsewhere in Europe.

There was no substantial protest to an indoctrination of Lutheran orthodoxy prior to 1700. From that date forward, an evangelical movement arising in Germany brought a call for a more intensely personal type of Christianity. Even so, forced infant baptism was practiced in Denmark until 1849.[5] Yet, where freedom of thought exists, legislation and government fiat cannot blot out the spiritual yearnings which arise from the secret chambers of the soul. It was a time of a religious awakening in northern Europe and America. Honest seekers of truth hungered to know the answers to life's most significant questions. The salvation of the soul received at least as much attention in the public discourse as that given to the safety of one's wealth. During the 1800s other Protestant faiths arose; the members of those faiths were called Protestant dissenters. As they grew more numerous, they became bolder. They were increasingly outspoken concerning religious choice and the resultant grievances imposed by second-class citizenship.[6]

Even in the 1850s, the question of a legally recognized or legitimate state church would be a barrier encountered by the first Latter-day Saint missionaries to Scandinavia. Religion was a matter of deep emotion, and many felt passionately about their religious beliefs—they identified with the traditions of their families. In Scandinavia, religion was seemingly interwoven within the fabric of national pride. Throughout much of Europe's history, throne and altar had been inextricably linked. It was part and parcel of a unified citizenry, a key element in the strategy of national defense against hostile foreign powers, for Europe was frequently on a war footing. The early Latter-day Saint missionaries who labored in Scandinavia, like Paul of old, had their faith tried by the testing experiences of persecution and prison.

In one sense, it was a cultural conflict. By contrast, in America modes of religious observance and institutional membership were voluntary matters. War had been an outgrowth of territorial and political disputes. People of all faiths volunteered and fought the enemy—foreign and domestic. America's struggle for independence was a war against an economically oppressive monarchy. It was not a quarrel seeking separation from the Church of England. From that remarkable revolution came a Constitution which safeguarded freedom of thought and will, where one could worship according to the dictates of conscience. Out of prior experience, America's Founding Fathers understood the hazards posed to personal freedom by a state church. The Constitution of the United States expressly prohibited the proscribing of a denominational religion. No taxes were to be used to support a particular denomination. Paradoxically, religion and active church membership in America seemed to flourish to a much greater degree than they did in Europe.

By the 1850s, European immigrants discovered a variety of religious affiliations in America. In large measure, Americans, though members of a number of different religious faiths, engaged in meaningful social and economic intercourse with each other. One man's money was just as good as another's. In most outward respects one could not distinguish the members of one religious denomination from another (At that time, the quaint dress of the Amish would have not been all that different from others). Commenting on European immigration in the 19th Century, Oscar Handlin wrote somewhat idealistically that Americans "associated with each other on terms of complete equality. There was, it seemed, no reason why a man should not change his church as freely as his hat. Indeed, to some immigrants it seemed that Americans were perilously near doing so all the time."[7]

Northern Europe's kings allied themselves with Luther's Protestant reformation, for it made patently good political sense to break Rome's hold on the hearts of their subjects. It was not a case of separating throne and altar, it was a matter of whose altar best fit the national interest. The national church allowed the Danish language to become better established, although Latin would remain the language of learning for many years. Royal marriages frequently were arranged on the basis of political hegemony, perhaps love would follow. Power, not romantic passion, was often the linchpin which made the marital match.

The royal marital maneuvering did not always work. There were those times when the in-laws posed a problem for a new monarch. For example, in 1648 Frederik III became Denmark's king. In the 1650s, he used his considerable political skills to oust from the Rigsråd two of his main adversaries. The two were the seneschal, (the agent in charge of the lord's feudal estate) Corfitz Ulfeldt, and the governor of Norway, Hannibal Sehested. Both men were married to Frederik's sisters.[8] Perhaps the old folk proverb which states that "blood is thicker than water" should be amended to acknowledge that blood is not thicker than power and money—at least, not in this case.

The kings foreseen by Daniel were busy attempting to expand their domain. They wanted to rule the world, at least as much of the world as they could take and hold. The taste of power tends to create an insatiable appetite for such. In the

great halls and the secret chambers of the royal palaces, sub-
terfuge, intrigue, conspiracy, and war were games with won-
drous possibilities. The earth was their chessboard, their subjects pawns to be spent in the quest for authority and dominion.
Bishops, knights, and castles all had their uses as well, and all
were used in the attempt to consummate royal objectives. In
their pursuit of the divine rights of kings, the actions taken were
frequently anything but divinely inspired.

The Protestant Reformation, coupled with the territorial
ambitions of Europe's monarchs, had been primary causative
agents leading to several centuries of European war. Europe
was a scene of continuing military conflict in the early 1800s,
much of it in which Denmark was embroiled. Denmark's initial
position in those years was one of neutrality, a position which
the British regarded as supportive of Napoleon. Admiral
Horatio Nelson bombarded Copenhagen on 2 April 1801 and
thereafter the Danes submitted to British searches of their ves-
sels. Nelson's success was facilitated by a lack of Scandinavian
cooperation. The Danes rejected a Swedish offer to fortify the
east coast of The Sound, the narrow strait between Denmark
and Sweden. Consequently, the British navy was able to sail out
of range of the guns of the Danish forts. Sweden's fleet was
detained by deficiencies and unfavorable winds at Karlskrona,
some 200 miles away.[9]

Denmark's continuing policy of neutrality and its refusal to
join a third coalition against Napoleon led to an 1805 bombard-
ment of Copenhagen. Then, during 2-4 September 1807,
Britain seized or destroyed Denmark's fleet and much of its
prowess as a trading nation. The aim of the British attack was
to prevent Napoleon from gaining control of the Danish navy,
thereby enabling the French emperor to cut off Britain's vital
Baltic trade. With the loss of their fleet, the Danes reluctantly
allied themselves with the French. Despite the efforts of Danish
gunboats and privateers, Denmark did not succeed in blocking
British convoys from proceeding through Danish waters. In the
end, Denmark found itself on the wrong side of that European
conflict and by 1813 was in state bankruptcy. The peace treaty

of 1814 resulted in Denmark's loss of Norway and Sweden. Wars can be economically devastating and this prolonged struggle was such for the Danes. The period following the Napoleonic wars was marked with economic stagnation. Trade and shipping declined while inflation rose sharply; Danish agriculture was hit hard by British import duties on corn. From 1818 onward, there was a marked fall in corn prices. Economic difficulties for Danish agriculture continued through the end of the 1820s.[10]

The 1800s were a time of economic and scientific change, although the rate of change was slow in comparison with the rate of technological change of the 20th Century. A servile agriculture had characterized the 17th and 18th centuries. Farm enclosure laws began in 1781 and by 1807 half of the farms were enclosed. Denmark gave tenants full legal protection against the lord of the manor in 1787 and formally abolished the status of serf in 1788—those who were tied to the land by *Stavnsbaand*. (*Stavnsbaand* is a Nordic word. In Norwegian and Danish it formerly meant: "An obligation to remain on a piece of land designated as your home." It was a very common provision in Denmark from 1733 to 1788.)[11] Emancipation from serfdom, a cruel relic of feudalism, rolled relentlessly eastward from Denmark to Bavaria and eastern Europe.

The practice of tying workers to the place where they were born (also called adscription), and not allowing them to leave without the landowner's permission, had been introduced to provide manpower for the militia. The system also provided the landowner with cheap labor. These social-political reforms led to a three-fold improvement of crop yields by 1807. Only the landless cottar class (peasants who were allowed to occupy a cottage and land in exchange for their labor) were still being ruthlessly exploited. There were other measures which regulated the labor services of tenant farmers. These laws made it easier for them to buy land. Certain manorial privileges were abolished such as the monopoly on stall-fed cattle.[12] (Feedlot or grain-finished cattle would be the equivalent in contemporary U.S. agriculture.)

By 1830, Europe's agriculture, its largest occupation, was shaking off the worst of the effects of its painful transition from a war-based to a peace-time economy. It had been an economically difficult period. Britain had become the most industrialized economy in the world. By 1830, only 25 percent of its population was engaged in farming.[13] In 1832, Norman Rothschild would declare that England was, in general, the bank for the whole world.[14] London had indeed become the financial capital for international commerce. Immigration, industrialization, and trade heralded the beginning of a new global economy.

Agricultural improvement was at the forefront in the changing character of the national economies of Europe. While there were substantial land additions to the agricultural production base in Hungary, Romania, and southern Russia, much of the growth resulted by raising productivity on farmland already under cultivation. Agricultural meetings and the *Journal of the Royal Agricultural Society* (founded in 1838) did much to further the application of scientific findings into agricultural practice.[15] Intensively operated small family farms began to produce a surplus as farmers manured and plowed the soils more deeply with enhanced plows and further implemented improved planting, cultivation, harvesting, and threshing techniques. Turnips, potatoes, clovers, and alfalfa were incorporated into the crop rotation. More forage was produced which enabled better winter feeding. This improved feeding, coupled with selective breeding, increased milk and meat yields per animal. With more milk available, cheese and butter production went up.[16] As animal agriculture became increasingly more profitable, the land base required for such operations resulted in larger farms with commensurately fewer opportunities for the younger sons to acquire a profitable farming operation. Necessity required that families look elsewhere.

By 1850, serfdom had virtually disappeared from Europe except in Russia and Romania. Scandinavia's agriculture involved animal, grain, and forage production.[17] There were vast coniferous forests in southern Norway and Sweden with 24 percent of Norway's land devoted to forests and three percent to cultivated lands and pasture. Some 73 percent of Norway was called inhospitable or nonproductive.[18] Consequently, the

Norwegians turned to their warm costal waters as fisherman and seafarers. It was a part of their Viking heritage. Even though the Norwegians exported fish to France, fishing by itself was inadequate to support a large population. In the 1800s, the lack of an agricultural land base restricted growth and economic opportunity. The manufacturing sector based on Norway's abundant waterpower resources lay in the future. Except for the iron industry in Sweden, most Scandinavian industry was small in scale.[19] It had been largely a matter of choosing to farm, fish the coastal waters, cut timber, or go to sea.

Denmark's soils and climate would enable the development of a highly productive agricultural sector, although the lands of its islands were more productive than the soils of the Jutland peninsula. The Danes were grain exporters. Despite Britain's earlier destruction of the Danish fleet at Copenhagen, by 1839 they had 1,600 ships. They were also in the international tariff business. Denmark controlled the entrance to the Baltic. Until 1857, foreign merchant ships dutifully cast anchor at Elsinore and paid their Sound Tolls to the Danish Crown.[20]

Even with the reforms, things were not easy nor favorable for Scandinavia's tenant and peasant farmers. They engaged in a survival style of farm management or subsistence farming rather than a risk-assumption strategy which typifies United States agriculture today. Generally, the tenant and peasant farmers had holdings which were too small and scattered to allow for mechanical cultivation. Their income situation made it difficult to accumulate capital. Usurious interest rates restrained borrowing to finance improvements or to adopt a more capital intensive farming approach.[21] Rather than capitalize equipment, the family's labor supply was substituted for machines. They carefully husbanded their finances. It was much harder for these folk than for those associated with, and part of, consolidated operations. Where land was scarce and wages poor and uncertain, people began moving toward the cities in search of better opportunities as artisans and laborers. By contrast, in Utah, threshing machines, a woolen mill, and other labor-saving devices were being purchased and operated cooperatively as such machinery could release additional men for missionary service.[22]

Military conscription in Europe had been a fact of life. It was a necessity. The several governments would have been unable to wage those long and difficult wars without it. Those wars had taken a deadly toll. The army was a risky vocation for the ordinary man with little opportunity for a conscript to advance. The officers generally were drawn from the nobles' sons—social privilege influenced economic opportunities. Life in the lower classes had limited and somewhat prescribed options—it was difficult. Even though these were nations with developing economies, other places held greater promise. Europe's lack of economic opportunity created an environment where the adventuresome among the lower classes were stirring. They began looking for improved financial possibilities, even if it meant going elsewhere. There was a resurgence of personal energy and individual initiative. It was an economic renaissance, and from across the Atlantic, America beckoned.

Land in America's plains and prairies of its Upper Midwest and its Great Basin was one of its many abundant natural resources. Hardworking immigrants could become part of the landed gentry, although in America it was not called that. It was a nation undergoing profound religious and social change. America's opportunities and its way of life appealed to able folk endowed with a sense of adventure, who yearned for a better life for their families. There was greater freedom for personal decision making. They could avoid Europe's quarrels. The movement across the Atlantic would profoundly affect Scandinavia and the United States.[23]

The reign of Frederick VII of Denmark brought other significant reforms. French political philosophy and its attendant "republicanism" infiltrated Denmark. The new constitution, adopted in 1849, limited the powers of the king. It created an elected legislature, the Rigsdag. The peasant representatives appeared to form a unified party, but that was not the case with other parliamentarians. In the political center were the liberals with no real party structure. Their heterogeneous mix included a large group of academics, who even then were difficult to harness and direct into a functioning, unified whole. To the right stood a smaller group composed of older civil servants and landowners who were philosophically opposed to the new constitution.[24] Slaves were freed in the colonies. (Denmark's colonies in India and Africa were sold in 1845 and 1850.)[25] The constitution made provision for religious dissenters, or those who wished not to affiliate with the state church. While religious liberty was a matter of constitutional law, the popular will lagged behind the ideal. Consequently, there was active resistance to the religious views of the nonconformists, to those who were not a part of the state church. The Danish liberals were insistent that the well-paid clergy would have to make the case for the state church without the help of the police.[26]

Arnold Friberg's painting *Mormon Preachers*. © Intellectual Reserve, Inc. In 1856, Danish artist Christen Dalsgaard wrote regarding the painting on which the Friberg painting is based, "Two Mormons in their wandering have come to a carpenter's cottage in the country where by preaching they seek to win adherents."

The legal provisions for religious freedom were more advanced in Denmark than in Norway and Sweden where the matter of religious choice took longer in coming to fruition. Some within the state church viewed with alarm any attempt to educate peasants beyond the minimal requirements of religion. Education had the potential to create social disruption. Knowledge was a key factor in maintaining power; it was something to be jealously guarded and tightly held. The right to print and distribute the Bible in Danish had been the prerogative of a clergy-controlled institution. Early Latter-day Saint missionaries found only a few honorable exceptions among the clergy regarding the diffusion of the Bible among the populace. Consequently whole neighborhoods, with the exception of the church or priest, were virtually without copies of the Bible.[27]

The new Danish Constitution provided for freedom of the press. It was one of the freedoms which had been vouchsafed in the American Bill of Rights. That freedom had been of vital importance to the successful preaching of the restored gospel of Christ in America. It was also a freedom needed in Scandinavia. Without the protection of freedom of the press, any publication of new religious materials would have been reduced to a clandestine effort. Such had happened before when various reformers made the effort to translate the Bible from Latin into the national languages of Northern Europe. For the Latter-day Saints, the publication of The Book of Mormon and the Doctrine and Covenants in Danish was absolutely necessary. It had been mandated by the Lord. The revelation of God given through the Prophet Joseph Smith directed *that every man shall hear the fulness of the gospel in his own tongue, and in his own language, through those who are ordained unto this power, by the administration of the Comforter, shed forth upon them for the revelation of Jesus Christ.*[28]

From America to Europe came new religious preachers saying salvation required that the individual must seek to know the will of God, that a prayerful consideration of the scriptures is a part of that process whereby one comes to know God, and Jesus Christ whom He has sent. Beyond the truths found in the Bible, these Latter-day Saint missionaries made another especially bold declaration. They proclaimed God had revealed a new volume of sacred scripture, the one foreseen by Isaiah; it was that voice speaking out of the dust.[29] It was the very stick of Joseph as foretold by Ezekiel, the companion scripture to the stick of Judah.[30] In their exhortations, Latter-day Saint missionaries taught the gospel of Jesus Christ using both the Bible and The Book of Mormon.

These new preachers of righteousness understood that resident within the Book of Mormon was a power which changed lives, for it had changed theirs. It was the Latter-day Saint missionaries' witness that Jesus of Nazareth was and is the Christ, and that He, as the Risen Lord, personally ministered to America's ancient inhabitants. They declared there had been a restoration as was foretold by Peter, the chief apostle of the Early Christian Church. Peter had boldly urged his recalcitrant countrymen to *repent and be converted, that their sins might be blotted out, when the times of refreshing shall come from*

Early proselyting efforts in Denmark as depicted by C. C. A. Christensen in his painting **"Preaching the Gospel."**

the presence of the Lord; and He shall send Jesus Christ which was before preached unto you; whom the heaven must receive until the times of the restitution of all things, which God had spoken by the mouth of all his holy prophets since the world began.[31] With Peter-like boldness, these missionaries proclaimed the long-promised restoration had begun. The Second Coming of the Messiah was at hand. The gathering of Israel had begun. Their case was compelling, their passion persuasive. The Reformation had paved the way for the Restitution. And they, like the ancient apostle, found many who believed.

The two decades since 1837 had been difficult days for the Latter-day Saints. They had undergone periods of persecution and serious financial distress. They had received little, if anything, for much of their real property in consequence of their expulsion from Missouri and the exodus from Nauvoo. Their removal from Illinois and the beginning of the colonization of the Great Basin required resources. In 1846, President James K. Polk requested the Mormons raise a battalion to help fight the war with Mexico. Five-hundred of their most able young men undertook the march from Council Bluffs, Iowa, to San Diego, California, the longest march of infantry in the history of the United States. Even when faced with such severe hardship, the leaders individually and the Church collectively were diligent to remember the new covenant—The Book of Mormon.[32] The Danish translation of the Book of Mormon, begun in Nauvoo in 1844, was completed in 1851 in Copenhagen.

The years of European revolution and upheaval had brought periods of social unrest and religious persecution. Yet, in the best tradition of Viking adventurism, the Danish desire for individual freedom had opened the way for other thinking, for new ideas, for a new faith. Europe was experiencing a religious revival. In part, that spiritual awakening was foreign led. Though the times were trying and difficult, there were meek and humble souls who sought the peaceable things of the Lord's kingdom. And the spirit of that conversion brought the breath of spiritual fire into their souls.

NOTES

1. Johansen, Blem, Dahl, Schou, Brandt, Kofoed family-tree database-information; May 5, 1999, p. 2 of 3.

2. Johansen, et al., Kofoed family-tree..., p. 2.

3. Johansen, et al., Kofoed family-tree..., p. 2.

4. Jackson K. Sauvarin, *The Family Name of Sauvarin*, Privately published by Jack and Noeline Sauvarin, 24 Cleland Crescent, Blockhouse Bay, Auckland, New Zealand, 1999, pp. 12, 19.

5. Rick Burns, Personal telephone communication, 29 January 2001. Burns is the Director of the Danish Immigrant Museum, 2212 Washington Street, Box 470, Elk Horn, Iowa. 51531.

6. John Walsh, "Religion: Church and State in Europe and the Americas," in *The New Cambridge Modern History, Volume IX: War and Peace in an Age of Upheaval*, 1965, p. 176.

7. Oscar Handlin, *The Uprooted*, 2nd Edition, Back Bay Books, Little, Brown and Company, Boston, 1979 pp. 112-13.

8. Carsten Wulff, editor and Flemming Axmark and Preben Hansen, co-editors. "Denmark," published by the Royal Danish Ministry of Foreign Affairs, Department of Information, Asiatisk Plads 2, DK-1448, Copenhagen K, 1996, pp. 436-37.

9. T. K. Derry, "Scandinavia" (Part B) "The Low Countries and Scandinavia," in *The New Cambridge Modern History, Volume IX: War and Peace in an Age of Upheaval*, 1965, pp. 484-85.

10. Carsten Wulff, et al., "Denmark...," p. 448.

11. Petter Svanevik, Personal E-mail communique, 22 January 2001. Petter Svanevik is a Norwegian who serves as a translator for the LDS Church.

12. T. K. Derry, "Scandinavia...," p. 482.

13. R. M. Hartwell, "Economic Change in England and Europe. 1780-1830," in *The New Cambridge Modern History Volume IX, War and Peace in an Age of Upheaval*, Cambridge at the University Press, C. W. Hawley, editor, 1965, p. 31.

14. R. M. Hartwell, "Economic Change in...," p. 46.

15. A. R. Hall, "The Scientific Movement and its Influence on Thought and Material Development," in *The New Cambridge Modern History Volume X, The Zenith of European Power*, 1830-70, Cambridge At the University Press, 1960, p. 23.

16. R. M. Hartwell, "Economic Change in...," p. 34.

17. R. M. Hartwell, "Economic Change in...," p. 35.

18. Samuel van Valkenburg and Ellsworth Huntington, *Europe*, John Wiley and Sons, Inc. New York, 1935, p. 236.

19. R. M. Hartwell, "Economic Change in...," p. 51.

20. R. M. Hartwell, "Economic Change in...," p. 52.

21. A. R. Hall, "The Scientific Movement...," p. 23.

22. William Mulder, *Homeward to Zion: The Mormon Migration from Scandinavia*, University of Minnesota Press, Minneapolis-London, in cooperation with Brigham Young University Press, 2000, p. 81.

23. By 1881, the drain of energetic, thrifty, intelligent Danes to America had risen to such a level that it was creating some hostility in the Danish press toward America, according to a letter from U. S. Consular officer M. J. Cramer to U. S. Secretary of State William Evarts. There was also complaint that republicanism was spreading among Danes who were unable to emigrate, thereby engendering dissatisfaction with large standing armies and consequently the heavy taxation necessary to support the military. See William Mulder, Op cit, p.326, endnote 86.

24. Carsten Wulff, et al. "Denmark...," p. 450.

25. Carsten Wulff, ct al. "Denmark...," p. 448.

26. William Mulder, *Homeward to Zion...*, p. 41.

27. William Mulder, *Homeward to Zion...*, pp. 40-43.

28. D&C 90:11.

29. Isaiah 29:4.

30. Ezekiel 37:16-17.

31. Acts 3:16-17.

32. D&C 84:57.

Chapter 3

SCANDINAVIA: A FRUITFUL BOUGH BY A WELL

We now turn to those Scandinavians who became a part of the 7th Handcart Company experience. To understand the driving force in their lives, it is necessary to consider the changes which result when one makes the sacrifices attendant in converting to a new religious faith, a faith arising out of a new revelation, a faith which requires sacrifice to attain salvation. The faith of those new Mormon converts had been tempered in the forge of adversity, a forge fueled by the hot coals of persecution and hardship. So steeled, like the devoted disciples of old, these new fishers of men went to the farms, the shops, the fishing boats, the villages, the towns, and the cities of Denmark, Norway, and Sweden. Theirs was a magnificent message. It was the glorious news that God had again spoken from the Heavens, that He had revealed Himself to prophets, as He had done in ancient times. It was a stunning message, a sharp break with traditional orthodoxy, yet it was an inclusive message, intended for everyone, men and women and families. Its power changed lives. That power fueled unquenchable fires of faith. It called for sacrifice on behalf of the cause. One preeminent doctrine taught by the Latter-day Saints was that the gathering of Israel was at hand, and the new converts were encouraged to assemble with the saints in the stakes of Zion.[1] Unquestionably, the advent of Mormonism disrupted the religious status quo.

It may have been an overt manifestation of Viking tradition which produced the fierce national pride that caused some in Scandinavia to view those who became American immigrants as traitors, as unfaithful sons.[2] Local priests who saw the tithe offerings dwindle and the number of empty pews increase were understandably alarmed. While the harvest would prove great, not all in Scandinavia received the message with gladness. There was resistance,[3] but then, why should one expect the new doctrine to be received differently in Copenhagen and Oslo than it had been received centuries earlier at Capernaum and Jerusalem? It has never been easy to believe in living prophets. Even a mortal Jesus, whose ministry was conducted in the midst of many miracles, encountered serious and conspiring detractors as He walked the pathways of Palestine. Opposition in the matter of religion seems to be the natural order of things.

The first Mormon missionaries to Scandinavia came to Copenhagen, Denmark in 1850. They were Erastus Snow and George Parker Dykes of America, John Erik Forsgren of Sweden, and Peter Ole Hansen of Denmark.[4] Brigham Young ordained Erastus Snow an apostle 12 February 1849 and at the following October Conference had given Elder Snow the assignment to open the work in Scandinavia. George P. Dykes and John E. Forsgren had served in the Mormon Battalion, Dykes as 1st Lieutenant of Company D and Forsgren as a private in the same company. Both had marched all the way to California. In addition, in the 1840s, George Dykes had done extensive missionary work among the Norwegians in the Midwest and had presided over the Ottawa, La Salle County, Illinois Branch of the Church, a unit comprised of a group of Norwegian emigrants who had joined the Church in that area.[5] John Forsgren and Hans Christian Hansen had been sailors when they heard the gospel preached in Boston. Hans wrote his brother, Peter Ole Hansen, who was residing in Copenhagen, concerning the new faith. In 1844, Peter, unable to find any Mormons in Denmark, came to America at his brother's urging to investigate Mormonism and to see a prophet. Hans and Peter Hansen arrived in Nauvoo some time after the assassination of the Prophet Joseph Smith. Brigham Young, in his capacity as president of the Quorum of the Twelve Apostles, set Peter O. Hansen to work on a Danish translation of the Book of Mormon.[6]

There had been other missionary work among Scandinavians in the United States. Scandinavian branches had been organized in Illinois, Iowa, and Wisconsin. One of those units, the Fox River Branch, sent Endre Dahl with 100 head of sheep and cattle along with a little cash to Nauvoo as a building contribution for the temple. Endre Dahl met the Prophet Joseph Smith on a street. Joseph invited Brother Dahl to come to his home. Dahl declined saying he was a very simple Norwegian, unworthy to enter the Prophet's home. However, Joseph Smith prevailed and persuaded Dahl to go with him, for he had seen more in Endre Dahl than Dahl had seen in himself and his fellow Norwegians. Not long thereafter the Prophet Joseph told his cousin, George A. Smith of the Quorum of the Twelve Apostles, "that the Scandinavians would in time come to play a significant role in the Church."[7]

These four initial missionaries, seasoned leaders in their own right, determined to begin the work in Scandinavia following the pattern used successfully in England. An organization of Baptist dissenters was found. This congregation was led by the Reverend Peter C. Mønster, a Baptist reformer who had been persecuted and imprisoned for preaching Christianity as he believed it. On 16 June 1850, the missionaries began to attend Reverend Mønster's services. They became friends with him and his congregation. Reverend Mønster shared with the missionaries the account of his struggle to teach new religious doctrine in Denmark. He recounted that he had used his time in prison to learn to read and speak English.

On Tuesday, 18 August 1850, Elders Snow and Dykes visited the Honorable Walter Forward, U.S. Minister to Denmark. Elder Snow had a letter of introduction from U.S. Senator James Cooper of Pennsylvania. The American diplomat, an attorney and a former member of Congress, had served as Secretary of the Treasury in the cabinet of President Harrison. He and Senator Cooper were personal friends. Walter Forward had received the appointment as U.S. Charge d' Affairs to Denmark from President Zachary Taylor.[8] Elder Snow described Forward as a "frank and generous gentleman of the old school." He cordially welcomed the elders, "made a number of enquiries about the Mormon people and their religion," and being generally acquainted with their history, "expressed himself liberally" regarding "the unhallowed persecutions they had suffered in America." Forward promised that he would render them any aid which was within his power to give.[9]

Erastus Snow was not a political novice. He had served as an early member of the Council of Fifty, a group of some fifty prominent men who had been given the charge of helping build the kingdom of God on the earth, but not in a sense that they would control the priesthood. One assignment given the Council of Fifty was to electioneer on behalf of Joseph Smith's 1844 candidacy for President of the United States. Erastus Snow possessed considerable oratorical skill. He had taken part in framing the Constitution of the Provisional State of Deseret, and at the time of his departure for Scandinavia was a member of the Legislature. En route to Denmark, he spent time in Washington, DC, listening to the intense debate regarding slavery and California's admission to the Union. His journal noted that he and Lorenzo Snow attended many of the exciting Congressional debates on these issues in which Messrs. "Calhoun, Clay, Webster, Cass, Benton & Douglas participated."[10] Apparently the two apostles had been assigned to lobby the Congress for Deseret's admission to the Union. However, the Compromise of 1850 brought not statehood to Deseret, but territorial status to a geographically smaller Utah.

It was not long until Walter Forward had an opportunity to demonstrate that he was as good as his word. Some three months after Elder John E. Forsgren's arrival in Sweden, he was expelled from his native land—he had begun to have success. His preaching had attracted the attention of the Swedish press. People began to flock to see and hear him in public and private meetings, and some Swedes requested baptism. In what was essentially a clandestine operation, the Swedish police took him by night, paid his passage, and placed him on board an American ship bound for New York. The Swedish officials requested that the captain not allow Forsgren to land until the ship reached the port of New York. However, the Mormon missionary soon won the friendship of the ship's captain. When the American vessel called at Elsinore to pay the Danish toll tax, Elder Forsgren disembarked with the captain's assistance only to be apprehended by Danish police acting at the request of the Swedish consul. Authorities in Stockholm, fearing that Forsgren would cross the strait and reenter Sweden in the south, had arranged by prior dispatches to counter any such eventuality. Elder Forsgren produced his American passport and claimed the protection of Mr. Forward who had just come to Elsinore from Copenhagen. Elder Snow recorded in his journal that America's minister to Denmark quickly came to Elder Forsgren's assistance, "effected his release, repudiating the aspersions of his enemies, and accompanied him to Copenhagen, where he arrived in good health, full of joy and the Holy Ghost, having been absent from us about three months."[11]

Andrew Jenson wrote that initially "Elder Snow urged that no one be baptized, but rather held them back, advising a more thorough investigation. Finally, however, the Lord warned him in a dream to do so no longer."[12] On the evening of 12 August 1850 in the clear waters of the Öresund [The Sound], just outside the ramparts of Copenhagen, Erastus Snow baptized 15 people, the first fruits of Mormon missionary preaching in Denmark.[13] Baptisms in Copenhagen became frequent. Christian Christiansen, who seven years later would captain the 7th Handcart Company, was among those baptized on 17 August 1850.[14] Within two months, many of the former Baptists had joined the new church. Reverend Mønster initially had been very friendly and somewhat inclined toward Mormonism. He read the Book of Mormon and Parley P. Pratt's *A Voice of Warning*. He taught baptism by immersion. The introduction of that doctrine made the preaching task easier for Elder Snow and his companions when they taught the absolute necessity that baptism by immersion for the remission of sins must be performed by those who held divine priesthood authority. As Reverend Mønster saw his flock decimated by conversion, his hesitancy to join The Church of Jesus Christ of

Latter-day Saints turned to doubt, and then to outright opposition toward the new faith and the Mormon elders.[15]

According to one biographer, Erastus Snow had proceeded carefully, seeking to minimize the possibility of alarming the Lutheran clergy, the government, or others who might organize the ignorant in mass protests against Mormonism. He was not after spectacular conversions. They did not hold public meetings. Rather it was in the homes of humble seekers where they taught the message of the Restoration, of the gathering of Israel to Zion in the tops of the mountains, where the mountain of the Lord's House would be built, and that all nations would flow unto it.[16] For many, the concept of a new Zion "was as a magnet attracting raw metal."[17] These were common folk. Many were poor and came from the ranks of the working class. They were laborers, mechanics, and peasant farmers who worked the lands belonging to the nobles. (According to one non-Mormon study, the vast majority of Danes who immigrated to America during this period came from the agricultural proletariat.)[18]

While discretion was warranted, Elder Snow and his companions had come at a most opportune time. The transition from feudalism to capitalism resulted in social disruption. Economic survival forced hard choices. People were of a mind to consider making changes. The Danish Constitution of 1849 made religious choice legally possible. Had Mormon missionaries come in 1839, the year of the second apostolic mission to Great Britain, things would have been extraordinarily difficult. Fascinatingly, the call to open Scandinavia had not come then. Undoubtedly, the economic opportunities afforded in America, and innate desire for a farm and home of their own, must have influenced the religious decision made by some Danes. In a real sense, those who controlled the land were, in large measure, those who controlled the country. It seems likely, however, that those early Scandinavian converts for whom the primary motivation for changing faiths had been centered in economic improvement rather than the quest for theological salvation, were found, probably disproportionately so, among those who ultimately remained in the American Midwest, for the handcart-

and-ox-team test seemingly sifted out those caught in the cares of the world.

On 17 August 1850 Elder Snow wrote an extensive missionary report to the First Presidency. He declared the "Spirit of the Lord" seemed to have led him to Copenhagen, that his time there had served to convince him the impression had been correct. He described Copenhagen as a city of 140,000, the seat of learning in northern Europe, and the most influential town in the kingdom. He told that until recently Denmark had been governed by an absolute monarchy, that Lutheran clergy had the superintendency of all primary schools and public instruction for the nation, except that certain privileges had been granted to the Jewish community, and to foreign mechanics who had been invited into Denmark. He reported that previously, proselyting against the Lutheran Church had not been permitted. He wrote of the prior persecutions of Mr. Mønster who had been imprisoned six different times for a total jail time of three years. Elder Snow reported that French philosophy, infidelity, and republican principles were increasing in Copenhagen and throughout Denmark. Then he wrote that at the death of the old king, the heir to the throne had been held at bay until a new constitution or "Grundlov" was adopted, ratified, and signed 5 June 1849. The constitution created the Rigsdag, or parliament, which resulted in as much political freedom for the Danes as was enjoyed presently in England. He indicated the outlook for religious freedom was not so good for Norway and Sweden. He described the Danes as a kind and hospitable people, who were given to a higher tone of morality than existed among the corresponding classes in England and America, and that if he was not mistaken in his feelings, the "Lord has many people among them." He wrote that many of the believers had received visions, dreams, and manifestations of the Holy Spirit, and that some reported they had seen, in vision, the missionaries before they came.[19]

On Tuesday, 24 September 1850, Elders Snow, Dykes, Forsgren, and Hansen spent the day in a council meeting in the spirit of prayer. During that meeting, "agreeable to the admonitions of the Holy Ghost,"[20] it was determined that Elder Hansen should commence the revision and rewriting of the Book of Mormon with an eye toward preparing it for publication. Peter O. Hansen's first effort at translating the Book of Mormon after his arrival at Nauvoo had centered heavily on Christ's resurrected ministry among the inhabitants of ancient America. Elder Snow would travel to England to procure the means needed to publish the Danish translation. Elder Forsgren was to labor in and around Copenhagen, while Elder Dykes was to proceed to Aalborg to open the work on Jutland.

One 1850 convert was Dorothea Christiane Thranum Christensen. That same September 24, she brought her 18-year-old son, an art student, Carl Christian Anton Christensen, to the home of Peter Bcckström to hear Elder Dykes on the matter of religion. Dykes lived at the Beckström home. It was late when he returned. The conversation terminated after an hour when young Christensen requested baptism. On 26 September 1850, just two days later, C. C. A. Christensen was baptized by Elder George Dykes in the waters of The Sound just north of Copenhagen.[21] Similar approaches of finding dissenter congregations and meeting in homes were used in Aalborg, and a second branch of the Church was established. With increasing strength, and using some of the new converts as missionaries, the missionaries spread across Denmark and over the Skagerrak to Risor, Norway by September 1851. Among those effective missionaries called to Norway was C. C. A. Christensen, who served as president of the Brevig Conference from 1855 to 1857.

On Monday, 26 April 1852, Willard Snow, a brother of Erastus Snow, arrived in Copenhagen to assume the presidency of the mission. In July, he received a letter from Johan F. F. Dorius which told of difficulties in Vendsyssel. Dorius had been holding a missionary meeting at the home of a local farmer. Lawless men came into the farmer's home and began pricking Dorius with awls, breaking up the meeting. Having succeeded in driving Dorius from the house, they vigorously pursued him, beating him with sticks and clubs, soiling his clothes with his own blood. Johan was able to make it into another home where he was washed, anointed with oil, and put to bed. The mob broke into the second home, tore away the bedding covering Dorius, and dragged him into the fields with the manifest intention of throwing the nearly naked missionary into a nearby creek. An unseen power prevented them from carrying out their design, and the mob dispersed. Dorius reported that he was healed by the power of God so that he was able to preach and baptize the next morning.[22] The awls used to attack Dorius were pointed hand tools with sharp, fluted blades. Awls were used for piercing leather and wood. Depending on how hard they struck him, the wounds could have been an inch or more deep. Given their usual use, the possibility of tetanus infection was real. Perhaps the bleeding spared him that. Considering those factors, his rapid recovery seems miraculous.

In August 1852 the Brevig Norway Conference was organized with Christian J. Larsen as president. Among others, Larsen was assisted by Elders Johan F. F. Dorius, Johan August Ahmanson, and Ole Olsen, all recent Scandinavian converts. Jeppe P. Folkman, a priest from Bornholm, Denmark, was one of those sent to Norway to assist with the labor.[23] A number of highly effective missionaries were called from among the new converts and the work gained in momentum and intensity.

Two early converts were Icelanders, Thorarinn Halflidason Thorason[24] and Gudmund (Gudmandur) Gudmundsen. Gudmundsen, born 23 March 1823 to pious parents, was the youngest of ten children. He had come to Denmark at age 16 to learn goldsmithing. Following completion of his apprenticeship, he continued on in Copenhagen where he had worked for some seven years as a goldsmith when he learned of the Mormons. One Sabbath day he attended a Mormon worship service where Elder Erastus Snow and his companions spoke. Gudmundsen believed the doctrines they taught, declaring as Paul had done anciently, that the gospel of Christ was the power of God unto salvation. He was baptized 15 February 1851 by Peter O. Hansen. At an 18 April 1851 fast meeting held in Copenhagen, Gudmund Gudmundsen was ordained a teacher by Erastus Snow and called to preach the gospel in Iceland. His companion was Thorarinn H. Thorason who had been ordained a priest. They returned to Iceland. During his years in Denmark, Gudmund's parents had died. While his brothers and sisters rejected his message, several others believed. Thorason baptized a husband and wife, Benedikt and Westmanöen Hanson. In consequence of this success, Icelandic legal authorities prohibited further open preaching and confined the missionary effort to those who would hear them in private. However, the missionaries were not subjected to mob violence, for the Icelanders abhorred lawlessness. At some point, Thorason ceased active missionary work when he encountered opposition of a different type. Mrs. Thorason hardened her heart against her husband's religious labors and burned his books.[25]

During December 1851, Thorason accidentally drowned in a fishing accident. For a time Gudmundsen labored alone. He was left with two baptized but unconfirmed members. Gudmundsen wrote Copenhagen reporting the death of his companion and stating that 24 individuals desired baptism. Elder Snow was saddened by the report. In addition to mourning Thorason's death, he was troubled by the memory that when he had ordained young Gudmundsen a teacher, the Spirit had whispered that he should ordain him an elder, but he had given the inspiration no heed, for the young man seemed so lively and enthusiastic, whereas Thorason appeared more thoughtful and reserved. Elder Snow turned his thoughts toward a suitable replacement. Peter O. Hansen volunteered to go to Iceland. When he applied for a Icelandic visa, Copenhagen officials discovered that Hansen was going to Iceland to serve as a missionary and denied him the necessary papers.[26] Gudmundsen remained without authority to baptize until Elder Johan Peter Lorentzen[27] arrived with instructions to ordain Gudmundsen an elder. Gudmundsen served in Iceland from April 1851 to July 1854. Nine individuals were baptized as a consequence of his service in Iceland.[28]

The Latter-day Saint faith encountered opposition and met with serious detractors. Unless someone is seeking a better, more fulfilling way, with an enhanced measure of Divine assurance that his life is pleasing to God, there is resentment when another suggests that what he has previously believed is incomplete. Religion has the capacity to evoke powerful emotions. If those emotions are not held in check by love, tolerance, gentleness, patience, long-suffering and brotherly kindness, then attitudes which reflect mistrust, misunderstanding and ignorance can dominate. Where negative attitudes persist toward those who believe differently regarding the salvation of the soul, then abuse and persecution can result. On 22 June 1851 a mob vandalized the small hall in Aalborg, Jutland, where the Latter-day Saints met. The branch president, Hans Peter Jensen, the owner of a manufacturing business, had been a leader in another faith prior to his conversion. When Elder Dykes returned from Hamburg to check on the branch's progress he was astonished to find the door ripped from its hinges, part of the walls torn down and the interior strewn with wreckage. A policeman summoned Elder Dykes to the mayor's office. The mayor warned the missionary to get out of Aalborg, that he could not promise protection for an hour. Dykes quickly boarded a steamer bound for Copenhagen.[29] Hans Peter Jensen's life was also in peril; he fled Aalborg to save his life. Despite the difficulties, the branch continued to grow. Among those who joined the Church in Aalborg in 1851 were Christen Jensen Olsen, his wife, Anne Nielsen Pedersen, and their family, including Christen, Anne Kirsten, Metta, Christina, Karen Marie, and Nicoline.[30]

In Norway, teachers of religion formed the principal opposition to the Mormon elders. Unable to prevent the loss of members of their flocks to the new faith by argument or Biblical rebuttal, not infrequently, the clergy turned to civil authorities and officers of the law for assistance.[31] Elders Johan Ahmanson and Jeppe Folkman spent four days in jail in Brevik, Norway, in September 1852. The Norwegian authorities in Frederikstad confiscated the passports and ordination certificates of Elders Larsen and Dorius. Missionaries Svend and Christian Larsen were jailed in Frederikstad Prison. Instead of the damp, dark cell they had envisioned, the Larsens where placed upstairs in the citizen's room, the equivalent of an American debtor's prison. With them were a Jacobsen and a Jensen, two Methodist dissenters, professional ship captains, who in their religious zeal had been jailed for disturbing the peace. Elders Svend and Christian Larsen had been incarcerated for similarly trumped-up charges.

During the course of their missionary service in mid October 1852, Svend and Christian J. Larsen stayed overnight at the home of Emil Larsen in Vaterland. They had "scarcely got up the next morning when the Underbyfoged, or mayor's deputy, a Mr. Fjeldstad, accompanied by a police officer appeared." The elders were requested to accompany these officers to the mayor's office. Upon entering, they were informed they were prisoners. When Christian Larsen asked on what charge, he was informed that it was because he had administered the sacrament and preached. He asked for the privilege of getting his clothes and arranging his affairs. The officers said he could send for his clothes. Recognizing that further protestation would be fruitless, Christian accompanied the officers to the courthouse where he was remanded to the Borgerarresten or citizen's jail. Svend was retained at the mayor's office where he was requested to explain the principles of Mormon belief. In a straightforward manner, Elder Larsen accommodated their request. To his surprise, his testimony regarding the Restoration and its associated doctrinal explanations did not change officialdom's attitude toward the missionaries. The mayor announced: "I am compelled to arrest you. You will have to follow the officers." Svend Larsen had neither baptized nor administered the sacrament in that region. He was convicted by the power of his personal witness. To the mayor Elder Larsen declared: "If it were not that I am being arrested for the sake of the testimony of Jesus Christ, you would find it no easy task to get me into prison." He then willingly went to prison where he and Christian would be held for the next five and one-half months. Of their imprisonment, Christian Larsen wrote: "I rejoice at being counted worthy to suffer for the gospel's sake, like my co-religionists in far-off America; but I felt grieved in my spirit when I thought of the many noble souls who were anxious to learn the many things pertaining to the kingdom of God, and that I was now deprived of the opportunity to instruct them."[32] It may have been that Christian Larsen was familiar with Acts 5:40-41 which, in part, reads: *And when they had called the apostles, and beaten them, they commanded that they should not speak in the name of Jesus, and let them go. And they departed from the presence of the council, rejoicing that they were counted worthy to suffer shame for his name.*

It was not long before they were joined by others. The next day, Saturday, October 16, Elder Johan F. F. Dorius was arrested and taken to Frederikstad court at noon where he was sentenced to prison. Officer Fjeldstad conducted him to jail. In the afternoon their number grew again with the incarceration of Elder Peter Beckström who had been arrested in Vaterland. Again, Fjeldstad was the jailer. To his credit, he, his wife, and family treated the prisoners kindly, granting them all privileges possible under the law.[33]

Johan Andreas Jensen[34] was born 16 November 1795 near Frederikstad, Norway. When he was five years old his father died. He went to sea and during the next 25 years rose from cabin boy to the captaincy of a large ship. His voyages took him to nearly all parts of the world. In 1849, Captain Jensen became deeply impressed with religion. He must have been inspired with Jesus' admonition for he gave nearly all of his goods to the poor and followed Him. In zealously preaching repentance, he rebuked the king and the state church. Jensen's religious fervor vigorously stirred the ire of the civil authorities, who cast him into prison, thereby giving him time to consider his ways.

The first Latter-day Saint converts in Norway had come from the Methodist dissenter group to which the captains Jacobsen and Jensen belonged. When the somewhat cantankerous Jacobsen was transferred elsewhere, Captain Jensen, still imprisoned, embraced the gospel. He had been moved by the elders singing the songs of Zion and their subsequent testimonies of the truth of what they taught. On Sunday 24 April 1853, Johan Jensen was moved to tears and with great emotion declared his conviction that what they had taught him was true. Upon his release from prison, Johan Andreas Jensen was baptized.[35] The five and one-half months the elders spent in prison were highly fruitful. Others heard their singing on New Year's Eve. (For a time all of the elders assigned to Norway were imprisoned at Frederikstad.) Carl Widerborg, a merchant, heard their message and argued at the capital for their release even before he was baptized a member of The Church of Jesus Christ of Latter-day Saints. If the civil authorities believed they could slow or stop the work from progressing, they were mistaken. The Frederikstad Branch doubled in size during the time the elders were incarcerated.[36] The jailer's daughter, Grete Sophie Fjeldstad, was among those who joined the Church. Grete's niece, Jacobine Erika Ask,[37] who was largely raised in the jailer's residence, was baptized in 1863 and immigrated to Utah in 1875. Unwittingly, by providing food and housing for the jailed elders, the Norwegian government had subsidized the Mormon missionary effort.

By legislative action or governmental policy, the Scandinavians had, in large measure, allied themselves with the church which had come of Martin Luther's efforts to reform the Catholic Church. Religion became the sole prerogative of a state church. Those who joined other faiths were seen as law breakers. The advent of Latter-day Saint missionary work in Norway brought particularly severe opposition. Not only were missionaries arrested and imprisoned for preaching, converts also were arrested and cast into prison, or put into the stocks for having joined the Church.[38] In 1853, the Supreme Court of Norway ruled that Latter-day Saints were not to receive the legal protection granted to other dissenting Christian faiths. The preaching of Mormonism and the performance of its gospel ordinances were offenses punishable by fines and imprisonment.[39] There was determined resistance to a new doctrine which said that in America there had been a restoration of the gospel of Jesus Christ. Norwegian authorities who thought such drastic measures as jailing the Latter-day Saint missionaries in Frederikstad prison[40] would stop the preaching of gospel had missed the relevant lesson recorded in The Acts of the Apostles. In a similar situation, the venerable Gamaliel had spoken plainly to the Pharisees and Sadducees. With directness he commanded the Jewish leadership to put the apostles forth a little space . . . *Refrain from these men, and let them alone: for if this counsel or this work be of men, it will come to naught: But if it be of God, ye cannot overthrow it.*[41] Converts and missionaries went courageously forward. Great things would be asked of them, and great things were willingly given.

Elder C. C. A. Christensen was jailed in Drammen, Norway, in March 1855 for preaching the restored gospel. Elder Johan F. Dorius was also arrested on similar charges about the same time. Magistrates frequently fined the Mormon missionaries for preaching the gospel and baptizing their converts. When unable or unwilling to pay the fine, the missionaries were allowed to "atone for the fine by bread and water imprisonment."[42] Christensen spent his time reading ecclesiastical history in order to become a more effective missionary. He composed poetry on the walls of his cell. In Christiania, police officers became increasingly friendly. They said: "Let the Mormons alone; they are peaceable and well disposed; they do not make us any trouble."[43] Jailers seemed to become more tolerant. Over time, some officers developed a grudging respect for the Mormon elders as they saw new converts abandon alcoholic beverages and other vices and become upright citizens. Jesus had provided the test for determining religious truth when He admonished skeptical listeners, that *if any man will do his will, he shall know of the doctrine, whether it be of God, or whether I speak of myself.*[44] As their fellow countrymen adhered to a rigorous standard of personal conduct, numbers of local officials began disregarding sanctions against the Mormons, allowing them an increasing degree of religious freedom. Norwegian district magistrate, Niels Torbjornsen of Kil, not only refused to jail the missionaries, but was converted to the new faith by their preaching despite the opposition of his son who succeeded him in the civil post.[45]

When Gudmund Gudmundsen returned from missionary service in Iceland he continued to serve in Denmark. While laboring in Kalundborg, he was arrested and imprisoned for seven weeks. When his accusers were unable to establish any case against him other than he had preached the gospel and baptized several people, he was released from prison and, against his will, immediately drafted into the army. The Kalundborg police conducted him to Copenhagen where he was issued a uniform, firearm, and saber and placed in military training. The imprisonment had left him physically out of condition, and Gudmund found Danish military training "exceedingly hard."[46] After 13 months of military duty his friends raised and gave him three rigsdaler[47] to buy an exemption from further military duty. When Danish authorities refused to accept the three rigsdaler, he gave the money to the poor. At some point, Gudmundsen became ill and was hospitalized. He used the hospital time to preach the gospel to his ward-mates. Among his converts was an army corporal whom he baptized before leaving the hospital. After a lengthy hospital stay, the physician and battalion general pronounced Gudmundsen unfit for military service because of a weakness of his lungs.[48] It was a fortuitous misdiagnosis. Among Gudmundsen's Danish converts were Niels Jorgensen Garff, Marie Jacobsen Garff, and their family.

In a Scandinavian Mission conference which commenced 28 December 1854 Elder Erik G. Erikson, who had been laboring in Sweden, reported that he had met with considerable opposition from the clergy and the civil authorities. He declared that Sweden was a difficult place to labor "because the laws would not permit men to worship according to doctrines laid down in the Bible." Nevertheless, there had been some success in Sweden's middle provinces, and one convert had been baptized in Stockholm.[49]

The Scandinavian winter of 1854-55 was bitterly cold. The sea waters of The Sound froze entirely over. The ice was of sufficient thickness that people could cross the frozen strait between Sweden and Sjælland on foot or even with teams. At its narrowest place, the strait is about 16 miles wide. The frozen sea prevented the arrival of various goods, causing shortages with resultant higher prices. It was the middle of April before sea traffic could continue from Copenhagen, and still later before steamers could run regularly between Stockholm and Christiania. The halting of sea traffic must have been a major factor contributing to high unemployment among the laboring class. Consequently, the laboring class suffered considerably. Many of the new Latter-day Saint converts were poor, their circumstances difficult.[50] In the midst of these tremendous difficulties, seemingly there were those who remembered and were comforted by the instruction Moses had given anciently, *When thou art in tribulation . . . turn to the Lord thy God [and be obedient to His voice] For the Lord thy God is a merciful God, he will not forsake thee . . ."*[51]

Devoted missionaries were undeterred by the terrible winter. Elder Canute Peterson departed from Stavanger on Norway's west coast 11 November 1854. His eastward journey to Christiania took him over the peninsula's rugged, snow-covered Telemark mountains. There was no other way to reach the Norwegian headquarters of the Scandinavian Mission. On 2 January 1855 he and Knud Nielsen, whom he had hired as a guide, traveled 45 miles through the mountains on snowshoes. It was a cold blustery day. The drifting snow made the journey perilous. The exertions of that day negatively impacted his health ever after. Arriving in Christiania, Elder Peterson assumed the presidency of the Brevig Conference.[52]

The missionary work pushed into the Danish countryside. Among the forests and fields of Sjælland were the thatched-roofed houses of Sorø, Denmark. In 1855, Latter-day Saint missionaries found and taught Hans and Ellen Christensen and her sons the restored gospel at Ellen's ancestral home, Nykobbel. On 11 May 1856 the new converts went to a nearby pond at night and were baptized members of The Church of Jesus Christ of Latter-day Saints. The clergy, their neighbors and perhaps relatives were disappointed at their choice of a faith. Yet, despite opposition, Sorø must have been a place rich in the believing blood of Israel. In 1856, Christen Dalsgaard, a Danish artist, painted "Mormon Prædikanter" [Mormon Preachers] and in part, said of it: "Two Mormons in their wandering have come to a carpenter's cottage in the country where by preaching . . . they seek to win adherents." An etching of this painting on display in 1994 at the Wilford Woodruff Building of the LDS Missionary Training Center in Provo, Utah, identified the scene as "Sorø 1856." Arnold Friberg has done a modernization of Dalsgaard's work. "Nykobbel House of Sorø" is similar to the cottage portrayed in Dalsgaard's painting.

The Book of Mormon was first published in English in 1830. Twenty-one years later, on 22 May 1851, the last sheets of the Danish translation were turned over to F. E. Bording, a Copenhagen binder. Bording had agreed to print 3,000 copies for 1,000 rigsdaler, or about $500 U.S. Elders Hansen and Snow had worked at the task for seven months. While Addison Pratt and others had been called to the French Polynesian Mission in the South Pacific, apparently no translation of the Book of Mormon had been undertaken there. Elders Snow and Hansen had been assisted in the Danish translation by a Miss Mathiesen, a teacher of several languages who subsequently joined the Church. Neither missionary's written account gave her first name, although an Ane Cathrine Mathiesen was listed on the records of the Copenhagen Branch in 1851. To what extent her assistance helped is not clear. Elder Hansen was of the opinion that she wanted it written in the popular style, and he was decidedly opposed to such a rendition.[53]

On 18 April 1857 a company of Scandinavian Latter-day Saints sailed from Copenhagen aboard the 238-ton *L. N. Hvidt*,[54] bound for England. The journal of Nicholai Sorensen indicates the *L. N. Hvidt* lay at Larsen's dock—probably a part of the Custom House Wharf, the usual point of departure in the 1850s. In addition to being the chief port, Copenhagen[55] was the Scandinavian headquarters of the Church from 1850 to 1905.

United by a common faith, varying challenges would confront some of the Scandinavian Latter-day Saint passengers that morning. For example, Ola Nielson Liljenquist was a master tailor and a burgher of Copenhagen. Liljenquist had served a number of years as a Scandinavian missionary. From 1853 to 1857, he presided over the Copenhagen Conference. He performed another great service for the Church by personally underwriting passport security for many Latter-day Saints during the 1852-57 period. Liljenquist could have been imprisoned for underwriting expenses beyond his personal ability to cover such costs as were incurred in Copenhagen by Latter-day Saints bent on going to Zion. Audaciously, he staked his reputation with Copenhagen authorities and Danish passport officials in the matter of the Latter-day Saints being able to sustain themselves. Without adequate financial support in Copenhagen, the people would have been returned to their villages and towns at local expense. By 1857, the new converts had grown in reputation with Danish authorities who said they would rather have Liljenquist's endorsement than that of other wealthier men, for the Mormons cared for their own people, and they had never had the slightest difficulty with any individual he had sponsored. Counsel Gendrup of Denmark had handled some 900 Mormon passports. Often he had aided Ola N. Liljenquist when circumstances were difficult. On one occasion Gendrup said to him: "Mr. Liljenquist, should you arrive in a better heaven than I, will you not think of me?"[56] He said that as they were stepping into a cab, a horse-drawn hack, to drive down to the steamboat landing, a mob attempted to take their four children from him and his wife, Kristina. The mob would have succeeded had the police not intervened. Their children were Nicholai Theodore, Olaf Oscar, Clara J. Josephine, and three-month-old Harold (Harlad) Frithoif.[57] Liljenquist would serve as assistant interpreter for the voyage of the *Westmoreland*.

Three Olsen sisters, Karen Marie, Christina, and Nicoline, were among those who boarded the *L. N. Hvidt*. Other members of their immediate family had emigrated earlier. Their brother, Jens, as a lad of 14, had gone to America with John Erik Forsgren's Company on board the *Forest Monarch*. Their father, Christen J. Olsen, a very early Danish convert, had intended to take his entire family to Zion, and had sold his land and home to make the journey. Then he was called to serve a mission by Elder Erastus Snow. The financial sacrifice associated with that call eliminated the possibility that Christen could take his family to America together. In December 1853, Christen; his wife Anne; and daughters Mette (23), Elsa Marie (13), and Niels Christen (7) sailed from Aalborg for England. They were part of the Christian J. Larsen Company on board the *Jesse Munn* which sailed from Liverpool 3 January 1854 and arrived in New Orleans 20 February 1854. Mette died in early March 1854 as they were coming up the Mississippi River and was buried in St. Louis, Missouri. Karen Marie, Christina, and Nicoline had to remain in Denmark. They were to come later as their financial circumstances permitted.

As Karen Marie Olsen was to board the *L. N. Hvidt*, she met a test of a different type. She had a serious suitor of whom she was deeply fond. He was madly in love with her. He begged her not to go. He saw the whole venture as foolhardy and unnecessary. On that April day, he brought to the dock a bag of gold pieces. He pled that she not go and pledged to give her everything he owned if she would remain in Denmark and marry him. Given the affection she felt for him and the perilous nature of the long journey, it must have been a heart-wrenching decision. Karen knew of Mette's death, but may not have known that perhaps as many as 200 of a total of 700 Scandinavians of the Christian J. Larsen Company had died, many of them from cholera.[58] Nevertheless, the fire which burned within her soul outweighed the affectations of her heart. Karen Marie and her sisters were determined in their quest for Zion.[59]

Among others boarding the *L. N. Hvidt* was Jacob Bastian, born 14 March 1835 in Sunbyvester, Amager, Denmark. Amager is a small, arrowhead-shaped island, adjacent to and just south-southeast of Copenhagen. Bastian was a descendant of hardy Hollanders who had sought refuge in Denmark from Spanish oppression during the 17th Century. They had come to Denmark at the urging of Christian IV, King of Denmark. Christian IV was an active supporter of the Protestant cause. The Danish monarch also wanted the Dutch immigrants to produce farm products for Copenhagen, his capital.

Jacob's father, Bastian Sorensen, had been a seaman in his youth and early manhood. Sorensen used the moderate fortune made at sea to purchase a farm at Sunbyvester, Amager. His mother, Margaret Olsen, was a daughter of one of that island's landed gentry. Their marriage had been opposed by her family as they considered Bastian to be of lower social and economic status. He and Margaret had eleven children, of whom ten were sons. Jacob was the fifth child. Bastian Sorensen died in 1846. At 14, Jacob graduated from school and then spent six months studying the Bible under the direction of a Lutheran priest; following this, he was confirmed a member of the Lutheran Church. After the death of his mother in 1852, Jacob spent time as a ship's carpenter apprentice and as a ship's carpenter at sea.

Among his schoolmates was Gertrude Peterson, the daughter of a widow-broker. She had been his favorite partner in the dance and had been his "chosen lady" when he won the "barrel king" competition.[60] Gertrude was described as beautiful, intelligent and refined. In 1854, Gertrude was baptized a member of The Church of Jesus Christ of Latter-day Saints. Jacob initially was attracted to the Church because of his affection for her. (Her name is also given as Gjertrud Peterson and Petersen. Given her Danish origins, it may have been Pedersen.)

Jacob joined the Church in January 1856. He attempted to teach his brothers the gospel, but they ridiculed the notion that religion was more important than wealth and social station. Jacob and Gertrude determined they would marry and go to America. Because there was a state church in Denmark, they asked the Lutheran priest to perform the ceremony. The priest refused because they were Mormons. They must have remembered the Master's admonition to "turn the other cheek," for Jacob's conversion to Mormonism had not been shallow. He and Gertrude consecrated all of their means to the 7th Company to assist others who desired to go to Zion, but otherwise would not have been able to go.[61]

Anders Christian Christensen, was born 4 September 1808 at Mijgdale Hjorring, Denmark. His wife, Sophie Marie Petersen, was born 13 March 1814 at Snells, Triested, Denmark.

Anders received an elementary education after which he was apprenticed to a neighbor's farm. That approach was considered a superior method for gaining vocational experience, and was preferred over working on one's father's farm or going to college. Anders and Sophie, their daughter Anna Margreta, and son Peter Christian, joined the Church in 1854. They were owner/operators of a farm and two grist mills. For his time Anders was considered relatively well-to-do and was given the title of Anders Christian of Sharendal. For more than two years following their baptism they provided free board and lodging to all of the Mormon elders serving in their locality. They also had given the necessary means to enable six fellow Saints to immigrate to Zion. In 1857 others wanted to go who had no way to finance the journey. Once again, Anders and Sophie Marie provided the money for another six Latter-day Saints to go to America. Their generosity meant they would pull a handcart rather than cross the plains by wagon train. Just prior to their departure, the elders blessed them that "after their arrival in the 'promised land' Sophie Marie would be blessed with a son in spite of her advanced years."[62] Their oldest daughter, Christiania, decided to remain in Denmark. In an act of faith, they placed money in the bank to provide means sufficient for Christiania's immigration, should she choose to follow them to Zion.[63]

Mads Christensen and his family were from the village of Blands near the eastern shore of Lolland. Born March 24, 1825, to Christen Andersen and Karen Marie Hansen, Mads was the fifth of 13 children. In addition to learning the skills of carpentry and cabinet-making, Mads was a dairy farmer who grew hay and grain, primarily barley for livestock feed, and rye which was ground into flour at the village mill and used for bread making. Mads and his family made butter and cheese. The excess skim milk, whey, and buttermilk by-products, along with grain, were fed to raise their hogs. They also grew vegetables and fruit. They produced some flax for linen and kept some sheep for wool. Clothing, bed, and table linens were made by the womenfolk from these products. Geese and ducks were kept for meat and for their down feathers from which Danish families made featherbeds and duvets. Chickens were raised for eggs and meat. The excess production was sold at the town market or traded for goods and supplies needed by the family. The diet was supplemented with fish from the Baltic. Sustained rain at harvest time created problems with the grain crops. If conditions were seriously wet and humid as the grain approached maturity, they had to contend with ergot infection, a dark fungus which attacks the cereal's seeds. To prevent development of the fungal infection during wet years, the heads of grain had to be picked individually from the stalks of straw, placed in baskets and carried to the barns and house where they could be spread out to dry.[64]

The prolonged ingestion of ergot-contaminated cereal grains produces a toxicity in humans and livestock, called ergotism. It causes vasoconstriction by direct action on the muscles of the arterioles, thereby resulting in a reduced blood flow. Ultimately thrombosis develops. In cold climates, such as those of Scandinavia, the body extremities are predisposed toward developing gangrene. Ergot also acts to stimulate the central nervous system, which is then followed by depression. Therefore, care was taken to protect the grain crop for their health depended on it. Bread was a principal component of the daily diet. If made from flour which had been ground from contaminated grain, there would have been a prolonged ingestion of the fungus. Farms were not large, and farm families attempted to be self-sufficient. The season's grain crop would have been stored in a granary where it would be used until the following year's harvest. In short, the farmer would have drawn from the same source each time he went to the mill to have grain ground into flour. While they did not understand the biochemistry and physiology of the disease, they knew full well the dangers posed by ergot-infected grain, and consequently took great pains to avoid it.

Despite the heavy load of farm work, the children of Christen and Karen attended school from ages seven to fourteen. In those years the schools were administered by the

Lutheran Church, and the Lutheran tradition was deeply ingrained among the people.

Mads was deeply religious. His faith in God had been apparent from early childhood. He had been taught to pray and believed deeply in the efficacy of prayer. He went often to secluded places in the woods or near the seashore to offer up his oblations to God. He told of one such incident as follows:

"To the nearest of my recollection, when I was about ten years old, I was in the field when the Spirit moved me to go and pour out my soul in prayer to my God. In accordance to this spirit, I went into the woods to a secret place and bowed me down upon my knees and called upon God. My prayer was that I might have happiness of living on the earth in a time of the power of the Lord like it was in the days of Jesus and the apostles; a time when the same gifts and graces would be bestowed upon men and the spirit of revelation might again be sealed upon the children of men as in the days of Pentecost; a time when man could stand forth and testify to the goodness of God and be called upon by the power of God to prophesy in the name of Jesus of things yet to come. After my prayer I looked towards heaven and beheld the heavens open and it appeared to me that I beheld the Lord surrounded by many holy beings. This satisfied me for the time being."[65]

When Latter-day Saint missionaries came, Mads again turned to prayer and he accepted the new faith—the restored gospel appealed to him. Maren, his wife, did not oppose Mads in his enthusiastic choice of a new faith, but she was reluctant to abandon her church. However, she was decidedly opposed to those who fiercely opposed the missionaries. Once, when a mob gathered in Blands determined to flog a missionary, the elder ran to the Christensen home and requested that he be allowed to hide from his pursuers. Maren was home alone, but she took him in, locked the home's outside door and hid him in her wardrobe. By this time the mob had surrounded her home. Danish law severely punished those who forcibly entered the house of another. The mob kept trying to get her to open the door long enough so they could take the elder. Maren refused. The mob threatened to get an officer of the law to compel her to open her door. To that threat she replied that she respected the law and that if the appropriate authority came, she would open the door to him, but she would not condone violence or lawlessness. Some time passed while the mob talked among themselves. Ultimately they recognized they could not frighten her and they dispersed. After the last of the mob had gone, a thought flashed through her mind: "Had she suffocated the missionary by locking him in such a tight space?" Hurriedly opening the wardrobe, she found to her great relief that he was well and profoundly grateful for the protection she had provided.[66]

Mads and Maren's first child, a son, Rasmus Peter, was born 9 December 1856. His mother wanted him baptized and christened in the Lutheran church, but Mads would not consent. He said children were to be given a name and a blessing, but baptism was not performed until the child reached the age of accountability. Religion became a matter of serious reflection and searching prayer. On 23 January 1857 Mads, Maren, and Mads' mother, Karen Marie Hansen Andersen, were baptized members of The Church of Jesus Christ of Latter-day Saints by Elder Niels Rasmussen. When they determined to sell their farm and immigrate to Zion, Karen determined she would go with them. Their remaining time in Denmark was short. They were among those who boarded the *L. N. Hvidt*.[67]

A party of 41 Danish saints[68] had sailed from Rønne, on the island of Bornholm, 11 April 1857, on board the sloop *Ane Maria Kristina*. The sloop's skipper was Andreas Ellebye. Hans Kofoed (also variously spelled as Kofoed or Koefoed or Kofford) was a key leader among the Bornholm saints.[69] He had been very much involved with the missionary effort there. In a census taken when Hans was 22, his occupation was listed as "gunner;" he was a part of the Bornholm militia.[70] A Kofoed family tradition indicates he had been a hunting companion of the Prince of Denmark. While that is probably incorrect, there was a Royal Danish Hunting Preserve on the Isle of Bornholm.[71]

Hans brought his large family to America, including his 72-year-old mother, Else Kirstine Kofoed, who was blind. Hans' wife, Cecelia, was three months pregnant. With them were their nine living children and other family members.[72] According to the Emigration Register, Hans paid 1,320 Royal Dollars for his family's passage.[73]

The Kofoed family was from Arnager Branch, the cradle of Mormonism on Bornholm. It was at Arnager that the first five Latter-day Saint converts on Bornholm had been baptized. One of those five was Else Kirstine Kofoed. During the evening of 2 December 1851 the villagers of Arnager had defended the missionaries against a mob saying the elders had "taught them correct principles, therefore, we will defend them." Most of those men who defended the elders on that occasion joined the Church shortly thereafter and immigrated to Utah.

Tradition has it that Hans Kofoed had been a burgermeister, or mayor, at the appointment of the king. His handsome team of horses pulled his official surrey around the island.[74] One evening he came on a mob of people who were throwing eggs at two men. In the line of duty, he stopped the incident and learned the two men were Mormon elders. He took them to his home, arranged for them to clean up, and talked religion all night. Hans Kofoed believed and joined the Church.[75] The Danish census of 1855 provided for the declaration of religious affiliation. There were 175 inhabitants in 48 families residing in Arnager. Of those counted in the census, 63 individuals were Latter-day Saints.[76]

Kirstine Mathilde Funch from Bornholm would not turn 17 until May 2. If Kirstine was not an orphan, then she left all of her immediate family in Denmark. Her baptismal date of 30 June 1858 may be an indication that her decision to join the Mormon cause was not acceptable to her parents, that she had been required to leave home for the gospel's sake. Her conviction as to Mormonism's divine truth resulted in uncommon courage.

Other saints with Bornholm roots were shoemaker Jens N. Holm, his wife, Margreta, and their daughter, 13-year-old Margreta Christina; Niels Thuesen (Dorcheus), a carpenter, and his wife, Engelke Kirstine (Angelica Christine) Lund. Their children, John Nicolas (14), twin daughters, Laura Christine and Julia Margreta (11), and Anna Frederikka (7) seem to have been born at Copenhagen. The Thuesens had lost two sons in infancy. Their family had been baptized 23 December 1854. Unknown to them that day on the dock was that Julia would die in June.

Niels Otto Mortensen, his wife, Maren Kirstine, daughter, Maren, and son, Hans Peder, were among the emigrating Danish saints. They had known Erastus Snow during his service as mission president. Niels believed in the doctrine that the children of Israel were to be gathered to the mountains of Zion. He and Maren Kirstine were leaving the graves of two sons who had died as infants. Niels was a weaver and a well digger. Yet as hard as he worked, they had not been able to go altogether as a family, so two daughters had been sent with earlier companies. Anne Margrette, the first of Niels' family to become interested in the Church, had gone to America as a part of a Latter-day Saint company which had been under the leadership of Peter O. Hansen, one of the first four Scandinavian missionaries. The Hansen company crossed the Atlantic to New Orleans on board the *James Nesmith*. Anne Margrette traveled safely to Utah with an ox-team company.[77]

Unknown to Niels and his family, as they boarded the *L. N. Hvidt* that April morning, was the loss of their daughter, Bodil Malene. She had gone the year previous in the care of the Jens Nielsen family. Bodil and the Nielsens were members of the James G. Willie Handcart Company. A bitter early winter storm struck during the fall of 1856, catching the Willie Company in the high country of present-day Wyoming. The wind-driven snow had reached a depth of nearly two feet when the company halted at Rock Creek Hollow in a desperate attempt to find shelter from the terrible October storm. Nine-year-old Bodil went out to gather brush for kindling a fire. "Returning, she reached her cart, with the brush in her arm. There she died, frozen to death. Starvation and bitter cold drained from her emaciated body the life she had fought for."[78] Exacerbated by a lack of food and winter clothing, the bitterly cold weather contributed to the loss of 19 percent of the Willie Company. Bodil was buried in a common grave of 13 handcart pioneers who perished that awful night at Rock Creek Hollow. In the aftermath of the company's struggle for survival, someone failed to notify her parents.

Helsina Hjetting Bohne was a widow with four sons: Jens Carl J., Henrik Morten, Sophus Morten, and Joseph Smith, and daughter, Anna Sophia. Her children ranged in age from thirteen to two years old. Her single, 26-year-old younger sister, Mette Maria Hjetting, was among those who boarded the *L. N. Hvidt* that April morning. Helsina's husband, Carl Frederick Bohne, had died in the Baltic Sea near Russia in 1854. Yet in the future, Helsina would marry a second time to Svend Larsen, the former pilot whose boat, *The Lion of Zion*, plied the harbors of Denmark and Norway on missionary errands and who, as a consequence of his missionary preaching, had been jailed in Norway's Frederiktadt Prison.

There were Norwegian and Swedish saints. The Frantzen family were a part of a group of 31 Norwegian Latter-day Saints who had embarked 11 April 1857 from Kristiania (Oslo), Norway, on board the Norwegian steamship *Viken*. The sea was calm and the passage to Copenhagen took but one day.[79] Christopher Hultberg (Hulberg) and family were among those from Sweden. Copenhagen, the headquarters of the Scandinavian Mission, was the assembly point for the voyage to England. Hans and Ellen Christensen and her two sons, Poul and Niels, left Sorø in early April 1857 to be ready to go.[80] They may have been in the same Sorø group as the Nicholai Sorensen family.

Nicholai and his wife Line (Magdelena or Malena Olsen) Sorensen had nine of their children with them. Their oldest child, Catherine Sophie, baptized 29 March 1857, remained behind for a time. She and her husband, Andrew Andersen, followed them to Utah in 1858. They also left the graves of sons, Soren Christian, who had died at eleven years, and Nicolaisen, a boy who had been stillborn. Nicholai was a farmer and a wheelwright. For a time as a young man, he played violin in the Tivoli Orchestra of Copenhagen. His 60-acre farm was quite large for that time. They kept milk cows, horses, sheep, chickens, and grew hay and wheat. Nicholai employed both workmen and a dairy maid on his farm. He admitted apprentices to his shop where wagons and other farm implements were repaired in addition to the manufacture of coffins, new wagons, sleds, spinning wheels, etc.[81]

Their son, Isaac Sorensen, wrote that as a lad he had herded cows, sheep, and lambs, that he had learned to plow and harrow, mow hay with a scythe, and cradle wheat. He started school at age seven and went every other day until he was fourteen. He could read well before he began school. During his years of attendance he "learned considerable history, wrote a fairly good hand, and could solve all ordinary problems in arithmetic."[82] This was the extent of his formal schooling.

Nicholai and family were devout Lutherans when the Latter-day Saint missionaries found them. Isaac said the coming of the missionaries radically changed the aims and purpose of their lives. Over a period of several months, the entire family embraced the new faith. "Abraham and Isaac were baptized June 18, 1855; father, mother, and Marie in September; Jacob and Christian and Christina soon thereafter. Sena [Kristine or Stine] and Henry [Henrik] were not old enough then [to be baptized]." Peter [Peder] and Sophia were not converted until later. They were living away from home. Isaac wrote that his older siblings "were exposed to the usual ridicule which was by no means lacking in our neighborhood. Still, by degrees, the whole family working faithfully on them, they accepted the gospel and longed to go to Zion."[83]

NOTES

1. Isaiah 11:11-12.

2. William Mulder, *Homeward to Zion...*, p. 45.

3. *The Deseret News Church Almanac 1997-98*, pp. 316-17, states there was heavy persecution waged against members as the missionaries pushed into every corner of Denmark. In Aalborg in 1851, a mob vandalized the hall where the Latter-day Saints were meeting.

4. Deseret News 1997-98 *Church Almanac*, Salt lake City, Utah, 1996, p. 316.

5. A more detailed account of this mission can be found in Joseph Smith, *History of the Church*, Volume V, pp 394-95, published by the Church by Deseret Book Company, Salt Lake City, Utah, 1960.

6. William Mulder, *Homeward to Zion...*, p. 9.

7. William Mulder, *Homeward to Zion...*, p. 8.

8. Zachary Taylor's appointment of Walter Forward as Charge d' Affairs rather than Ambassador is politically intriguing, since as ranking diplomat he was effectively the acting ambassador.

9. Andrew Jenson, *History of the Scandinavian Mission*, Deseret News Press (1927), Salt lake City, Utah p. 6.

10. Karl N. Snow, Jr., "Erastus Snow: The Call to Denmark, the Mission and the Publication of the First Non-English translation of the Book of Mormon," a talk given to the Mormon History Association's annual meeting, held at Aalborg, Denmark 29 June 2000. Karl Snow cites Erastus Snow's Journal and the Biographical Directory of the American Congress as historical source material for activities in Washington, DC, and the first name of Senator Cooper. Senator Cooper was an attorney by profession. He had served in both the U.S. House and Senate. In 1850, he chaired the Senate Committee of Indian Affairs. Indications are that Cooper was familiar with the West and sympathetic to the Mormon petition for statehood. Karl N. Snow, Jr. is Erastus Snow's great grandson.

11. Erastus Snow, *One Year in Scandinavia*, Liverpool: Published by F. D. Richards, 15 Walton Street, 1851. Printed by R. James, South Castle Street. Taken from pp. 10-11, which are entitled, "An Extract from the Private Journal of E. Snow."

12. Andrew Jenson, *History of the Scandinavian Mission...*, p. 7.

13. Andrew Jenson, *History of the Scandinavian Mission...*, pp. 7-8.

14. Andrew Jenson, *History of the Scandinavian Mission...*, p. 8.

15. Andrew Karl Larson, *Erastus Snow: The Life of a Missionary and Pioneer for the Early Mormon Church*, The University of Utah Press, Salt Lake City, Utah (1971) pp. 212-13, 218.

16. Isaiah 2:2-3.

17. Andrew Karl Larson, *Erastus Snow...*, p. 219.

18. John Bodnar, *The Transplanted: A History of Immigrants in Urban America*, Indiana University Press, Bloomington, (1985), p. 17.

19. Andrew Jenson, *History of the Scandinavian Mission...*, pp. 8-9.

20. Andrew Jenson, *History of the Scandinavian Mission...*, p. 15.

21. Richard L. Jensen and Richard G. Oman, C. C. A. Christensen 1831-1912: *Mormon Immigrant Artist*, 1984, The Church of Jesus Christ of Latter-day Saints, Salt Lake City, Utah pp. 3-4. Andrew Jenson, *History of the Scandinavian Mission...*, pp. 15-16.

22. Andrew Jenson, *History of the Scandinavian Mission*, p. 55.

23. Andrew Jenson, *History of the Scandinavian Mission*, p. 57.

24. In some accounts the name Thorason is not given.

25. Andrew Jenson, *History of the Scandinavian Mission*, p. 25.

26. Andrew Jenson, *History of the Scandinavian Mission*, p. 25. Jenson uses the term passport, rather than visa. In today's parlance, passports are granted by the country in which one holds citizenship, and a visa is granted by diplomatic officers of the nation one wishes to visit. Iceland was a possession of Denmark until 1918, so Danish authorities were within their rights.

27. The Lorentzen name is given as Johan T. in a *Church News* editorial of February 3, 1979, but is given as Johan Peter on p. 78 of Andrew Jenson's *History of the Scandinavian Mission*. In the biography of Peter Niels Garff, an account written by his descendants, the name is given as John T. Sorensen.

28. *Peter Niels Garff*, a biographical account of his life written by his descendants, see pp. 13-14. Privately published by the family of George Peter and Tryphena B. Garff. January 1983. A copy is in possession of Peter Niels Garff's great grandson, Robert Garff.

29. Arnold Irvine, *Deseret News* article under the date of 24 June 1967, headlined "Aalborg Mob Wrecks Mormon Chapel," dateline 22 June 1851.

30. Rebecca Wright Snow Payne, *A Resume of the Life of my Grandmother*, [Karen Marie] *Caroline Olsen Wright*, privately published, June, 1978, p. 3.

31. Andrew Jenson, *History of the Scandinavian Mission*, Deseret News Press, Salt Lake City, Utah (1927) pp. 101-102.

32. Andrew Jenson, *History of the Scandinavian Mission*, pp. 62-63.

33. Andrew Jenson, *History of the Scandinavian Mission*, pp. 64-65

34. In 1984, one of Johan Andreas Jensen's great-grandsons, Elder Russell M. Nelson, was called as a member of the Quorum of the Twelve Apostles. Prior to his call to the apostleship Dr. Nelson had been a pioneering surgeon and researcher in the matter of open-heart surgery.

35. Russell Marion Nelson, *From Heart to Heart, An Autobiography*; in Chapter 2, "From Europe to Ephraim," p. 7.

36. Don H. Smith, E-mail copy of a paper on "Johan August Ahmanson" given at the Mormon History Association meetings in 1999, pp. 3-4 of 8 pages.

37. John M. Madsen of the First Quorum of the Seventy is one of Jacobine Erika's descendants. Don H. Smith, "Johan August Ahmanson...," p. 5 of 8.

38. *Deseret News Church Almanac 1997-98*, p. 369. One can get a flavor of the persecution by reading "Love Is Its Own Reward" by Laird Roberts in the February 1978 issue of the *New Era*. This article is a fictionalized account of a true incident in family genealogical records.

39. Richard L. Jensen and Richard G. Oman, *C.C.A. Christensen 1831-1912: Mormon Immigrant Artist*, Op cit., p. 6.

40. Ronald T. Halverson, Personal Communication, 13 December 2000.

41. Acts 5:34, 38-39.

42. Andrew Jenson, *History of the Scandinavian Mission*, p. 103. The fines as recorded in Jenson's history are given in "speciedaler."

43. Andrew Jenson, *History of the Scandinavian Mission*, p. 103.

44. John 7:17.

45. Jensen and Oman, *C.C.A. Christensen 1831-1912...*, pp. 6-9.

46. Peter Niels Garff, *A Biographical Account...*, p. 15.

47. Count Ulrik Ahlefeldt-Laurvig of Denmark states the Rigsdaler was derived from the German Reichstaler which was the head coin in Germany and Northern Europe. The Scandinavian coin-convention set the value of 1 Rigsdaler as equal to 2 Danish Kroner. The exchange rate as of this date is 1 U.S. dollar equals 8.40 Danish Kroner. Personal communication, 29 April 2001.

    A Rigsdaler was a large silver coin used in Denmark during the 18th and 19th centuries. It was derived from the German Reichstaler of the 16th century and ranged in value from 50 cents to over one dollar U.S. currency. Initially worth three Danish marks, the rigsdaler later increased in value to four and finally to six marks. Each mark was worth 16 skillings and a skilling was worth 12 pennings or three hvid.

    Source materials for the possible value of the "rigsdaler" were *Webster's New 20th Century Dictionary of the English Language*, The World Book Company, New York, 1941, p. 1471, see "rixdollar" and coinage information provided courtesy of The Royal Danish Consulate General, 10877 Wilshire Blvd., Suite 1105, Los Angeles, California 90024, telephone 310-443-2090. Mulder's Homeward to Zion, Op cit., p. 78 gives the value two rigsdaler to one U.S. dollar.

48. Peter Niels Garff, *A Biographical Account...*, p. 15.

49. Andrew Jenson, *History of the Scandinavian Mission*, p. 101.

50. Andrew Jenson, *History of the Scandinavian Mission*, p. 102.

51. Deuteronomy 4:30-31.

52. Andrew Jenson, *History of the Scandinavian Mission...*, pp. 102-103. Jenson states on p. 78 the Norwegian Mission was known as the Brevig Conference.

53. Karl N. Snow, Jr., *"Erastus Snow, The Call to Denmark...,"* pp. 7-9; endnote 28.

54. Conway B. Sonne, *Saints on the Seas: A Maritime History of Mormon Migration 1830-1890*, University of Utah Press, Salt Lake City, 1983, p. 41. A screw steamer is driven by a screw propeller, an early form of a ship's propeller, where an Archimedes screw is used to produce thrust by accelerating a flow of water.

   The *L. N. Hvidt* was an iron hull screw steamer with three masts, one funnel, and overall measurements of 171' x 23' x 11'. Owned by the General Danish Screw Steamship Company of Copenhagen, she had been built by James Henderson & Son at Renfrew, Scotland, and apparently was first launched in 1857. Renfrew has long been noted as a place of shipbuilding and boiler making.

55. Carsten Gram. *Church News* of September 18, 1993, p. 8. *Deseret News*, Salt Lake City, Utah.

56. This quotation is from Liljenquist's personal journal which was quoted by William Mulder, *Homeward to Zion...*, p. 130.

57. *Autobiography of Ola Nielson Liljenquist, Westmoreland* (April 1857) *Mormon Immigration Index–Personal Accounts*. The full names of the children and their birth years are given in the ship's roster as posted in the *Mormon Immigration Index*, The Church of Jesus Christ of Latter-day Saints.

58. *Mormon Immigration Index–Personal Accounts, Jesse Munn* (January 1854), *Autobiography of Svend Larsen and Reminiscences and Diary of Hans Jensen Hals.*

59. Rebecca Wright Snow Payne, *A Resume of the Life...*, pp. 4-6.

60. According to Arthur L. Crawford who wrote a biographical sketch of his grandfather, Jacob Bastian, Jacob had entered dancing school at age nine. At 12, he and his partner were one of four couples selected to dance before the Crown Prince of Denmark. Three times he won the honor of Barrel King, a competition associated with an annual Danish holiday. A cat was placed into a sealed barrel and suspended some 10 feet in the air. Competitors mounted on fast horses would ride at the barrel and strike it with a cudgel. The one successful in striking it the hardest freed the cat and was named the "Barrel King." His chosen lady would then advance, place a crown on his head, and decorate him with her colors. *Biographical Sketch of the Life of Jacob Bastian* by Arthur L. Crawford, March 1917. Bastian died 22 April 1924. A copy of this

sketch was provided by the Charles Castleberry family of Sandy, Utah.

61. Arthur L. Crawford, *Jacob Bastian...*, p. 2.

62. Eileen C. Cooke, Personal Communication, 17 May 2001. Eileen C. Cooke is a great granddaughter of Anders Christian and Sophie Marie Christensen. Her grandfather, Anton Christopher Christensen was born 5 November 1859 in Riverdale, Utah. Eileen Cooke said the blessing pronounced on her great grandparents by the elders is an oral tradition in their family. No doubt it was remembered because of its remarkable nature, for all indications were that she was well past her time for child bearing; she was 45 years and 8 months of age when Anton Christopher was born, 20 years since the birth of her previous child.

63. *A Sketch of the Lives of Anders Christian Christensen and His Wife, Sophie Marie Christensen*, pp. 1-2. This manuscript is privately held by his descendants and used courtesy of Eileen C. Cooke and her brothers, Val R. Christensen and Allan R. Christensen. Christiania Sophie was born 31 August 1834. She was baptized a member of The Church of Jesus Christ of Latter-day Saints on 19 September 1855, four months after the baptisms of her parents and siblings.

64. Phyllis Christensen, *Mads Christensen 1825-1914.*, pp. 1-2. An undated manuscript in possession of descendants of Mads Christensen family members who provided a copy to the author.

Large gas-fired grain dryers are a technology developed in the latter half of the 20th Century. However, even now such technology is not an affordable option for small farmers in the Third World. For example, Filipino farmers dry their threshed rice on the paved roads of their province during the hot, sunny part of the day.

65. Phyllis Christensen, *Mads Christensen...*, p. 4.

66. Phyllis Christensen, *Mads Christensen...*, pp. 4-5.

67. Phyllis Christensen, *Mads Christensen...*, p. 5.

68. According to Jimmy B. Parker (*The Life Story of Hans Ancher Kofoed*, Privately Published 1982, pp. 21-22) the Bornholm newspaper states there were 41 Latter-day Saints while 39 Saints are listed in the Scandinavian Mission's "Emigration Register." Parker quoted the Bornholm news article as follows: "Last Saturday between two o'clock and three o'clock P.M. 41 Mormons sailed from Rønne (Bornholm) to Copenhagen with the sloop *Ane Marie Kirstine* with Skipper Andreas Ellebye. They were from different places on the island and were on the way to the Mormon State of Utah in North America. One man had besides a wife and nine children (some of whom were sick), his old and blind mother with him on this long and dangerous journey."

69. Count Ulrik Ahlefeldt-Laurvig writes that today "there are very good Royal Hunting Grounds on Bornholm. It has always been a tradition that the Royal family, now the Prince, each year goes to Bornholm on

the Royal Yacht to shoot roe deer." Personal communication, April 29, 2001.

Jimmy B. Parker, *The Life Story of Hans Ancher Kofoed...*, p. iii, states that Kofoed is the spelling that Hans apparently preferred and used it for most of his life. The Mormon Immigration Index gives the spelling as Kofod. Except for the immigration information in the appendices, this account will use the spelling preferred by Hans and his descendants.

70. Jimmy B. Parker, *The Life Story of Hans Ancher Kofoed*, Privately Published, 1982, p. 3.

71. Scandinavia has two kinds of deer, the lordly red deer and the agile, smaller roe deer which is very graceful and an accomplished jumper. According to Ronald T. Halverson (Personal Communication 30 April 2001) they are very much like the deer in America, only smaller. The difference in size is similar to the difference in size between America's White-tailed deer and its Mule deer. The latter is so named because of its large ears.

72. Jimmy B. Parker, personal communication 25 April 2001. Parker has been a professional family researcher and has researched and written extensively *The Life Story of Hans Ancher Kofod*. Parker said the Lieutenant General role which is Kofod family tradition has not been proven.

73. Jimmy B. Parker, *The Life Story of Hans Ancher Kofoed...*, p. 22.

74. Jimmy B. Parker, *The Life Story of Hans Ancher Kofoed...*, p. 13.

75. Jimmy B. Parker, *The Life Story of Hans Ancher Kofoed...*, p. 13. While the tradition of Hans being a mayor has come down through several branches of the Kofod family, it has not been definitely proven. However, it does seem to be quite certain that Hans defended the missionaries.

76. Jimmy B. Parker, *The Life Story of Hans Ancher Kofoed...*, p. 16.

77. History of Niels Otto Mortensen of Systofte, Denmark. The sources for this eight-page historical sketch are given as Eleanor Bruhn, Mae Wilden, Margaret Dustin, Samuel Carson Mortensen, Frank Otto Mortensen, Vern C. Mortensen, Virginia Mortensen Lowe, and the Journal of the Iron County Mission. A copy was provided to the author by Marlene Mortensen Burton, Parowan, Utah. Anne Margette is listed as Nielsen on the passenger roster of the James Nesmith, but in Utah followed the U.S. naming system and used the name Mortensen.

78. Gordon B. Hinckley, "True to the Faith," *The Ensign*, The Church of Jesus Christ of Latter-day Saints, May 1997, p. 66.

79. *Reminiscences and Journal of John Frantzen, Westmoreland* (April 1857), *Mormon Immigration Index–Personal Accounts*. In a 25 April 2001 telephone conversation, Jim Parker, who has researched and written of the *Westmoreland* company, said there were 31 Norwegian

Latter-day Saints. Conway B. Sonne's *Saints on the Seas: A Maritime History of Mormon Migration 1830-1890*, University of Utah Press, 1983, p.48 is the source of the sailing and arrival dates and the name of the steamship, *Viken*.

80. Clare B. Christensen, *The Life Story of Ellen Andersen Christensen*, p. 1, Christensen Family Files.

81. A. N. Sorensen, Editor, "The History of Isaac Sorensen: Selections From a Personal Journal." *Utah Historical Quarterly* XXIV:51, Utah State Historical Society, 337 State Capitol, Salt Lake City, Utah (1956).

82 Sorensen, *The History of Isaac Sorensen...*, p. 51.

83. Sorensen, *The History of Isaac Sorensen...*, p. 51.

Chapter 4

FAREWELL TO DENMARK

Nicholai Sorensen left a journal account which details the group's departure from Denmark. Beginning with the date of 14 April 1857, he recorded the following:

We left Haugerup. We got up at 4:30 A.M. We had plenty to do to pack all of our belongings. I was together with Jacob Nielsen at about 8:00 A.M. when some of the children came and made a very loud noise. So to make peace with these godless people, I had to give up my watch to the ringleader, a very lively girl that would not give up till she got her wishes fulfilled. We packed all our belongings on Jens Nielsen's wagon and left for the station. I, Peder, Abraham, Niels and Jens Johansen left to go to Sorø to get our passport in order in order to say farewell to some of our friends there. The time went quick and at 12:30 noon we were all ready. Jacob Jensen came with some of his family. We had a big snow storm on the way to the station. When we got to the station we were met by a large crowd of friends and relatives that came to bid us farewell. We had a good visit with them. -12:30 P.M. the train came and we all said a sad farewell to each other. We boarded the train and I lifted up little Stine so her Aunt Mette could see her for the last time. At least for a long time. We got to Copenhagen at 5:00 P.M. and stayed at a hotel located on Vestergade 16. Here we were made very welcome and had a very good time.[1]

April 15th. In Copenhagen we had plenty to do to take care of our luggage and money matters. We also had to buy some articles we needed. In the evening we all met for an evening prayer. This made me feel very good.

April 16th. I got up at 6:15 A.M. and finding out I forgot something back in Haugerup, I boarded the early train back there. I arrived back on the noon train having completed what I went to take care of. When I got back to Copenhagen our Maria was ill and we had to get a doctor.

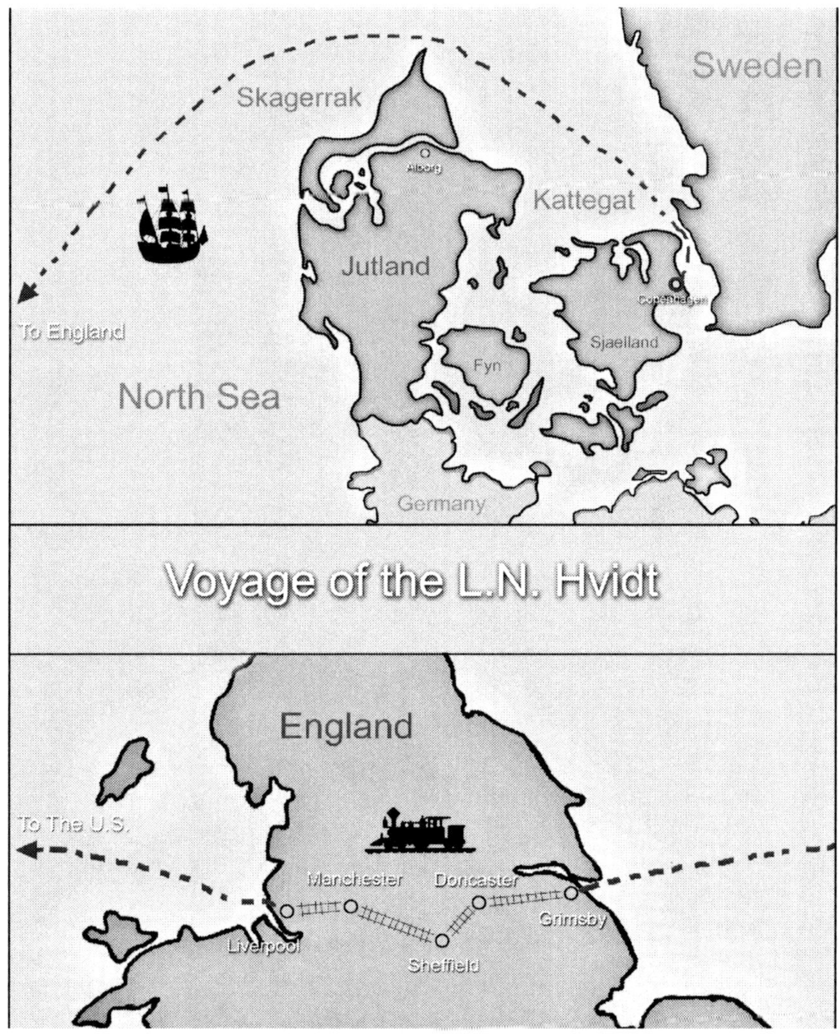

Map by Jeremy Munns

April 17th. We got up early and was very thankful to find out Maria was better. There was still some things to take care of.

For many, it had been necessary to come early. Mid-19th century transportation and communications meant more time was needed to get people assembled and organized, even though waiting in Copenhagen consumed much-needed finances. This is but a sample of those who boarded the ship that morning. Each family and each group must have had a unique story to tell. There must have been worries, doubts, anxieties. Yet, faith overcame fear.

Hector C. Haight,[2] president of the Scandinavian Mission, served as presiding officer for the 536 Latter-day Saints on board the *L. N. Hvidt*. These Latter-day Saint converts had great affection and respect for their church leaders and missionaries. Evidence of that love can be found in the names given to children born after the parents' conversion. For example, given names included the following: Erastusina, Haightina, Josephina Brighamina, Josephine, Joseph Smith, Hyrum Smith, John Willard, and Brigham Nephi.[3]

That April morning, 536 Latter-day Saints marched up the gangplank. Amid goodbyes and waving handkerchiefs, the *L. N. Hvidt* cast off its lines. Away from the fishing boats moored in Copenhagen's picturesque canals and out into The Sound steamed the *L. N. Hvidt*. The green tower of "Our Savior's Church,"[4] erected to commemorate the triumph of Christianity in Denmark, faded from view as they sailed over the horizon. The greening fields of Denmark's spring slipped away, replaced by the blue of the sea. Pangs of homesickness and seasickness must have tempered the sense of adventure, but there was no turning back—they were committed. They sailed north through the Kattegat, swinging west around the tip of Jutland, which they passed on April 19,[5] across the Skagerrak, and into the North Sea where they headed southwest towards Grimsby. It was symbolically a final farewell to Scandinavia. They, like the family of Lehi of old, were bound for the "land of promise."

Nicholai Sorensen recorded the following:

April 18th. I got up at 5:30 A.M. It was a beautiful dawn breaking forth and it filled our hearts with thanksgiving to our heavenly Father for all his blessings and for this day when we were on our way to Zion. I wrote a letter to my sister Mette in answer to a letter she wrote on the 17th . The morning went fast and at 10:00 A.M. we said goodbye to the people at Larsen's dock, where the ship, *L. M. Whit* [*L. N. Hvidt*], lay that we were going to take to England. When we got there, to my horror, we found some lady had taken little Stine with her. Not knowing if it was one of our Church members or some other I was worried and started looking all over for them. After awhile I got word they were back and my heart rejoiced and I thanked my Heavenly Father for all his goodness to us and for the safe return of little Stine. We all stayed on the dock till about 12:00 when we all went aboard the ship. We left Copenhagen at 1:45 P.M. The sea was very calm and the weather beautiful. We soon passed Faldboden and Trekroner. We enjoyed ourselves very much this very calm and beautiful afternoon. We went to sleep that night happy and thankful for all our blessings and prayed for the safety of our ship and the ones that had care of it.

April 19th. This morning's sky was bright red. We made good speed until the afternoon when it started to blow. The ship began to roll and nearly everyone got seasick. Little Stine, Peder and myself was the only ones not sick so me and Peder was plenty busy taking care of the rest.

April 20th. After a very bad night we welcomed the morning. It was still blowing quite hard. Some of the sick started to move about. In the evening we made our beds up on deck but did not sleep very good.

April 21st. The morning came forth beautiful. The weather was good. We were all happy as we were told that by noon we would be able to see land. This also was true. Everybody was happy and not any would say they felt seasick. About 2:00 P.M. our ship docked at Grimbye [sic], England. At 3:30 P.M. we were permitted to go on land. We were taken to a hotel that was fixed up to receive emigrants. Here we could get hot water and we made us some coffee and sandwiches. One of the men had to sleep in an out building where corn was kept as there was no more room at the hotel.[6]

There is no other body of water quite like the North Sea, for it is often treacherous and unpredictable, and this crossing had been made in particularly rough conditions. Landing in England, 12-year-old Niels Christensen asked his mother "why the land in England rocked?"[7] Another passenger, Lars Christensen, said the *L. N. Hvidt* had to battle the North Sea whose waves showed great strength. Everyone was ordered below deck where there was nothing but floor to lie on. It was very crowded and almost everyone was seasick. "When [they] landed everyone needed a good cleaning up."[8]

Landing at Grimsby[9] on the afternoon of April 21,[10] the Scandinavian saints were greeted with the quaint sounds of Lincolnshire's dialect. (Unknown to them at the time, that lack of facility in English would prove to be an obstacle between the Scandinavian saints and Scotsman James P. Park who would receive the assignment to captain the 7th Company in Iowa.) Grimsby is 15 miles southeast, and on the opposite side of the Humber River, from the more notable Kingston upon Hull. (694 miles across the North Sea from Copenhagen). Sorensen's comment that the *L. N. Hvidt* company spent the night at a "hotel that had been fixed up for immigrants"[11] indicates financial considerations were paramount. Although Grimsby may have been a cheaper place to spend a night; it also may have been the harbor where the *L. N Hvidt* had docking rights. Unquestionably, these pioneers were husbanding their resources.

Two Danes, C. C. A. Christensen and Carl C. N. Dorius, who had been serving as missionaries in Norway, came directly from Norway to Hull, England. From 1855 to 1857, Christensen served as president of the Brevig Conference which placed him in charge of the work in Norway. Hull was a large port with extensive docks, the oldest of which had been constructed in 1775. Ships from Hull helped defeat the Spanish Armada in 1588. In subsequent centuries, Hull became noted for its warships. In 1857, Britain was the world's dominant sea power. One can only guess at the emotions and thoughts of the adults and the children. They must have been filled with the wonder of it all.

April 22nd. We got up at 5:00 A.M. We had been told that we were to take a trip to Liverpool at 6:00 A.M. (Here I will say our time was one hour ahead of English time.) We left at 7:30 A.M. for Liverpool. The fields were green and some things planted had all come up. This told us they were a month ahead of us in Sjælland. The cattle were out grazing. We rode over fields, rocky places and between mountains, through cities and countries, through tunnels eight times. The longest one a mile long. It sure went a lot faster than we were used to in Denmark. At 3:00 P.M. we arrived in Liverpool. We were shown to a hotel and given something to eat. We were shown our rooms and spent the night there.[12]

The Scandinavian saints crossed England by train, via Doncaster, Sheffield[13] and Manchester, arriving at Liverpool's Brunswick Station.[14] The journal record written by Nicholai Sorensen reports contrasts between England and Denmark. His description of the fields and the advance of the season in England is indicative of a farmer's keen interest in those types of things. The English fields were green and had cattle grazing in the pastures. Some of the newly planted crops were up. The spring season was a month ahead of Sjælland. He captured it all. The family's success was dependent on him being alert to nature's window of opportunity, and Nicholai had been a successful Danish farmer. His journal description notes the hills, mountains, and rocky places of England. These topographical differences had come as an abrupt change from the flat, fertile plains of his native Sjælland. Upon their arrival in Liverpool, the Scandinavian Saints were lodged in a cheap hotel, indicative of their modest material circumstances.[15]

On the morning of April 23, after a breakfast of coffee and all the French bread they could eat, the saints and their baggage were taken to the *Westmoreland*.[16] Each family was given their passport. Most Scandinavians were unable to read them for the passports were written in English. Nicholai Sorensen wrote they "had very nice beds to sleep in, three to a bed. Husband, wife, and one child in each."[17]

Liverpool, then the European headquarters of the Church, was an industrial and maritime boom town for it had become a principal point of embarkation for American-bound emigration. It had made a successful transition from being the northern hub of a notorious three-cornered trade involved in human trafficking called the Liverpool Triangle. In the 18th Century, sailing ships operating out of Liverpool carried trinkets and cheap cotton goods to West Africa where they were exchanged for African slaves. Those slaves were then taken to the West Indies were they were traded for sugar, cotton, rum and other goods which were then transported back to England. In addition to Europeans bound for America during the 1850s, Liverpool's streets were alive with Irish emigrants and sailors from many nations who were seeking unsavory diversions from the sea. Called a haven of churches, it was also home to houses of sin. Of it one visitor said, "In Liverpool decent chaps owned ships, fairly decent chaps broked cotton, almost decent chaps broked corn—the rest just didn't exist."[18] There was an economic chasm between Liverpool's rich and poor. It rivaled London as a commercial center, and as a port city was several days shorter sailing time to America than was London due to delays encountered in the English Channel and the River Thames. Yet as a port, not everything was favorable, for its tides could range up to 29 feet and winds were often contrary. While it had extensive docks, not infrequently they had to be approached by disembarking into a smaller boat given the wide fluctuations of the tide.

According to the 1851 census, Liverpool had 376,065 inhabitants. In 1854, Rasmus Nielsen, a Latter-day Saint from

Denmark who sailed for America on board the *Benjamin Adams,* wrote there was no end of things to see in Liverpool: huge stores, factories, and buildings not equaled in Denmark. The most wonderful thing about Liverpool was the shipping. "I think there are 100 harbors and 1,000 ships in each," he wrote. Cotton goods, porcelain, glassware, lemons, and citron were described as very cheap, "but eating is very dear." There were great butcher shops with beef priced at 7 cents and pork at 8 cents [a lb]. They did not see rye bread at all, but wheat bread was everywhere. The English also mixed oat and cornmeal together. Reports indicate the Danes were especially fond of rye bread, while the English were more inclined toward wheat. While in Liverpool the Benjamin Adams Company purchased $1,000 worth of canvas for making tents for their use in America.[19]

People tend to eat that to which they have become accustomed. Rye was one of the chief cereals grown in northern Europe. Though it repays careful farming practices, rye does better than other major cereals on poor or very sandy soils. It is able to withstand considerable degrees of either soil acidity or alkalinity and is less exacting in its soil fertility requirements than is wheat. The soils of western Jutland are sandy whereas loam soils are more characteristic of eastern Jutland and the Danish islands. Norway's glacial soils tend to be shallow and poor. During the 1850s an understanding of the science of soil fertility was just beginning. Hence, rye tended to outproduce other major cereals on soils lacking in fertility, and Scandinavians had become accustomed to eating rye bread. The Scandinavians would discover that on America's rich virgin soils, the principal cereal grains grown were wheat and corn, with lesser amounts of barley, oats, and rye.

Orson Pratt of the Twelve presided over the affairs of the Church in Europe. His, or the Church's, address was 12 Islington, Liverpool. There were those in the company who were acquainted with his writings, for several of his tracts had been translated into Danish, and some of his sermons had appeared in the Scandinavian Mission periodical.[20]

In March 1857, Carl Christian Anton Christensen and Carl C. N. Dorius sailed directly from Kristiania (Oslo), Norway, to Hull, England. They were among the Latter-day Saints who joined the *Westmoreland's* passenger company at Liverpool. Carl Christian Anton Christensen, a simultaneously apprenticed decorative painter and student at the Danish Royal Academy of Art, had joined the Church in 1850. He was 18 years of age when baptized. Filled with missionary zeal and eager to share the news of the gospel's restoration, he was called in 1853 to serve as a missionary, first in Denmark and afterward in Norway. Among other young Danish converts also called as missionaries were two brothers, Carl Christian Nikolai Dorius and Johan Frederik Ferdinand Dorius. The three would become life-long friends as well as sub-captains over 16 handcarts each in the 7th Company. In 1857, they were released from their missionary labors and given permission to immigrate to Utah. Also among the *Westmoreland's* contingent were three young women, whom the three missionaries planned to marry upon their arrival in Salt Lake City. Johan Dorius, however, was in Copenhagen and sailed on the *L. N. Hvidt*, as did Karen Frantzen, his bride-to-be.[21] Johan Dorius' mission to Norway had resulted in a period of incarceration at Elverhoi. Perhaps a condition of his release may have been that he leave Norway.[22]

The journey from Europe to the mountains of western America required tremendous financial sacrifice. Then, in 1855, Brigham Young initiated a daring change in the immigration pattern. Where all previously had gone west by ox-team, they would now attempt a bold experiment of going west by handcart. Rather than land in New Orleans and go up river to St. Louis, Missouri, and Florence, Nebraska, the immigrant companies would disembark at an eastern port city and cross the eastern United States by rail to Iowa City. This change would reduce the severe climatic stress of the lower Mississippi basin as well as shorten the time at sea. It would also reduce the possibility of cholera—a constant threat to river travelers. In September 1855, President Young had written the European mission president directing the implementation of this change in the mode of crossing the plains. In addition to the rigors of walking and pulling handcarts across 1,300 miles of plains and rugged wilderness, for skeptics there was another element of risk inherent in using the new approach. It would be another seven months before the Chicago and Rock Island Railroad reached Iowa City on 21 April 1856.[23]

Many new converts could not afford to come on their own. During prior years, the Church had provided assistance through the auspices of the Perpetual Emigration Fund. The poor were not to be left behind. Such had been Church doctrine since the exodus from Nauvoo.[24] Consequently, through contributions and other means, a revolving fund was established to aid in their coming to Zion. Then, as the emigrants paid back the funds to the Church, others could be helped to emigrate. That fund was called the Perpetual Emigration Fund. However, such funding would be unavailable for assisting emigrants in 1857. Brigham Young had written Orson Pratt in 1856 stating that monies in the Perpetual Emigration Fund had been exhausted. One source of Perpetual Emigration funds was the ferrying business along the Mormon-Oregon-California trail system. In those areas administered by the Territory of Utah, charters to conduct business were issued by the territorial government. These charters stipulated that 10 percent of the ferrying proceeds were designated for the Perpetual Emigration Fund. That provision was a sore point with non-Mormon operators and their political allies. The economic situation was further aggravated by a lower level of cross-country migration during the 1855 and 1856 seasons. Consequently, there was fierce competition between Mormon and Gentile operators for the diminished ferrying trade.[25]

President Young instructed Elder Pratt there must be no more borrowing of money to supplement the Fund, and then making up the deficiency by taking funds from the tithing contributions. Brigham Young wrote that "we truly feel to assist the poor Saints to come to Zion" as indicated by the previous practice of the Church, but that it was not wisdom to pursue the gathering of the poor to the exclusion of all other facets pertaining to the building of the kingdom of God. In conformance with that policy, Elder Pratt announced in the 27 December 1856, *Millennial Star*: "This office will not send any P. E. Fund emigrants to Utah, during the year 1857. All funds that the Company can command will have been exhausted in discharging the heavy liabilities incurred in sending out over two thousand souls, in the year 1856."[26] Like their "Captain of old,"[27] the missionaries had taught the gospel of Jesus Christ to the humble folk of Scandinavia, who, despite meager financial means, were rich in faith. Earlier companies of Latter-day Saints from Great Britain and Scandinavia had been beneficiaries of the Funds, but the 7th Company was not so aided. Yet they were among those of Europe fired with the desire to gather with the Latter-day Saints in the mountains of the American West. In a spirit of quiet Christian generosity, those with greater means sacrificed to help those who would otherwise be left behind.

Individuals and families who could finance their own transportation to Utah were encouraged to emigrate. Those who planned to go west by handcart would need to send to the Church's European office $12.50 for each railroad fare from Philadelphia to Iowa City, and $15 per person to purchase the handcarts and outfitting supplies necessary for crossing the American plains. These deposits were to be in the Liverpool office by 1 February 1857. The fare for the ship's passage was in addition to these amounts.[28] For those who planned to go west by team, the cost would approximate $275 for "one wagon with bows, yokes, and chains, four oxen, and one cow—perhaps two."[29] For purposes of comparison, in those days gold was valued at $20 per ounce.

The Latter-day Saints who steamed to England aboard the *L. N. Hvidt* were a part of some 2,000 who sailed from Europe under Mormon auspices in the spring of 1857.[30] Initially, Hans and Ellen Christensen had planned to complete the journey to Utah by ox team. The disposal of their holdings had provided sufficient funds to do that. At some point, however, they determined to consecrate all they had to a common fund to assist others who were destitute, and to undertake the trek west by handcart.[31] Of the 2,000 immigrants in 1857, some 566 planned to travel by handcart, and 311 by team. The remaining Latter-day Saints would remain either in the eastern United States or on the frontiers of what are now the mid-western states until they could earn sufficient money to outfit themselves for the journey to Utah.[32] Sacrifice was required to get to Zion, and additional sacrifice would be needed to build Zion. Though a formidable undertaking, those filled with faith were undaunted by the challenge.

Prior to joining the *L. N. Hvidt* company at Liverpool, C. C. A. Christensen wrote that he and Carl Dorius met and heard Orson Pratt speak on the topic, "The Patriarch Jacob blesses his two grandsons, Ephraim and Manasseh." They were impressed and thrilled with the venerable Apostle, with his great kindness and dignity. He had illustrated his remarks by laying his hands upon the two young men as though he were the patriarch and they were Joseph's sons. Though they understood but very little English at that time, they seemed to capture the gist of what he said.[33] What other activities Christensen and Dorius were engaged in during the time after their arrival in Great Britain and prior to the arrival of the Copenhagen company were not given. With little facility in English, it must have been an adventure to find their way about Liverpool, buy something to eat, etc. Perhaps they were in the company of Elder John Kay, for he had served with distinction in the Scandinavian Mission.

While C. C. A. Christensen and the two Dorius brothers had intended to wait until reaching Salt Lake City to marry, Church leaders counseled them and two other engaged couples not to wait. Obedient to direction, with Elder John Kay officiating, C. C. A. Christensen married Elise Rosalie Haarby of Fredrikschald, Norway; Carl Dorius married Ellen G. Rolfson of Risor, Norway;[34] Johan Dorius married Karen Frantzen of Norway; Lauritz Larsen married Anna Maria Thomson; and Jacob Bastian married Gertrude Pedersen, aboard the *Westmoreland* in Liverpool Harbour on April 24.[35] Risor and Fredrikschald are on opposite sides of the Oslofjord and were among the first towns proselyted by Latter-day Saint missionaries. Fredrikschald is now called Halden.[36] The first four men are titled "Elder" whereas Bastian was referred to as "Brother." It may be a reference to recent missionary service, or it may be indicative that Bastian had not yet been ordained an elder, an office in the Melchizedek Priesthood of the Church. Elise Haarby had been baptized in September 1854. She was the first female member of the Frederikschald Branch of the Church.[37]

NOTES

1. Nicolai Sorensen, *Account of Journey From Haugerup, Denmark to Salt Lake City.* The journal account is from the Sorensen family archives, and is used as a courtesy of John W. Welch, a descendant. The Peder mentioned is given as Ole Peter and Abraham as Frederik Abraham on the *Westmoreland* roster. Little Stine is three-year-old Ingeborg Kristine. Jens Johansen is also listed on the ship's roster.

2. In 1976 Hector C. Haight's great grandson, Elder David B. Haight, was called to serve as a member of the Quorum of the Twelve.

3. See the *Westmoreland* Passenger Manifest.

4. Count Ulrik Ahlefedt-Laurvig states "Our Savior's Church was built in the 1682-1696 period in a Dutch Baroque style patterned after drawings by Lambert van Haven. The Spire was added in 1749-50." Personal Communication, 29 April 2001.

5. The date for passing through the Skagerrak is given in *Autobiography of Lars Christian Christensen, Westmoreland* (April 1857) *Mormon Immigration Index—Personal Accounts.*

6. Nicholai Sorensen, *Account of Journey From Haugerup...* pp. 1-2.

7. Clare B. Christensen, *History of Niels Christensen, Christensen Family Files.* The initial history was written in 1922 by Maud Driggs Christensen from incidents told her by Niels Christensen, her father-in-law and enlarged by his grandson Clare who heard many things from his grandfather as he worked alongside him on the family farm.

8. *Autobiography of Lar Christian Christensen*, Op cit.

   Records of their four-day crossing are limited. That is not particularly surprising. Even so ardent a record keeper as William Bradford, the Pilgrim leader, wrote less than 700 words about the *Mayflower's* ten-week voyage. In that light, Nicholai Sorensen's 386-word account of the four-day North Sea crossing could be considered voluminous.

9. Grimsby was a fishing port of ancient origin. It contained several medieval buildings, including a 13th Century church where King Richard I had held Parliament.

10. Nicholai Sorensen, *Account of Journey from Haugerup...*p. 2.

Sorensen wrote that they docked at 2:00 P.M. and were permitted to go on land at 3:30 P.M.

11. Nicholai Sorensen, *Account of Journey from Haugerup*...p. 2.

12. Nicholai Sorensen, *Account of Journey from Haugerup*...p. 2.

13. Sheffield lies at the foot of the Pennine Mountains which at their highest elevations rise between 2,000 and 3,000 feet. West of the Pennines is the Lake District of Cumbrian Mountains, a domed, dissected area of ancient rocks. However, these English hills and mountains were but a humble foreshadowing of the majestic mountains they would encounter in the American west.

14. Nicholas J. Evans, Personal Communication, December 23, 2000. Evans states the train would have crossed England on the lines of the Manchester, Sheffield and Lincolnshire Railway via Doncaster, Sheffield and Manchester. The route would have taken them through the coal mining, steel and textile manufacturing region of central England. The Nicholai Sorensen account states they arrived at 3:00 P.M.

15. *Journal History of the Church*, 13 September 1857, p. 12.

16. *Diary of Matthias Cowley, Westmoreland* (April 1857), *Mormon Immigration Index–Personal Accounts*.

17. Nicholai Sorensen, *Account of Journey from Haugerup*...p. 2.

18. Dixon Scott, Liverpool, p. 51, and Edward Howell, *Liverpool As It Is* as quoted by Conway B. Sonne, *Saints on the Seas: A Maritime History of Mormon Migration 1830-1890*. University of Utah Press, 1983, pp. 35-35.

19. *Journal of Rasmus Neilsen, Mormon Immigration Index–Personal Accounts, Benjamin Adams* (January 1854), p. 2. Neilsen's journal was translated from Danish by his son, Christian Emil Neilsen, who told that his father had died coming up the Mississippi River 28 March 1854.

20. C. C. A. Christensen, "By Handcart to Utah: The Account of C. C. A. Christensen." Translated from Danish by Richard L. Jensen. *Nebraska History* 66:(4), 346, endnote 4, Winter 1985.

21. C. C. A. Christensen, "By Handcart to Utah: The Account of C. C. A. Christensen." Translated from the Danish by Richard L. Jensen. *Nebraska History* 66:(4), 333-35. Winter 1985. Hereafter this will be referred to as C. C. A. Christensen Account. *Reminiscences and Journal of John Frantzen*, Op cit.

22. According to Don Smith, personal communication January 9, 2001, a missionary, Johan Ahmanson, was incarcerated in Fredrikstadt Prison at the same time as was Dorius. A reading of Smith's paper on Ahmanson seems to indicate they may have been imprisoned at Elverhoi. Ahmanson became a part of the Willie Company. Ultimately, he became disaffected with the Latter-day Saints, brought suit against

the Church, and was awarded $1,000. His descendants include those who founded the Ahmanson Foundation in Southern California. Hafen and Hafen, *Handcarts to Zion...* p. 289, list him as John Ahmanson on the Willie Company roster.

23 Stanley B. Kimball, "Sail and Rail Pioneers before 1869." *BYU Studies* 35:2 (1995), see pp. 19 & 23. Kimball said that "eleven pioneer companies totaling 4,121 immigrants had landed at East Coast ports and had taken one of several rail and river routes west to the trail head." (see p. 21.) Therefore, the use of rail transportation was already underway before 1856.

24. D&C 136:8: *Let each company bear an equal proportion, according to the dividend of their property, in taking the poor, the widows, the fatherless, and the families of those who have gone into the army, that the cries of the widow and the fatherless come not up into the ears of the Lord against this people.*

25. John D. Unruh, Jr., wrote that one non-Mormon objection to the ferrying businesses was "that the Mormon charters contained stipulations that anyone erecting public ferries without permission of the Mormon authorities were liable to fines up to $1,000, to be collected for use by the Territory of Utah. Indian agent Jacob Holeman doubted the constitutionality of a proviso that specified that 10 percent of ferrying proceeds—most of which came from non-Mormons—were earmarked for the Perpetual Emigration Fund." (John D. Unruh, Jr., *The Plains Across*, University of Illinois Press, Urbana and Chicago, 1983, pp. 286-87.) Not only had the demands been great for P. E. Funds in 1856, there are indications that cross-country migration was down in 1855-56, and that non-Mormon entrepreneurs were competing vigorously for the ferry trade. A case can be made that one of the underlying causes of the Utah War was "Gentile" entrepreneurial jealousy over the success of their Mormon business competitors. Non-Mormon allegations regarding restraint and monopoly of trade were further enhanced by vicious rumors of treason. Those disparaging charges, which found listening ears in Washington, DC, were fundamentally rooted in the fertile soil of non-Mormon economic discontent. Interestingly, Unruh states that "only in the Mormon domain were service facilities reasonably well regulated." (*The Plains Across*, p. 293.) When a climate of suspicion is coupled with an economic downturn, where "Gentile" businesses were struggling to survive, it became fashionable to blame the Mormon competitors for their difficulties. There is a similar, albeit a more horrendous example, found in 20th Century world history. Consider the vicious attitudes toward and confiscatory actions taken by Nazi Germany in the 1930s in the matter of Jewish banks and businesses. During periods of severe financial stress there are people who, when unrestrained by ethics and moral values, become cruel, mean, and terribly nasty.

26. LeRoy R. Hafen and Ann W. Hafen, *Handcarts to Zion: The Story of a Unique Western Migration, 1856-1860.* University of Nebraska Press,

Lincoln and London in association with The Arthur H. Clark Company, Spokane, Washington, 1960; pp. 148-49. The Hafens cite the *Millennial Star* of 27 December 1856 (XVIII:821).

27. That expression is taken from Cyrus H. Wheelock's hymn, "Ye Elders of Israel." (#319, *Hymns of The Church of Jesus Christ of Latter-day Saints*, 1985, Deseret Book Company, Salt Lake City, Utah.) The hymn was published in the *Millennial Star*, 11 April 1857. Apparently Wheelock composed it either while serving as a missionary in Great Britain or shortly thereafter, for he was part of a company of 14 returning missionaries under the leadership of Elder Franklin D. Richards of the Twelve, who overtook the Martin Handcart Company on the evening of 7 September 1856. (This is according to a report written by F. D. Richards and Daniel Spencer, published as Appendix C in the LeRoy R. Hafen and Ann W. Hafen text: *Handcarts to Zion*, pp. 218-19.) Sung by Latter-day Saints on board the *George Washington* as they set sail from Liverpool 27 March 1857, it remains a favorite hymn of missionaries to this day.

28. The cost of ocean passage does not seem to have been preserved for the *Westmoreland* in remaining documents. However, it is given as follows for the *George Washington* which sailed March 28, 1847 from Liverpool for Boston: All adults, who were passengers from eight years and up, £4.5; from one year to eight, £3.5; all infants were one shilling. *Diary of Amos Milton Musser, George Washington* (March 1857), *Mormon Immigration Index–Personal Accounts*, p. 1. The fares would have been similar, although it could have been a little higher since Philadelphia was a greater distance. In the 1850s the £ sterling was equivalent to $5.00 U.S. Gold was valued at $20 per ounce. Gold prices fluctuate in the world's commodity markets. However, if one prices gold at $270 U.S. per ounce, the cost of an adult passage in December 2000 would be $243.00 U.S. dollars. These emigrants were traveling under Spartan conditions.

29. Hafen and Hafen, *Handcarts to Zion...*, p. 149; and *Millennial Star 27* December 1856, XVIII: 822.

30. Hafen and Hafen, *Handcarts to Zion...*, p. 149.

31. Clare B. Christensen, *History of Niels Christensen...*, pp. 1-2.

32. Hafen and Hafen, *Handcarts to Zion...*, p. 149.

33. C. C. A. Christensen, *By Handcart to Utah...*, p. 336.

34. Ronald T. Halverson said that his great-grandmother, Ingeborg Frederiksen or patronymically, Ingeborg Knutsensdatter, came from Risor, and that Risor was the first place in Norway where the Latter-day Saint missionaries taught the restored gospel. (Personal Communication 13 December 2000.)

35. *Journal of Matthias Cowley Emigrating Company, Westmoreland,* (April 1857), *Mormon Immigration Index– Personal Accounts*. Cowley and the Richard L. Jensen translation of C. C. A. Christensen's account

(p. 336) give the name of Christensen's bride as Ellen Rosalie Scheel. There was no Scheel on the passenger manifest. Other sources, including an account by James Jensen, give her name as Haarby. The passenger manifest spells her name, Harbye. The reason for the seeming contradiction is that Scheel was her biological father's name whereas Haarbye or Haarby was her stepfather's name. She usually used her stepfather's name as her maiden name, but for her marriage she used Scheel, her legal name. (see Richard L. Jensen and Richard G. Oman, C. C. A. Christensen: 1831-1912 *Mormon Immigrant Artist* published by The Church of Jesus Christ of Latter-day Saints, Salt Lake City, Utah 1984, p. 9)

People are sometimes known by different names during the course of their lives, a condition which may have been intensified in Scandinavia because of the patronymic system and a language barrier. It was probably a case of Danish, Norwegian, and Swedish speakers giving their names to English scribes. There were bound to be mistakes. Whoever spelled the names of my ancestors used Swedish spellings. For example, they are listed as Hans and E. Christianson, Paul and Nils Peterson on the passenger manifest. About a year after coming to Utah, they determined to use the American custom and adopted their father's surname, Christensen rather than Pedersen, and Poul began spelling his name Paul.

36. C. C. A. Christensen, *By Handcart to Utah...*, endnote 6, p. 346.

37. From the obituary of Elise Rosalie Haarby Christensen published in the 12 May 1910 issue of the *Ephraim Enterprise*.

Chapter 5

OUT INTO THE ATLANTIC

Beginning with later trans-Atlantic crossings of 1855, and essentially all voyages departing from England thereafter, Mormon immigrant ships sailed toward the American ports of Boston, New York, or Philadelphia rather than New Orleans. This shortened the time at sea with its attendant risks and poor diet. Sea fares were probably lower, although there would have been the cost of railroad tickets. Most importantly, they avoided the oppressive (some called it murderous) heat and humidity of the southern Mississippi River Basin. Those hot, humid conditions of the lower Mississippi constituted a serious physiological stress for Northern Europeans, and stress renders the body more vulnerable to disease. To minimize the impact of that stress, earlier Mormon immigrant companies crossed the Atlantic Ocean and Gulf of Mexico during the cold and dangerous winter months which was much more risky than a springtime crossing given the severity of the winter storms. The *Westmoreland's* spring sailing enabled the Scandinavians to avoid the dangers of a winter voyage, and yet they arrived in America's Midwest in time to reach Utah by early fall.

Peter Neilson (Nielsen) had been a member of the 1855 Scandinavian company under the leadership of Peter O. Hansen, which sailed to New Orleans on board the *James Nesmith*, and then came up river on *The Oceana*. He recorded there were a number of deaths coming up the Mississippi. Arriving at St. Louis, Neilson wrote, "We were met by our beloved brother, Elder Erastus Snow, who said we had been prospered in our voyage." Then, alluding to the deaths in the company which occurred as they steamed up river, Elder Snow said the Prophet Joseph Smith had predicted the time would come when it would be unsafe for the Latter-day Saints to come by the Mississippi River route, that they would have to come by New York.[1] Fascinatingly, only two more Mormon immigrant companies would land at New Orleans. By late February 1855, Latter-day Saint Atlantic travelers were docking at the major seaports of the eastern United States.

The *Westmoreland* was a quality ship, built in 1851 during the heyday of the American clipper and packet ships. By this point in maritime history, the construction skills of American shipwrights were unsurpassed. Ships of this period had been built for speed and strength, and profits were influenced by the number of crossings. Their daring captains and crews challenged the Atlantic in all seasons with a maximum of canvas in weather which sometimes would not allow the crew to go aloft and take in sail. Where the seamen had been impressed into service or had been taken by treachery, tough, brutal officers frequently disciplined reluctant crewmen with fists and belaying pins.[2]

Robert R. Decan, who captained the *Westmoreland*, had been the ship's skipper since 1854. An experienced seaman, he

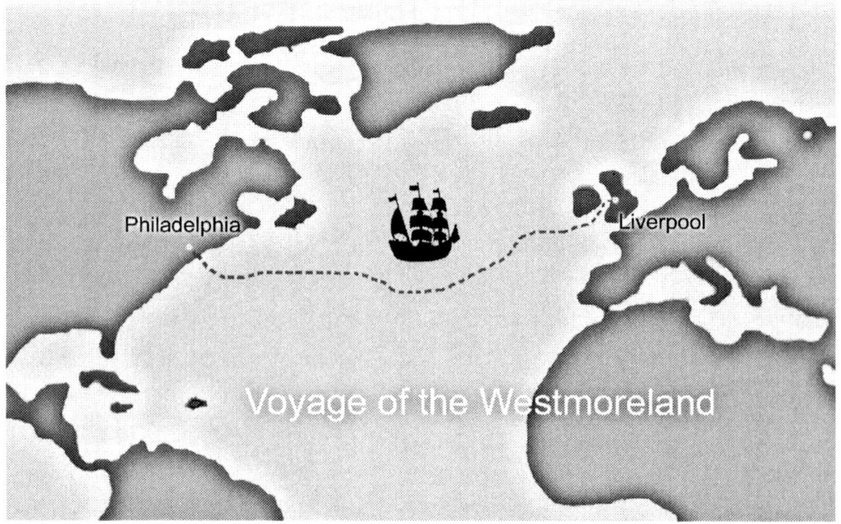

Map by Jeremy Munns

had previously commanded the 339-ton bark *Sultana* in 1848; in 1849, the 624-ton *Champlain*; in 1851, the 738-ton ship *Shenandoah*; and in 1852, the 816-ton ship *Saranak*. The *Westmoreland* was 999 tons, 170' x 36' x 18'.[3] She was a two-decker with three masts, a square stern, a figurehead, and was built of oak with iron and copper fastenings.[4] Her owners were John Burton and John R. Penrose of Philadelphia.[5]

The presiding officer or president of the Latter-day Saint company on board the *Westmoreland* was Matthias Cowley. Ultimately, his son, Matthias Foss Cowley, and grandson, Matthew Cowley, would both serve as members of the Quorum of the Twelve. From Philadelphia, Cowley told something of the voyage in a letter reporting his stewardship to Orson Pratt. He also kept a dairy. A journal of the "Emigration Company" was kept either by him or by a clerk under his direction.

On April 24, while moored in the River Mersey (a 16-mile navigable estuary which empties into Liverpool Bay), alongside Waterloo Dock, Liverpool, British port authorities cleared the *Westmoreland* for embarkation. The ship was pronounced in very good sailing condition, clean, and comfortable.

The Select Committee of the House of Commons on emigrant ships in 1854 had paid particular attention to the matter of emigrant ships and their passenger complements. Charles Dickens documented that concern in a footnote to the account he had written regarding the Latter-day Saints on board the Amazon in June 1863. He wrote:

> After this Uncommercial Journey was printed, I happened to mention the experience it describes to Lord Houghton. That gentleman then showed me an article of his writing, in *The Edinburgh Review* for January, 1862, which is highly remarkable for its philosophical and literary research concerning these Latter-day Saints. I find it in the following sentences:—"The Select Committee of the House of Commons on emigrant ships for 1854 summoned the Mormon agent and passenger-broker before it, and came to the conclusion that no ships under the provisions of the 'Passenger Act' could

be depended upon for comfort and security in the same degree as those under his administration. The Mormon ship is a Family under strong and accepted discipline, with every provision for comfort, decorum, and internal peace."[6]

Earlier in the day, Nicholai Sorensen, Olsen and N. Nielsen and a few others went shopping in Liverpool. They purchased "six loaves of English bread and a looking glass."[7] The Presidency of the British Isles "favored them with a visit." Elders Orson Pratt and Ezra T. Benson had been among those who had come. Everything seemed in readiness.

By 1849, Great Britain lifted a trading ban which it had pre-

"Emigrant Ship" 1867 by C.C.A. Christensen, © by Intellectual Reserve Courtesey of Museum of Church History and Art, Salt Lake City, Utah. Two features about it suggest that it may have been the *Westmoreland*. The field of stars indicates something of a circular pattern, which depicts the flag of the period when California was the newest state. While admitted to the Union in 1850, California was still the newest state in 1857. Between 1858 and 1867, six more states were admitted, and the stars were in more of a block arrangement. The other feature is the black star on the foresail. For a time the *Westmoreland* was assoicated with the Gurion Line which used a black star inside a white diamond on a blue flag as it's symbol.

viously imposed on foreign competitors seeking to do business with its colonies. The American merchant fleet was poised to take advantage of such liberalized conditions, and it made handsome profits for ship owners. The 1850s, the decade before the Civil War, were years of dynamic immigration and lucrative trade for the United States. It had begun with the California gold rush. South of the 49th parallel, the Oregon territory was being settled by pioneering American farmers. In the political race to determine who would control Oregon, the pioneer settlers outdistanced the British fur-traders. The Great Basin was being colonized. The first Mormon pioneers arrived in southern California in December 1849. The United States organized territorial governments in those areas heretofore considered Indian Territory. The Compromise of 1850 created two large territories: Utah and New Mexico. (Ultimately all or parts of the states of Arizona, Colorado, Nevada, New Mexico, Utah, and Wyoming would also be carved out of those territorial jurisdictions.) Visionary Brigham Young was thinking of a railroad, of using the Missouri-Yellowstone river system and other waterways, as well as other more rapid means of transportation than ox-teams and handcarts to bring new Latter-day Saints west.[8] It was a time of great vitality. The 7th Handcart Company, indeed all Latter-day Saint immigration, was an important part of it. They were building the kingdom of God, "far away, in the West."[9]

About 8 A.M. on Saturday 25 April, the anchor was weighed and a small steamer pulled the *Westmoreland* down the Mersey and into deeper water. Favorable winds caught the sails of the three-masted *Westmoreland*, and she sailed out into the Irish Sea. Food was distributed to the passenger complement. There was ½ loaf of bread to each passenger and 1 lb. of pork per week per person. Some began to get seasick.[10]

The sails were able to remain as initially set by the pilot until May 9.[11] For the "set of the sails" to remain unchanged until May 9 meant the winds had remained steady and favorable. The captain's log would tell whether they went north past the Isle of Man or sailed south into the Atlantic via St. George's

Channel. From Cowley's diary, it appears they sailed south.[12] Wind and fog would have influenced the initial choice of direction. Back then, the best of weather information was rudimentary. A seasoned captain and crew and the blessings of the Lord were vital to a successful voyage; prayer was an important part of the passengers' routine.

The Atlantic was then the world's most important commercial highway with dangers to match. Its prevailing winds were westerlies. In the language of the seafarer, the westward passage to America was called the uphill crossing. Under sail, in the face of the wind, the ship's officer barked the orders: "Heave to, boys," and the tack was changed from starboard to larboard, or port, as it is known today. Out toward the Atlantic they sailed, where for centuries Europe's quarreling captains and kings had fought deadly battles for supremacy of the sea. There were those on board who'd had firsthand experience with Europe's wars. Now, in a period of international calm, a new sea power was emerging. The national ensign flying from the *Westmoreland* had red and white stripes with a field of blue adorned by 31 silver stars. These Scandinavians were to be part of the effort to add another. Out on the sea the billowing sails tugged at the halyards, the canvas snapped, the wind's kick blew a salty spray into their faces. Curious lads watched the captain and his officers use the instruments of celestial navigation, with only the company's instructions and the language barrier between the officers and a thousand boyish questions. They were underway.

During the evening meeting April 25, a letter from Orson Pratt was read, announcing Cowley's appointment as president. The appointments of Cowley and his counselors, Henry Lunt and Ola N. Liljenquist, were sustained unanimously. The company was organized into four wards with a president over each, namely George W. Thurston, 1st Ward; Lorenzo D. Rudd, 2nd Ward; Christen Larsen, 3rd Ward; and Carl C. N. Dorius, 4th Ward. Prayer meetings were held in each ward every night and morning, and at noon as far as the Church officers could make it convenient. Each Sunday was set apart for fasting, praying, and preaching. Schools were organized in each ward for educating the saints in English. A musical company was organized and, for diversion, they sometimes played music and danced. Occasionally, they held interesting and amusing dialogues and criticisms.[13]

Instructions were given as follows: Lamps should be lighted as soon as it was dark, and put out between 9 and 10 P.M. All wards should have evening and morning prayers as a unit. All should retire by 10 P.M. and arise at 6 A.M. The cooks will make the fire at 6 A.M. and "put it out at seven o'clock at night." When the saints arose in the morning they were to clean themselves and all around their berth. No one was allowed behind the second cabin.[14] In the case of storm they were not to go up on the poop deck, an enlarged superstructure at the ship's stern above the level of the main deck. Sufficient fresh air was to be maintained in the cabins, but the windows must not be opened on the weather side. They were not to associate with the sailors, and the sailors were not to be admitted below.

On April 27th Nicholai Sorensen recorded:

Got up as usual. Had prayer and as on other days we were given our allotment of water every morning at 10:00. We got more food given out. 13½ lbs. meat, 16½ lbs. beans, 16½ lbs. rice, 16½ lbs. flour, 11 lbs. sugar, 11 lbs. oatmeal, 22 lbs. potatoes, 11 packages of tea, salt and pepper. The main problem now was to get some food cooked. Our kitchen was very small for so many.[15]

One instruction was as follows: "One ward will boil at [a] time and then boil for the whole day."[16] One assumes that the water was boiled for culinary purposes. What is not clear is whether it was also boiled for the laundry.

Of April 28th, Sorensen wrote:

The weather was quite ruff. The wind blew hard. A few of the brethren met in prayer to our Heavenly Father. Our prayer was answered. The wind stopped blowing and we were very thankful and happy. We were all up and about but mother. She was still confined to bed and was very sick. Henrik had a bad ear but felt pretty good. I felt fine. Not seasick at all. All was [sic] feeling pretty good except mother. She had trouble with Diarrhea rather than vomiting. Sister Liljenquist gave her a remedy that helped her a lot.[17]

On Wednesday 29 April, Cowley recorded that they had sailed under a fair wind, that water was served out today and every morning during the passage.[18] That entry, coupled with the instruction that "one ward was to boil per day for the entire day," may suggest water was being boiled for laundry. One historian wrote that fresh water seldom ran short on Atlantic crossings because rain refilled the water barrels. However, under conditions of adverse weather, given the large numbers of passengers who were crowded into the ship's hold, there were those voyages when the fresh water supply became a worrisome situation.[19]

On April 29 a band was organized. It consisted of three clarinets, six violins, two harmonicas, and one flute. They held a dance on the poop deck that evening.[20] Social activities helped break the monotony of the sea. Nicholai Sorensen's journal entry for this date told that he stood watch from 2:00 to 5:00 A.M., that being the first man up he was able to put on the tea kettle and had plenty of warm water when his family arose. His wife was still quite ill, but the "ship's doctor had given her some pills to stop the diarrhea." Henrik was given some powder for his earache, but it did not seem to help.[21]

Some preparations for the handcart journey were undertaken during the voyage. One of these preparations was making tents. It was less costly to purchase the canvas materials needed for their construction in England than in the United States. These materials were brought on board as a part of the passenger's luggage. The work to create them was a satisfying and productive diversion from the sameness of life at sea. Those blessed with nimble fingers, and those who had worked with canvas in other circumstances, proved to be especially valuable.[22] It was part of the process of becoming self-reliant. Those who were to make the Great Basin blossom and flower so that

Zion might arise and put on her beautiful garments,[23] had to be doers of the word, and not hearers only.[24]

As was the case with other trans-Atlantic voyages of this period, passengers cooked their own meals. Supplies were provided from the commissary by the steward, C. C. A. Christensen. "The provisions distributed each week to each family consisted of biscuits, potatoes, meat, bacon, flour, rice, peas, tea, sugar, etc."[25] Isaac Sorensen said, "The worst problem was diet." The biscuits were not palatable. Only Isaac's father, Nicholai, was able to eat the biscuits. He recalled they sold the biscuits they had remaining from the voyage on going ashore in America.[26] Lars Christian Christensen wrote that the food was not very good, that many could not eat the hard crackers (sea biscuits[27]). Lars ate no bread during the entire voyage. He reported there were some barrels of raw cracked peas.[28] The peas were apparently the only fresh-type produce on board.

Sea biscuits or crackers are also called hardtack. They were a simple dried bread, made from flour and water, and then baked, insofar as possible, to a moisture-free or desiccated condition. The lack of moisture reduced the likelihood that molds would grow and spoil them. In order to eat hardtack and not break a tooth, the biscuits had to be broken into small pieces and soaked in water. On many ships, the captain and his officers had freshly baked bread, while the crew and the passenger complement ate biscuits. Good fresh bread complemented by dairy products was an important part of the diet for Scandinavians. Fresh bread and dairy products were not available on the Atlantic voyage. Dietary change was another nutritional or physiological stress which undermined their physical strength, thereby making their health more vulnerable to other challenges during the arduous handcart journey.[29] The lack of dairy products for younger children so accustomed to having them in their diet would have rendered them especially vulnerable to disease. One wonders if the biscuits were also a contributing factor to seasickness.

Cowley's letter to Orson Pratt indicates they established organizational protocols for many activities such as the order of cooking, dealing out the provisions, building fires, etc. The *Westmoreland's* passenger officer list records that Jens P. Folkman and Gudman (Gudmund) Gudmanson were cooks. Apparently this meant they had the overall responsibility for directing the cooking and making the fires. Meal preparation on a family basis for 544 Latter-day Saints would have required considerable organization, given the size of the ship and availability of cooking facilities.

For much of the early voyage the winds were favorable. Nicholai Sorensen wrote that on April 30 they had "fine weather and the wind was just right and the ship made good speed." He was especially happy on May 1 for his wife had slept well and felt much better. They had a good wind, but it came from a direction which caused the ship to roll a good deal. He added: "So many of our belongings fell on the floor of the cabin. Those who had Parselin [porcelain] got most of it broken up."[30] He made an extensive entry for May 2.

> The night has been bad for me. I had been busy bringing pots and picking up things that was always falling down and rolling around on the floor. Most luggage was not fastened. I would say that most of them were just thrown about. I had fastened ours when we first went aboard. I had some rope with me from Sorø. We were given more provisions, bread, bacon, meat and potatoes. The weather was very good and all the sick was [sic] brought up on deck and here we were many hours. I got some of our bedding up on the deck and into the sun. Everyone enjoyed this day and all felt much better. It did mother a lot of good to be out in the sunshine and all the others that had been seasick. In the evening we as usual had prayer and our Brethren Robt. and L. Larsen spoke many enlightening things to us. Bro. Liljenquist also joined us. He also spoke and gave us many things to think about. Also reminded us that it was Fast Sunday the next day and wanted everyone to go to the kitchen to do the cooking needed as to be free all Sunday. He promised us we should have meetings at 10:00 A.M. and

also at 2:00 P.M. This made us all very happy and we all went to bed happy.[31]

On May 3 they had rain. Sunday meetings were canceled due to the rolling of the ship. All on board had to hold on to trunks, water buckets, cups, and saucers, for everything which had not been securely fastened moved about the ship. Lars Christensen described how a big breaker dashed over the *Westmoreland*, nearly rolling the ship on her side. He did not give the date, but his description[32] seems to fit that of Nicholai Sorensen's May 3 entry.

> At midnight we were all awakened by our belongings again being thrown around the floor. The ship was rolling very bad all day and we were not able to have our meetings.[33]

That afternoon, in the midst of those difficult conditions, a sister from Denmark, Marie Jacobsen Garff, the wife of Niels Jorgensen Garff, gave birth to a son.[34] The boy was named for the ship and her captain, Decan *Westmoreland* Garff. Decan Garff was the twelfth child born to Niels and Marie Jacobsen Garff. Seven of their children had died very young. One had been stillborn. Because of Marie's delicate health, and the fact Niels and daughter, Trina, were ill, the Garffs had brought with them a nurse and a midwife. (Karen Marie Petersen and Sophia Christopherson traveled with the Garff family as a unit under one ticket.) Niels Jorgensen Garff had been a tailor at age 19. By the time of his marriage at age 35 he is listed as a freeholder, a farmer who owned his own land. He had been released from Denmark's levying rolls in 1831 because he lacked capacity to serve in the military "due to being crippled in both of his hips." Niels J. Garff did not expect to live to see the valleys of the mountains in America's Great Basin. Convinced the journey would cost him his life, he nevertheless was determined to go, for he wanted his family to be in Zion.[35]

Nicholai Sorensen recorded the following:

> May 4th. This day did not promise to be any better. Big waves rolled over the deck and some water came

down on us. We were busy wiping the floors under the beds and all over. The day went as the others. Being of the Mormon faith we looked to the holy things and the promises to all the faithful that makes our lives worthwhile and makes us happy day by day . . .

May 5th. This morning the weather was a little better. Niels Jorgensen had been standing watch from 2:00 A.M. to 5:00 A.M. He told me there was a good fire in the stove and to bring the tea kettle so we could have some boiled water. I was soon upon my feet to help some of the others that were not feeling well. We were again given out provisions. Rice, flour, beans, sugar, tea, sennip and pepper. We also could have had some oatmeal and vinegar but we had some and so didn't take any. We were also given some fruit juice. In the afternoon all the sick was [sic] brought up on deck. The weather was very calm. The ship did not make very good speed as the wind had almost stopped blowing but what little we had helped the speed of the ship. We saw a lot of sea hounds near the ship. [Sea hounds or dog fish is a common name given to several small sharks such as the spotted shark or greater dogfish, the piked dogfish, etc.] A lot of them [the passengers] were bedding out on deck, drying in the sun.

May 6th. This morning the tea kettle did not awaken us. We had cooked two meals the day before and had used all our water that had been given out. Bro. Mikkelsen had saved two cups of water. He gave it to mother and me. At 6:00 P.M. all was [sic] called together for prayer meeting. I forgot to tell that we had been divided into four different branches. I was head of one of them. [This notation suggests that each ward may have been divided into branches.] We belonged to the second branch. Me, mother, Kirsten, Maria, Henrik, and Stine. We opened with song No. 29 and 30 in the outside room where the drinking water was stored.

Peder, Abraham, Isak, Jacob, Kristian and Niels were also in the same room. For two days we had no wind. It was for this purpose that we had met to ask our Heavenly Father to let it blow enough so the ship would make speed. Our prayer was answered and we all went to bed happy and thankful.

May 7. After a good night's sleep I woke at 5:00 A.M. Got up feeling happy although my clothes were all wet from being too warm and had been sweating. The weather was wonderful and the wind was just right. Niels and I were busy all forenoon fixing things. It being Sophie's birthday we were giving a special fine dinner, soup and meatballs. In the afternoon all had to meet to pay the tickets for the train fare across America. I paid $132.00 for my family. For the stay in Liverpool $4.20. Then there were some small debts to pay. Like money spent for drinks for the sailors that cooked for us from Copenhagen to Grimsby in England. You could give any amount you wanted to. I gave $.80. This was to be given back to us at the purchase of the rest of our tickets. Bro. Lauritz Larsen went around to each to see how many would like to learn English by having a class. We all signed up but mother and little Stine. Our President Kovlif was to have charge of the school. Another day went and we all were happy and thankful, especially as mother was much better and was able to be up most of the day.[36]

Friday May 8 the wind was from the east. Dawn had broken with a bright red overcast sky. The word about the ship was that they had reached the halfway point. At the request of Henry Lunt, they prayed for a stronger wind. During the night the wind freshened and blew strongly from the south. By the morning of Saturday May 9 they were under a strong south wind. It kept increasing until they were required to take in sail for the first time since leaving Liverpool. At one point they were making about 10 miles per hour.[37] About 10 A.M. the wind began to blow out of the west and came from that direction until night when it shifted to the southwest. The heavier winds increased the amount of seasickness, for the ship was pitching heavily. "The front would stand straight up from the water and then down again like it was going under the sun."[38] Of the morning of May 10 Nicholai Sorensen wrote he had been awake most of the night listening to the howling of the wind. They passed by four ships that day not far from the *Westmoreland*.[39]

On Monday, May 11, the winds remained contrary and they were four points off course. The account suggests they were getting water into the hold for provisions had to be moved. In the rough sea, while Nicholai Sorensen was putting the tea kettle on, the ship lunged so severely that his feet went out from under him. He hit his head hard against a box, hurting an ear. One leg was badly bruised. The injuries put him in bed for the day.[40]

On Tuesday, May 12, the wind was unfavorable and the ship's course was toward the north. Sadness struck at 3 P.M. when Karen Larsen or Larsdatter, the daughter of Lars and Anna Peterson [Ane Pedersen] died; she was buried at sea at 6 P.M.; the ship's position given as latitude 40o59, longitude 45o48. Of all the scenes cast in bronze or captured on canvas, there is none more poignant than a sorrowing family at the grave of a child. Yet a grave on land usually has some identifying features, forever etched in memory. Perhaps it is a grove of trees, a hill, or a secluded spot along the bank near a bend in the river. Somehow on land there is always the faint possibility that one day you might return to the place of tender remembrance, made sacred by the tears of disappointment, where an added measure of solace might be found. Burial at sea must have been even more difficult. For a small moment the little body lies in the weighted canvas bag, the weeping mother whispers a tearful goodbye, the board is lifted, and the body slides down into the watery deep, covered until the resurrection by the sameness of the sea. It is difficult to fathom the depth of the emotional wrenching. For some the mortal journey is very short. Karen had been born 21 February 1856 in Falster, Denmark, a small island of fertile lowlands to the south of Sjaelland.

Nicholai Sorensen recorded his wife was able to drink a little warm water and eat a little bread. She had suffered seriously with sea sickness. For dinner all they had to eat was rice mush. Their May 13 dinner consisted of peas. All of his family ate well except for 14-year-old Maria who, as yet, still had a poor appetite.

On Thursday, May 14, the leadership determined not to give out additional pork. They had come to the conclusion that eating the pork of the ship's stores was adversely affecting the Saints' health. The pork may have been a very fat, salty bacon. However, there seems to have been little alternative animal-protein foodstuff to replace it.

Nicholai Sorensen recorded that it was a wonderful morning for sailing. The sun was shining and the wind ideal for making good speed. All were invited to be on deck at 10:00 A.M. About ten it began to rain and hail heavily. At 1:00 P.M. The sun reappeared and they were able to bring all of the sick topside. It began to storm again at 5:00 P.M. and all passengers were ordered below to their cabins. The ship's crew was busy with the sails and conditions were precarious for a time. However, the storm abated and they held a church service that Sorensen described as wonderful. He wrote that it was the first time they had Brother Kovhy[41] with them. Brother Kovhy bore testimony and shared many faith-promoting incidents and Brother Liljenquist translated it in the Norwegian language. Many other men bore their witness of the gospel in a meeting which lasted until 9:30 P.M. when all passengers retired to bed.

Of May 15 Nicholai Sorensen wrote:

> I woke early. It was still dark so I just stayed in bed till it got light. As I usually did first thing in the morning was to get hot water ready for tea. The wind was good and we made good speed. At noon it started to storm and by afternoon it was really bad. Most of the sails had to be taken down but we still made good headway, more so than any time before. The storm was bad the rest of the night. The sea was very rough and the waves were very big and washed over the deck of the ship. The ship

rolled and we in our bunks rolled from side to side. I didn't sleep very much and was far from well.[42]

The heavy weather persisted on May 16. Many of the passengers were apparently seasick. Ephraim Gottfred Jensen, the infant son of Anders and Ingerline Jensen, died Sunday May 17th.[43] The ship would have been near the Newfoundland Ridge. He was buried at sea. An expression of sympathy to his mother, Ingerline, from Anna Peterson would have been especially comforting for she understood, perhaps as no other, the pain of saying goodbye at sea. Cowley's letter and diary record these events, evidence that he was a shepherd who watched over his flock. It is a lesson in leadership and recordkeeping.

A "General Conference" was held aboard ship May 17. The authorities of the Church were sustained by unanimous vote and cheering. The leaders collected $12 per adult and $6 for each child under eight and over one year for train fare from Philadelphia to Iowa City. They collected $5,572.04 for the purpose of expediting business upon arrival in Philadelphia. All that would not be expended for train fare from there to Iowa City would be returned to the saints. The advance preparation saved them considerable trouble in Philadelphia. An excellent spirit prevailed among the people who testified they had been greatly blessed and their journey had been a "Heavenly one to them."[44]

From Cowley's geographical reference points plotted against time, one can estimate the *Westmoreland* had sailed approximately 1440 nautical miles (1656 statute miles)—110 miles per day toward their destination. Since the wind had blown them north off course, they would have traveled farther than that.[45]

While this rate of speed seems slow by comparison to today's travel times, it was more than double the speed of the westward-bound *Mayflower*. The *John J. Boyd*, from whose passenger complement would come some of the 7th Handcart Company members, had been 65 days at sea during the 1855-56 winter. Fewer days at sea saved provisions. The challenges of obtaining fresh water, critically important in maintaining human health, would be lessened. There was apparently a daily water ration. One day, an ill and very thirsty ten-year-old, Martin Hansen, whose family's daily water ration had been consumed, insisted he be given a drink of water from the sea. Martin was unwilling to accept his parents' counsel, and after lengthy complaining on Martin's part, his father lowered a tin into the Atlantic and captured him a drink. Martin wrote, "I drank it and nearly strangled."[46] Shorter voyages meant there was less likelihood of developing scurvy or other problems endemic in lengthy voyages when fresh fruit and vegetables were unavailable. The *Westmoreland* had Doctor J. H. Davidge on board who, Cowley wrote, "Acted the part of a father to this people, in attending to the sick and afflicted among us."[47]

Monday, May 18, was warm and pleasant. It was a day of playing, performing music, and dancing on deck. Cowley attended the 3rd Ward prayer meeting. During the 1st Ward's evening prayer, the first mate, Mr. Whall, came and told them to stop their . . . singing. They were having prayers prior to retiring for the night. The captain severely chastised the first mate. Afterward the captain apologized to the Latter-day Saints, and told them to proceed as usual with their religious duties. Tuesday, May 19, the *Westmoreland* passed the *Ericson*, a New York mail steamship bound for Liverpool. On Wednesday, May 20, they passed another steamship and found themselves in very foggy weather. Nicholai Sorensen took his son, Henrik, to the kitchen to show him how they cooked their food. Henrik had not previously seen the kitchen as he had been in bed for much of the voyage. Heavy rain would prevent them from returning to their cabin for 1½ hours.

On Thursday, May 21, Cowley commenced writing his report to Orson Pratt in Liverpool, and noted that he had enjoyed eating oysters. He spoke at the Friday, May 22, prayer meeting of the 4th Ward on the principles of progress towards perfection. Cowley's letter to Orson Pratt is about 950 words in length. It reports that when 25 days out from Liverpool and within two days of Philadelphia they were "caught in calms and fogs for ten days." He praised Captain Decan for his clever management of the ship, and except for the calms and fogs they'd had a delightful passage. He wrote that "Captain Decan has proved himself to be a whole-souled man, and deserves credit and praise for his manly forbearance and gentlemanly conduct toward all passengers," that his abilities as a seaman cannot be surpassed by any.[48] Cowley's generous evaluation of Captain Decan seems well-founded.

Saturday, May 23, was calm and pleasant. The ship *Sir Robert Peel* was in view all day. The Saints spent Sunday May 24 bearing testimony and receiving instructions regarding preparations for landing. A good many fishing boats were in sight and at anchor. But the going was slow. By Wednesday May 27 they had been in six days of calm. They sighted the *Caroline*, a brig bound for Wilmington, North Carolina. (A brig is a two-masted, square-rigged ship.) The sighting of other ships was their major break in the sameness of the horizon at sea. The winds picked up on Thursday, May 28. In the afternoon they ran into a thick fog and the crew had to take in sail. Elders Cowley, Lunt, Thurston, and Rudd prayed in private for the fog's removal. Within a few minutes it had disappeared, and the light ship (used as a navigational aid in lieu of a land-based light house) off of Cape May came into view. There were several other ships near the entrance to Delaware Bay. A ship's pilot came on board at 9 P.M. to guide the *Westmoreland* safely up river to Philadelphia.[49]

As the *Westmoreland* was moving up the Delaware River, among many fine ships they passed was an American man-of-war, the *Minnesota*, which was bound for the East Indies.[50] James Jensen said: "As the emigrants beheld that emblem of national power, they raised their voices in loud intonations of cheers and hurrahs. The captain of the battleship returned the salute of welcome by firing the guns of the ship."[51] It was a wonderful welcome, a greeting greatly appreciated by the Scandinavian saints who were now to become naturalized Americans. Their first view of America, the shores along the Delaware, had been inspirational.[52] They were taken with the charm of Philadelphia. One wrote: "If any place in the world could give a foreigner an exalted impression of America, it was the scenery about that city."[53] Johan Dorius tells that on the afternoon of May 30 a steamboat began to tow them up river toward Philadelphia.[54]

On Saturday, May 30, between 6 and 7 P.M.,[55] while coming up the Delaware River, Jorgen Jensen Schram, an elderly brother from Vendsyssel, Denmark, died. Determined in his quest for Zion, and filled with faith in the righteousness of the cause, Jorgen Schram had come to America without relatives to support him in the effort. He was buried in a Philadelphia cemetery.

With sadness, Cowley reported another death to Orson Pratt. It was the assassination of Parley P. Pratt, Orson's brother, and fellow Apostle.[56] Parley P. Pratt had been murdered May 13 in Arkansas. Parley P. Pratt had composed a number of significant hymns of the restoration including "The Morning Breaks," "An Angel from on High" and "Come, O Thou King of Kings." He had been imprisoned with the Prophet Joseph in Missouri. His autobiographical account of the Prophet Joseph Smith rebuking the guards in a Missouri dungeon at midnight stirs people to this day. Now, like his friend, the Apostle with the poetic pen had gone to a martyr's reward. It came as a very great shock. While the Scandinavian converts had not known Parley P. Pratt personally, his book, *The Voice of Warning*, had been an important factor in arousing within them a desire for a new religious life. "That book," wrote one, "carried the conviction that the new message it proclaimed came from God."[57]

Martin Hansen remembered that it was raining when they arrived at the docks in Philadelphia.[58] The Scandinavian saints were welcomed by Angus M. Cannon who had come representing Elder John Taylor.[59] It must have been from Cannon that Cowley learned of Parley P. Pratt's assassination. Recorded in the appendix of the *Autobiography of Parley P. Pratt* is an extract from *The Mormon* of May 30, published in New York. John Taylor was its editor. That article announces the martyrdom of Parley P. Pratt. It is an eloquent tribute and biographical sketch of Elder Pratt's life. Undoubtedly written by John

Taylor,[60] and published in the May 30 edition of the paper, it seemingly explains Elder Taylor's absence at the arrival of the *Westmoreland*. One purpose of such Church leader visits was to give counsel and provide encouragement concerning the remainder of the journey to Utah. The Scandinavians found it comforting to have a capable leader come as a representative of the leading councils of the Church. Their needs would be addressed. They would learn what it was they had to do, and how they could accomplish it.

Accounts of ship voyages made by Latter-day Saints indicate that passenger deaths among their companies were relatively few. The *Westmoreland's* record was particularly excellent in that regard. Sensitive captains seemed to realize that a Latter-day Saint company provided a maximum opportunity for success with a commensurate minimization of problems. In 1855, the *James Nesmith* carried a company of 441 Latter-day Saints presided over by Peter Ole Hansen, one of the four initial missionaries to Scandinavia. Eighteen died during the crossing from Liverpool to New Orleans. Before they went up river to St. Louis, the *James Nesmith's* captain came to them and said this had been his most prosperous crossing of the Atlantic, "that in the future if I have my choice, I will bring none but Latter-day Saints."[61] In the trip immediately prior, the captain reported he had embarked with a thousand passengers, but no sooner had they put to sea than they commenced to drink, play cards, quarrel, and were filthy in their habits. Such behavior lowers resistance to disease, and disease took hold of the passenger complement. Seven hundred died and were buried at sea. The Captain also reported another earlier voyage with passengers of similar habits. On that crossing there were only 11 survivors out of an original company of 300 people. The Latter-day Saints understood that it was the strict observance of the principles of the gospel of Jesus Christ which had brought them safely through.[62] The testimony of the ship's captain must have called to remembrance the experience of the family of Lehi when his eldest sons, indulging themselves in "much rudeness," forgot for a time that Power by which they were crossing the many waters.[63]

NOTES

1. Family Records of Peter Neilson [Nielsen], Personal Accounts, *James Nesmith, Mormon Immigration Index*. Family Record (Ms 5345) pp. 5-9, 11; Acc #17756).

2. Charles Dickens in an 1863 essay entitled "Bound for the Great Salt Lake," published in his book, *The Uncommercial Traveller*, wrote of the practice of taking men against their will for service at sea. He stated: *Down by the Docks, they "board seamen" at the eating-houses, the public-houses, the slop-shops, the coffee-shops, the tally-shops, all kinds of shops mentionable and unmentionable–board them, as it were, in a piratical sense, making them bleed terribly, and giving no quarter. Down by the Docks, the seamen roam in mid-street and mid-day, their pockets inside out, and their heads no better."* (Charles Dickens, *The Uncommercial Traveller*...p. 218.) Polite society seemingly looked away from such blatant abuse of human freedom, apparently accepting that such servitude took vagrants and other less desirables off of the streets and made of them contributing members of the country's economy. The grog-shops were especially fruitful fields for finding unsuspecting seamen. Ready-to-wear clothing was sold at slop-shops, whereas gentlemen and ladies wore tailor-made. At tally shops, goods were sold on the weekly installment basis, or laid away until paid for. Until 1812, buyer and seller each kept a record of the payments by cutting notches, representing amount paid, on the edges of seasoned willow or hazel tally sticks. In a class-conscious society, shopping at such places was apparently considered somewhat degrading.

3. Ed. Note: On 5 February 2000 I toured the *H. M. Bark Endeavour* replica, as she lay moored at the Devonport, New Zealand pier. My initial impression was the *Endeavour* replica was a small, scaled-down ship. "No," said the guide, "at an overall length of 109 feet 3 inches, she is within an inch of the original." The *Endeavour* was a three-masted ship. Had her rope rigging been laid out in a single line, it would have measured 29 kilometers or 18 miles. At 170 feet by 36 feet by 18 feet, the *Westmoreland* was 61 feet longer, 7 feet wider and 7 feet greater in depth. That extra 7 feet meant a second deck. Captain James Cook began his voyage of discovery with 92 people on board. Given the *Endeavour's* head room of 4 feet, 7 inches in the Marine's Quarters, and 5 feet, 7 inches in a gentleman's cabin, they would have been terribly crowded. The Endeavour had a gross tonnage of 397 tons and a maximum breadth of 29 feet. 2 inches. The *Westmoreland* overall size of 999 tons was 2½ times greater, but they were carrying 544 passengers plus the crew. One can safely conclude those on board the *Westmoreland* were crowded. The frequent Church services and classes in English were important for helping maintain morale in such a tight fit. The organization, of necessity, would have been formal and highly efficient.

4. Conway B. Sonne, in *Ships, Saints, and Mariners: A Maritime Encyclopedia of Mormon Migration 1830-1890*, (University of Utah Press, Salt Lake City, 1987, p. 152) lists the materials used in construction of the *Westmoreland*. Ships of this period were frequently constructed of oak. Captain James Cook's *Endeavour* was built of oak with an elm keel, and most likely Baltic pine for her decks, topsides, masts and spars. In the early 1800s many masts and spars were made from New Zealand's kauri trees. Oak has a drawback. It is very susceptible to rot and to attack from marine borers, and particularly so in tropical waters. Cook's *Endeavour* sailed for 29 years, and it was finished. (see *Endeavour: Millennium Tour, Ticktock Publishing* Ltd., 1999, p. 2.) For many years the British Admiralty always built first a detailed scale model of the ship. The model was then taken to the king for his approval. The actual ship was then constructed from the pattern of the model. In one war with Holland, the Dutch sent fighting ships up the River Thames and captured a large British man-of-war. During the course of that battle, British seamen took the models out the back door and away from the fighting. It was Board of Admiralty policy that ship models were to be saved from the enemy even at the loss or capture of operating ships; that is, the models were considered more valuable than the ships themselves. (Personal communication with Jackson K. Sauvarin, 24 Cleland Crescent, Blockhouse Bay, Auckland, New Zealand. For nearly 60 years, Sauvarin has been a student of the history and construction of sailing ships, and is himself, a builder of exquisite model ships.)

   According to the Ships' History Branch of the Naval Historical Office, Washington, DC, (Personal Communication, 29 November 2000, telephone 202-433-3643), American shipbuilders of the 1850s may have used models, or perhaps more likely, half-models in the construction of sailing ships. (However, a wealthy ship owner may have had one built for display in his corporate offices.) There were/are in existence "Tables of Offsets" and "Tables of Spars and Sails" which were pretty much standard for the period and which were used in ship building. According to the Ships' History Office, "There is much concerning that period of which we now have little knowledge." Sonne (p. 152) tells that in 1873 the *Westmoreland* was wrecked by fire and sold at auction.

5. Conway B. Sonne, 1987. *Ships, Saints, and Mariners: A Maritime Encyclopedia of Mormon Migration 1830-1890*. University of Utah press, Salt Lake City, p. 152.

6. Charles Dickens, *The Uncommercial Traveller*... p. 230, footnote 1.

7. Nicholai Sorensen, *Account of Journey from Haugerup*... p. 2.

8. Hafen and Hafen, *Handcarts to Zion*..., pp. 151-52.

9. Hymn #30 "Come. Come, Ye Saints" verse 3. *Hymns of The Church of Jesus Christ of Latter-day Saints*, Deseret Book, Salt Lake City, Utah, 1985.

10. The *Westmoreland* may have been assisted down the River Mersey by a tug. The *George Washington* had been. If she was, it was not mentioned in records which are available on the *Westmoreland's* voyage.

Nicholai Sorensen, *Account of Journey from Haugerup...* p. 2.

11. Alice Neeley Moncur, 1916. History of Niels and Ingeborg Hansdatter Nielsen, LDS Historical Department. Req. No. 108006. Microfilm, call #9256. See pp. 112-19. The letter is reproduced in Allen C. Christensen's, *The Christensen Family of Sorø, Denmark and American Fork, Utah, U.S.A,* privately published in 1994 by Family History Publishers. Copies are on file at the LDS Church Historical Department. This letter is now a part of the *Mormon Immigration Index.*

12. Cowley gave positions for the following dates: Sunday, May 3, latitude 46°45, longitude 26°23; Friday, May 8, latitude 44°35, longitude 37°; Tuesday, May 12, latitude 40°59, longitude 45°48; Sunday, May 17, latitude 42°21, longitude 500°½. Had they gone north, they would have had to sail to approximately 55°30 north latitude to have cleared Ireland's northernmost point. The North Atlantic's currents and the colder ambient temperatures which would have been encountered farther north, and the greater distance required for the uphill crossing, all suggest the southern route.

Diary of Matthias Cowley, Westmoreland, Mormon Immigration Index.

Additional evidence to suggest the *Westmoreland* sailed south into the North Atlantic through St. George's Channel relates to the ocean currents of the North Atlantic. Sailing in a southwesterly direction would have aided the voyage by avoiding the North Atlantic Current, until they encountered the Gulf Stream, in the area where the Gulf Stream divides into the North Atlantic Current and the Azores Current. At that point, they would have turned essentially west or west-northwest, (the May 17 position might tend to indicate a west-northwest heading), cutting diagonally across the North Atlantic Current toward the Labrador Extension. The Labrador Extension flows to the southwest. (see Drainage Regions and Ocean Currents, *Reader's Digest World Wide Atlas,* Reader's Digest Association, Pleasantville, New York, 1984, p. 189.) They would have caught the Labrador near the Newfoundland Ridge or Basin, their position when the infant boy, Ephraim G. Jensen, died. By that point in the voyage they were heading southwest toward the Delaware Bay, with the Labrador Extension to aid them in the remaining days of the Liverpool to Philadelphia crossing. The several geographic positions given by Cowley in his letter to Pratt, coupled with the fact they did not fundamentally change the set of the sail from April 25 to May 9, seem to support such a course. Without Captain Decan's log, however, this is simply an educated guess.

13. Alice Neely Moncur, *History of Niels and Ingeborg...*pp. 112-19.

14. Second cabin can refer to either accommodations for ship officers of lower rank than the captain, or for second class passengers. The captain's cabin was usually a large compartment with windows at the stern of a sailing ship.

15. Nicolai Sorensen, *Account of Journey...* p. 2.

16. *Journal of Matthias Cowley Emigrating Company*, Op cit.

17. Nicolai Sorensen, *Account of Journey...* p. 3.

18. *Diary of Matthias Cowley, Westmoreland*, Mormon Immigration Index.

19. Kate Caffrey, *The Mayflower*, André Deutsch Limited, London, 1975, pp. 76-77. Regarding trans-Atlantic crossings, it was Caffrey's appraisal that no one drank water as long as wine and beer supplies held out. Clearly the Latter-day Saints on board the *Westmoreland* would have used water if for no other reason than their financial situation would have mandated drinking water, notwithstanding the doctrinal principles taught in Doctrine and Covenants Section 89. However, the voyage reports for the ships which carried large passenger complements indicate that in some cases, such as with the *John J. Boyd* which sailed from Liverpool 12 December 1855, they almost ran out of water and had, in fact, but one day's supply remaining when they landed at New York 15 February 1856.

20. *Diary of Matthias Cowley, Westmoreland*, Mormon Immigration Index.

21. Nicolai Sorensen, *Account of Journey...* p. 3.

22. Don H. Smith, E-mail communique, 16 January 2001. Dr. Smith states that tents had been successfully fabricated by the Martin Company. However, the Willie Company had been without the pattern, and that is one of the things which delayed them and prevented the Willie Company from getting an earlier start. Smith is of the opinion that tents were made on the voyage, but it is not mentioned in the *Westmoreland* reports because it would have only been done with those of nimble fingers, which is an explanation as to why the activity is not mentioned by most immigrants.

23. *Doctrine and Covenants* (D&C) 82:14.

24. James 1:22.

25. *Journal of Johan F. F. Dorius, Westmoreland* (April 1857), *Mormon Immigration Index–Personal Accounts*. The provisions list given for each adult on the *George Washington* was "132,[-] of water, 3½ ms of bread or biscuit, [-] of flour, 1½ ms oatmeal, 1½ ms of rice, 1½ ms of peas, 1½ ms of beef, 1 ms pork, 2 ms potatoes, 2 ounces of tea, 1 m sugar, a ½ of mustard, a ½ ounce of pepper, 2 ounces of salt, & 1 jill [sic] of vinegar. A barrel of flour was usually 196 lbs. jill of vinegar. [A

gill is ½ of a pint, or ½ cup or 4 fluid ounces.] The water was issued daily. The weekly allowance for the passenger complement was 20 barrels biscuit, 4 tierce beef, 4 barrels pork, 4 bags rice, 5 barrels flour, 5 oatmeal, 4 sugar, 4 barrels of peas, ½ chest of tea, ½ barrel of vinegar, besides pepper, mustard, salt, every Saturday." *Diary of Amos Milton Musser*, Op cit. A tierce is given as ⅓ of a pipe or 42 gallons. A pipe is a large cask equal to 2 hogsheads. A hogshead runs from 63 to 140 gallons, the U.S. measure being 63 gallons. A pipe equal to 126 gallons would contain 2 hogsheads of 63 gallons each. The U.S. volumetric measures were apparently being used on the *George Washington*. On that basis, a barrel of flour would have contained 196 lbs. The volume of a tea chest was indefinite. By construction, it was a light wooden box lined with either lead or tin. The expression [-] indicates the unit or measure could not be determined in Musser's account.

26. *Journal of Isaac Sorensen–Utah Historical Quarterly Vol. XXIV* (1956) p. 52. This account also states the Sorensen family arrived in Salt Lake City on 15 September 1857, and that they used oxen to go west. After Florence, they traveled most of the way to Utah with a handcart company, often camping with them at night. That report would indicate the family of Nicholai Sorensen went west with Matthias Cowley's wagon train.

27. For additional information on hardtack during the long voyage of the whaleship, *Essex*, see Nathaniel Philbrick's *In the Heart of the Sea: The Tragedy of the Whaleship Essex*, Viking–Penguin Putnam, Inc., New York, New York, 2000.

28. *Autobiography of Lars Christian Christensen, Westmoreland* (April 1857), *Mormon Immigration Index–Personal Accounts*. This family went west in the 7th Handcart Company. One problem that developed with sea biscuits or crackers on long voyages was they tended to become infested with weevil. As late as the time of Admiral Lord Nelson, a recognized sport was for sailors to tap biscuit bits on the table, and then place wagers as to which piece "walked away first." One of Columbus's sons reported that many crew members preferred to wait for darkness to eat as they would then not have to see the weevils in the biscuits or hardtack. (Caffrey, Op cit, p. 76.) Weevil infestation is not mentioned in the voyage of the *Westmoreland*. In all likelihood, it would not have been possible to resell weevil-infested biscuits, unless it was for livestock feed.

29. Amos Milton Musser, who helped nurse the ill on board the *George Washington* made an insightful comment about diet and health. Under the date of "Wed. April 1, 1857," he wrote: "Up till [-] past 2 with Mrs. Jenkins. All day engaged in working with the Saints. Oranges, lemons, red herring, preserves, & jams are very necessary things for [one] to bring along on a sea voyage." According to Musser's journal entry of a day earlier, Mrs. Mary Anne, wife of Thomas Jenkins, had given birth

to a "fine daughter . . . at 1/4 before 10 o'clock p.m." *Musser*, Op cit.

30. Nicholai Sorensen, *Account of Journey...* p. 3.

31. Nicholai Sorensen, *Account of Journey...* p. 3.

32. *Autobiography of Lars Christian Christensen, Westmoreland,* Mormon Immigration Index.

33. Nicholai Sorensen, *Account of Journey...* p. 3.

34. The ship's position was given as latitude 46º45, longitude 26º23.

35. Peter Niels Garff, *A Biographical Account...*, pp. 1-3.

36. Nicholai Sorensen, *Account of Journey...* p. 4.

37. It is not known if these speeds were in nautical or statute miles. Historically, sea speeds were determined by counting the knots against time as the weighted knots rope was allowed to run out.

38. Nicholai Sorensen, *Account of Journey...* p. 4.

39. Nicholai Sorensen, *Account of Journey...* p. 4.

40. Nicholai Sorensen, *Account of Journey...* p. 5.

41. No one named Kovhy is listed on the *Westmoreland's* passenger complement. Is Kovhy another individual whose name was inadvertently missed in the compiling of the *Westmoreland* company's roster, or is it a misspelling of Kofoed? Hans Ancher Kofoed was from Bornholm where some say Bornholm Danish sounds more like Swedish, a language situation which could possibly explain the need for the Norwegian translation.

42. Nicholai Sorensen, *Account of Journey...* p. 5.

43. Nicholai Sorensen, *Account of Journey...* p. 5; and the Cowley diary, *Westmoreland*, Mormon Immigration index. Latitude 42º21, longitude 55º0$\frac{1}{2}$.

44. Cowley diary, *Westmoreland*, Mormon Immigration Index.

45. One degree latitude or longitude equals 1/360 of the way around the great circle of the earth, or 60 nautical miles which is approximately 69 statute miles. In the 15-day interim between the birth of the Garff boy and the death of the Jensen's son, the *Westmoreland* had sailed 5.86 degrees south and 19.78 degrees west, One should note that the farther one gets from the equator toward the poles, the distance is lessened per degree longitude. That must be taken into account when making estimates of distances sailed.

46. Martin Hansen, *A Synopsis or Short Sketch of My Life*, p. 2. This account was written in longhand by Martin Hansen in his later years. A copy is in possession of Martin's grandson, Cecil Ray Hansen, of American Fork, Utah and is used with his permission. On the *Westmoreland's* immigrant roster, Martin Hansen's name is given as

Morten. No doubt he, like others, adopted the American expression for his name.

47. Cowley letter to Pratt.

48. Cowley letter to Pratt.

49. Cowley diary, Mormon Immigration Index.

50. Cowley diary, Mormon Immigration Index.

51. James M. Tanner, *Biography of James Jensen*, pp. 12-13.

52. C. C. A. Christensen, *By Handcart to Utah...* p. 336.

53. J. M. Tanner, *Biography of James Jensen*, pp. 12-13.

54. *Journal of Johan F. F. Dorius, Westmoreland* (April 1857), Mormon Immigration Index.

55. Nicolai Sorensen, *Account of Journey...* p. 7. Sorensen gives the time of death and that Schram was from Vendsyssel.

56. Cowley letter to Pratt.

57. J. M. Tanner, *Biography of James Jensen. Journal History of the Church*, 13 September 1857, p. 13.

58. Martin Hansen, *A Synopsis or Short Sketch...*, pp. 2-3.

59. Cowley's letter to Orson Pratt. Hafen and Hafen say that Angus M. Cannon came representing John Taylor. The Hafen text cites the *Jensen Journal History of the Church* as their source. Tanner's James Jensen account said they were welcomed by Taylor and Cannon. Johan Dorius's journal, *Journal History of the Church*, 13 September 1857, p. 23, states they arrived at the port of Philadelphia 31 May 1857 where the immigrants were welcomed by Elder Angus M. Cannon in the absence of Elder John Taylor. Cannon acted as emigration agent at Philadelphia. Cowley and Dorius have been taken as the definitive sources which is confirmed by *The Autobiography of Parley P. Pratt*.

60. On behalf of the Twelve Apostles, John Taylor wrote the tribute to Joseph Smith, Jr. which is now D&C 135. John Taylor assisted Parley P. Pratt's son, Parley P. Pratt in the publication of the *Autobiography of Parley P. Pratt*. Elder Taylor, in an addendum to the Preface said that "as Bro. Parley had brought the gospel to me, and as I have always entertained for him the most profound regard, I esteemed it a duty, due alike to gratitude and respect, to assist in having him properly presented before the community." *To The Public*—John Taylor. The *Autobiography of Parley Parker Pratt, Embracing his Life, Ministry and Travels*, edited by his son, Parley P. Pratt, Published for the Editor and Proprietor by Russell Brothers, New York, 1874.

61. *Family Records of Peter Neilson [Nielsen], Mormon Immigration Index*—*Personal Accounts, James Nesmith* (January 1855) p. 2.

62. *Family Records of Peter Nielsen, Westmoreland,* Mormon Immigration Index.

63. 1 Nephi 18:8-22.

<u>Chapter 6</u>

PHILADELPHIA TO IOWA CITY

The stay in Philadelphia was short. Arrangements for rail transportation to Iowa City, Iowa, and other necessities had been made quickly. Angus M. Cannon had acted as the emigration agent at the port of Philadelphia. The earlier financial arrangements and other preparations made aboard the *Westmoreland* had indeed expedited the process. Time was critical. While this was the 46th day since the Copenhagen departure, the most demanding part of the journey remained.

Henry Lunt's journal states that fares for adults were $10.50, half that for those between six and twelve, and free for those under six. They "traveled via Chicago and Baltimore and many places of interest."[1] The special Baltimore and Ohio[2] train took them south from Philadelphia to Baltimore, Maryland and then west to Wheeling, Virginia;[3] from Wheeling westward to Columbus, and then northwest toward Chicago; from Chicago they went west to Rock Island.[4,5]

The Saints had a zeal for Zion though, and the beginning of that long pull and push toward it awaited them at Iowa City. That is the issue which must have consumed their thoughts. Henry Lunt said that from Chicago they went to Rock Island where he and Cowley took the express to Iowa City to prepare things for the arrival of the immigrants.[6] They must have ridden the Davenport and Iowa City Railroad from the Mississippi River to the Iowa City terminus. They had not traveled west on a passenger train. Many year later, Niels Christensen would tell his grandson, Clare, that "it was wonderful riding in box cars with planks for seats."[7]

Four members of the company died during the rail journey.

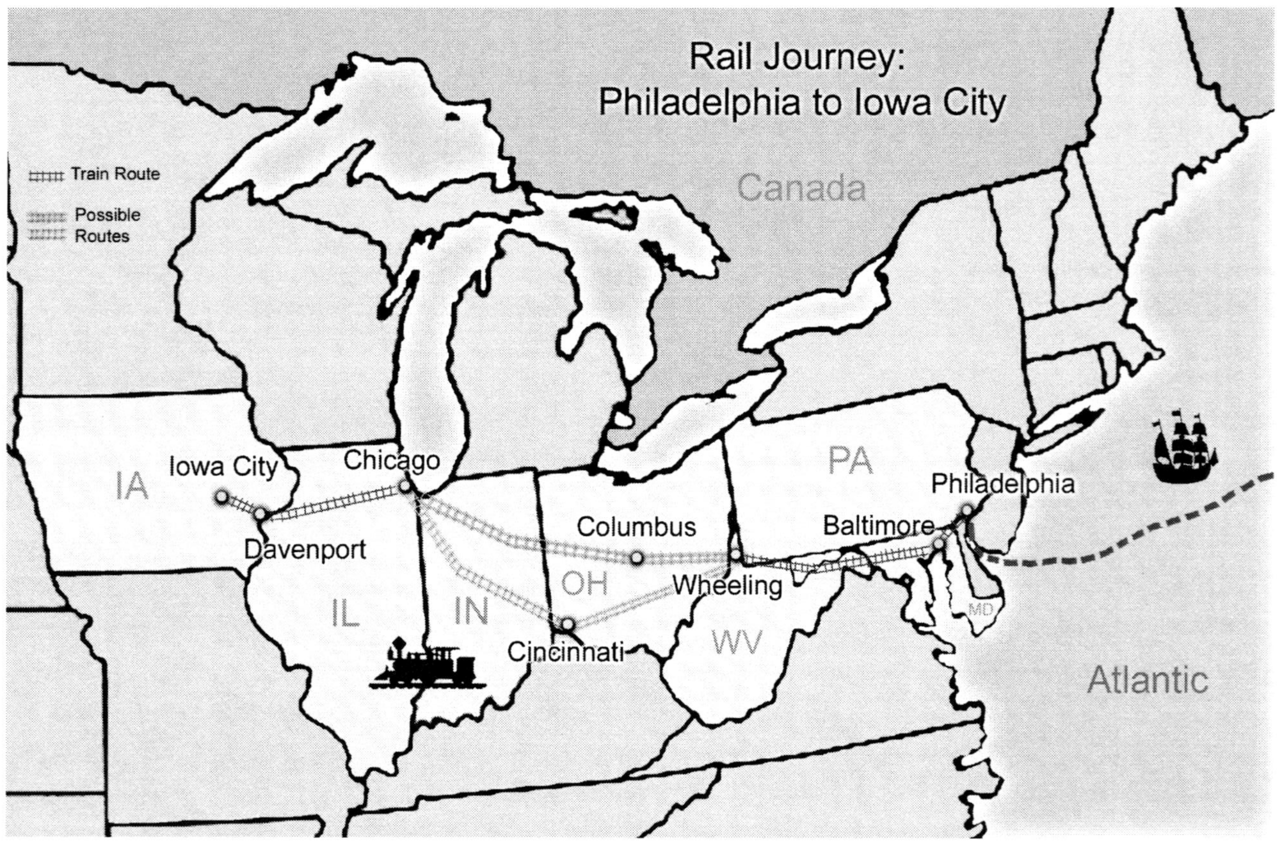

Map by Jeremy Munns

Three were children and the other was Hans Hammer, an elderly brother from Bornholm, Denmark.[8] It is left largely to conjecture as to when they died and where they were buried. Among other unanswered questions are the following: How was the company fed? Usually there was no rail-line food service until the train stopped at a station, and then a short opportunity existed to buy food from vendors. Had they packed food baskets in Philadelphia? A food basket would have been mainly bread, dried salted meats and perhaps some cheese, butter, and jam. In early June there would have been little available fresh fruit or vegetables. Were they able to purchase some fresh milk or buttermilk from vendors at the train stations? Did they carry water? Where did they sleep? Did they disembark the train at night, camp out, or lodge in cheap hotels, or ride on though the dark hours? If their experience was similar to the Saints who had come a month earlier on the *George Washington*, they rode on through the night, sleeping on their luggage or wherever they could find a spot to lie down, stopping to make connections, and to enable the steam-driven locomotives to take on water and fuel.[9]

In an 1862 account of the journey across Illinois, the state is described "a flat, fertile country. Hundreds of cattle [were] grazing on the prairies . . . . Stopped at a village and cleaned them out of bread."[10] Johan Dorius' account mentions the enjoyment of riding through the beautiful country which exhibits fertility, a land blessed by the Lord. Anna (Ana) Christine Jensen wrote that the train journey was not all pleasure. She told of changing cars at night and having to walk a distance in the darkness to meet the next train in the dark. The sick were carried by two men. One elderly man who was being assisted to the next connection dropped dead in his tracks. His mortal energy completely spent, he had laid down his life in the quest for Zion.

One evening they were turned out of the rail cars. Anna Christine and her family sat in the rain in front of a large building, but its doors were not opened. Some sat under umbrellas; Anna Christine's parents got under some "trussed work" for shelter. Anna Christine sat with her baby sister in her lap all night while the rain and mud ran down the hill and onto them. As dawn broke, they looked as though they had laid in a mud hole. With the coming of morning the door of a freight building was opened to them. There was nothing in it except a little straw and some rough goods. They went to an eating house for breakfast. Food was carried to the sick. Anna Christine saw a young man bring a cup of soup and sit down on the floor to feed a young woman who lay sick on a little bit of straw. She thought him especially thoughtful. Later she learned the ill woman was this man's sweetheart. Some of her family were ill and had to occupy an entire seat on the train ride. Others lay on the floor. One night Anna Christine had to stand. She hardly had room to lean against the window. "We were always glad to get off the train," she wrote. One car in which they rode was said to be a cattle car.[11]

One could now ask fascinating questions regarding life's daily activities concerning what for them must have seemed to be rather routine. All were going through it. There does not seem to be much mention of faith-reassuring experiences. Rather, it was an ordinary, pedestrian sort of thing that tested their desire and tried their faith. These Scandinavian saints apparently looked on the bright side. They seem not to have recorded in much detail their demanding trials, although they had them. The men, women and children of the *Westmoreland* company reflected dignity and determination. Perhaps those with especially keen spiritual insight may have recognized the train journey as another unique test of adversity, one of life's grinding, polishing trials. Yet, the paucity of written information about the 1,500 mile rail journey indicates it was not seen as a wonderfully different adventure.[12] It was simply the bridge between the waters of the sea and the sands of the plains.

On the afternoon of 9 June the Scandinavian saints arrived at the rail terminus in Iowa City. The week-long rail trip was at an end. They had apparently averaged some 145 miles per day.[13] Handcarts were obtained at the Iowa City train station. Jacob Bastian told his grandson they assembled their handcarts in

Iowa. They purchased the materials needed to construct the handcarts in the east and brought them on the train. Jacob's carpentry skills were highly beneficial.[14] The first step in the 1,300 mile journey west was the three-mile hike to the staging area at Clear Creek. They first had to cross the Iowa River. It is a large river, an important tributary to the Mississippi. It runs south-southeast from Iowa City until it fishhooks back to the northeast just prior to its confluence with the Mississippi. Eastern Iowa is a wooded hill and vale country. The Iowa River is in one of those deep vales. Clear Creek empties into the Iowa.

Clear Creek is aptly named. At a point northwest of the campsite, one can stand on the brow of the 30-foot-deep hollow which overlooks Clear Creek, and see distinctly the sand and pebbles in the bed of this quiet stream. Along the hollow's ridge was a pioneer cemetery for some who had died before the journey was through. The handcart campground is northwest, some three miles from where the train station would have stood.[15] There, among the beech, hickory, and maple trees, the grass and wild flowers of the Iowa prairie, the *Westmoreland's* passengers made camp. Tents were pitched in a circle; each tent accommodating up to 18 people.[16]

Clear, uncontaminated streams were sought after and much prized by early explorers and pioneers. Many who died on the way west fell victim to typhoid and cholera, both of which can be water-borne diseases. Cholera is caused by a bacillus generally carried into the body by contaminated water or food.[17] The bacillus releases powerful toxins which cause profuse diarrhea and vomiting, and deplete rather rapidly the body's mineral balance. The onset of cholera comes without warning.[18] Human health is promoted by an abundance of pure water. Water and salt requirements are sharply increased by strenuous exercise. Those dietary needs are further exacerbated during hot and humid conditions. The multiple stresses of hard physical exertion after a prolonged period of physical inactivity, inadequate nutrition, and a hot, humid environment to which one has not been acclimated, increases human susceptibility to any disease. Those were some of the physiological challenges which were just ahead for these Scandinavian pioneers. The matter of water purification was not so well understood then. Had it not been for the fresh, virgin nature of North America, the death toll could have been much greater.

On the late afternoon or early evening of June 9, the Scandinavian saints arrived at the Clear Creek camp. Others were already there. James P. Park, a Scotsman and returning missionary, had not gone west with saints who had come earlier on the *George Washington*. Christian Christiansen, an early Danish convert who had been serving a mission in the United States, was among those who greeted the Scandinavian saints. Of Christiansen, Johan Dorius recorded: "Here [at Clear Creek] I saw, among others, Brother Christian Christiansen, who had brought me into the Church."[19] Christiansen had immigrated to America on board the *Forest Monarch*—in the ship's company led by John Erik Forsgren. He had gone on to Utah in 1853. Then in 1855 he was called to go east and serve a mission in the United States. A part of his assignment was to assist with the immigration of on-coming Latter-day Saints.[20] Christian Christiansen was ordained an elder by Erastus Snow, the first Dane ordained an elder in Denmark. Elder Snow called Christiansen to succeed Elder Forsgren as president of the Copenhagen Branch, thereby allowing John E. Forsgren to devote all of his time to missionary proselyting.[21]

Not all of the *Westmoreland's* passengers would go west in handcarts. Some went under the leadership of Matthias Cowley in ox and mule-drawn wagons. Johan Dorius said that most of the immigrants crossed the plains with either the 7th Company or the Matthias Cowley wagon train. In addition to those who had earlier come to America, other Scandinavians would join them at Florence. Some would be left in Nebraska because of health. The family of Ola N. Liljenquist, the assistant interpreter, was among those who went west with Cowley's wagon company.[22] Ola, however, was assigned to go with Captain Park. Duty took precedence over personal considerations.

NOTES

1. *Henry Lunt Journal: Mission to England*, 9 September 1854 to 20 October 1859. Transcribed by Evelyn K. and York F. Jones, May 1999, Cedar City, Utah. Manuscript call #16466, LDS Archives, p. 17.

2. Except for Kimball's mention in "Sail and Rail Pioneers" (p. 19) of the opening of the first division of the Baltimore and Ohio Railroad in May 1830, he does not seem to identify Mormon immigrant companies as using this line. *The Journal of Henry Lunt* states it was the Baltimore and Ohio Railroad and he gave the fares amounts.

3. *Journal History of the Church*, 13 September 1857, p. 23. Interestingly, Stanley Kimball's "Sail and Rail Pioneers" does not attempt to trace the rail route of the *Westmoreland* Company.

4. Henry Lunt Journal..., p. 17.

5. Railroad building was a hot-ticket item on the 1857 political landscape. Several transcontinental routes had been proposed during the preceding decade. A southern route through Texas and the New Mexico Territory appeared to be the most practical and least expensive to build. President Buchanan was partial to the southern route. Unfortunately, the South lacked the political muscle to get the measure through Congress. Failing to get the southern route enacted, Jacksonian Democrats blocked the northern or central route on Constitutional principles, namely the federal government was not authorized to grant subsidies for internal improvements (Kenneth M. Stampp, *America in 1857...*, pp. 215-16).

6. Henry Lunt Journal..., p. 17.

7. Clare B. Christensen, *History of Niels Christensen...*, p. 1. Allen C. Christensen, *The Christensen Family History*, Op cit, p. 6.

8. Journal History of the Church, 13 September 1857, p. 23. The *Westmoreland's* passenger manifest gives 1793 as the year of Hans Hammer's birth. Jim Parker who has studied the Bornholm Saints identified Hans Hammer as the one who died on the rail journey. Telephone conversation of 25 April 2001. Parker's wife, Sherrie, descends from Hans Kofoed or Kofod who was an important leader among the Danish Latter-day Saints of Bornholm, Denmark.

9. Entries in the Diary of Williams Lawrence Hutchings, a passenger on the *George Washington* who traveled to Iowa City with a part of the passenger complement, indicate he traveled all night while lying on his luggage. Stops were made to wait for other train connections and to cross rivers such as the Hudson. Another passenger, Susan Melverta R. Witbeck, said stops were made at Buffalo, Cleveland, Chicago, and Rock Island. See Mormon Immigration Index–Personal Accounts, *George Washington* (March 1857).

10. Thomas Memmott, Journal (1 July 1862) quoted by Stanley B. Kimball in "Rail and Sail Pioneers," p. 26.

11. Anna Christine Jensen McRae's account is quoted by Jimmy B. Parker in *The Life Story of Hans Ancher Kofoed*, privately published by the Hans Ancher Kofoed Family Organization, Ogden, Utah, 1982, pp. 50-51.

12. Jimmy B. Parker, *The Life Story of Hans Ancher Kofoed...*, p. 50.

13. Kimball, "Sail and Rail Pioneers" p. 19, indicates the immigrant trains averaged about 12 miles per hour. Given that exact departure and arrival times are not known, and that stops must have been made for food, for water and fuel for the steam-powered engines, to change trains and crews, to bury the dead, etc., it would seem that when the train was moving they were probably making about 12 miles per hour.

14. Arthur L. Crawford, *Jacob Bastian...*, p. 2.

15. Clear Creek is in present-day Coralville, Iowa. The site of that handcart and ox and mule-team staging camp is now a part of the campus of the University of Iowa. Monuments erected jointly by the University of Iowa and The Church of Jesus Christ of Latter-day Saints tell its Mormon pioneer history. Native vegetation, trees, grass and wildflowers, are protected and becoming reestablished, so as to be an accurate botanical reflection of what the place was like in the 1850s.

16. Journal of Johann F. F. Dorius, *Journal History of the Church,* 13 September 1857, p. 23.

17. There is a report from the accounts of those who came aboard the *James Nesmith* in 1855 that indicates cholera may have been contracted in Leavenworth, Kansas, and Weston, Missouri, when cholera contaminated clothes were taken in as laundry by former *James Nesmith* passengers who were attempting to earn additional funds to help finance the journey west. See *Family Records of Peter Neilson* [Nielsen], Op cit., p. 3.

18. There is a description in the *Journal of Langley Allgood Bailey,* edited by Allen C. Christensen, p. 5, (a copy is on file along with the original journal at the LDS Archives) wherein the limited description of symptoms of a life-threatening illness fit those of cholera. He and his family were members of the 5th or Martin Handcart Company. At Clear Creek, they waited for two costly weeks while their handcarts were being finished. During those two weeks, Langley "learned to swim in the river." It would have been the Iowa River, or perhaps near the mouth of Clear Creek for Clear Creek is not deep enough for swimming at the campsite. While walking across Iowa, with its frequent August thundershowers, he was "taken down with a hemorrhage of the bowels . . . and was unable to walk." He ultimately lapsed into unconsciousness. His survival was miraculous, a gift of Divine Providence, in response to his mother's unwavering faith and a blessing by Elder Franklin D. Richards of the Twelve.

James Godson Bleak, 26, was also a member of the Martin Handcart Company. His journal entry for Sunday the 14th [September 1856] records: "While I was on Guard last night I was attacked with Bloody flux. Have been very ill all day." On Monday the 15th, he wrote: "We traveled 22 miles. I began to draw the handcart but was obliged to leave it. Brother Francis Webster very kindly persuaded me to get into his handcart and drew me 17 miles. Elder Hunter and the two sisters Brown very kindly drew me about four miles. For which kindness I feel grateful, and pray God to bless them with health and strength." His Tuesday the 16th entry recorded: "We travelled 9 miles. Through the blessing of God [I] was able to draw the Handcart to day but am still very ill." *The James Godson Bleak Journal*, Microfilm, Call #MS 14773, LDS Church Archives, Bleak, James Godson, 1829-1918, Journal, 1854 Feb.-1860. Bleak Feb. Bleak and his wife Elizabeth, 27, had four children: Richard, 6; Thomas, 4; James Jr., 2; and Mary, an infant. Francis Webster, 25, is believed to be the same man who spoke eloquently in defense of the decision of sending the Martin Company so late in the season. On that occasion he was in a group of people who became sharply critical of the Church leaders for allowing the Martin Handcart Company to start so late in the season with no more supplies and pro tection than could be afforded by a handcart company. When he could stand their criticism no longer, he arose and with great emotion, based on his own experience, refuted the critics. See p. 78 of *Our Heritage: A Brief History of The Church of Jesus Christ of Latter-day Saints* for an account of Webster's moving declaration of faith.

19. Journal of Johan F. F. Dorius, *Journal History of the Church*, 13 September 1857, p. 23.

20. Journal of Johan F. F. Dorius..., p. 23.

21. Erastus Snow, 1818-1888 Journals, Journal Book No. 5, \ December 1847—September 1850\ LDS Historical Department Archives, Thesfile Infobase p. 143. See also Andrew Karl Larson, *Erastus Snow: The Life of a Missionary and Pioneer for the Early Mormon Church*. University of Utah Press, Salt Lake City, Utah, (1971) p. 264.

22. J. M. Tanner biography of James Jensen. Op cit. 14. *Journal of Johan F. F. Dorius, Westmoreland* (April 1857), Mormon Immigration Index-Personal Accounts.

PART II

HANDCARTS WEST

Chapter 7

ACROSS IOWA

June can be hot and humid in Iowa—an apt description for June 1857.[1] It was a case of one extreme following another, for winter 1856-57 in America's Midwest had been severe and the spring season one of incessant rain and cold. In an April 26 letter begun on board the steamer *Envoy*, James A. Little wrote Orson Pratt that buds on the trees along the Mississippi were just beginning to appear, the grass was slow in starting, and that farmers in Iowa, Illinois, and Missouri had lost their winter wheat crop to the bitterly cold weather.

That terribly harsh winter followed hard on the heels of a poor corn harvest during fall 1856, thereby compounding the husbandry problems for livestock farmers. An abundant corn crop was the basis for successful livestock production. The shortage of feed resulted in the loss of thousands of cattle and hogs. Well-fed livestock can handle much lower ambient temperatures than those which have inadequate feed and must paw for forage in snow-covered meadows or in the woods. Therefore, finding cattle and mules in trail condition was difficult, even though the oxen had been purchased under an agreement which stipulated they should be well-fed until May 1. Some oxen and mules had to be driven 300 miles to get them to Iowa City. Those combined conditions resulted in high prices for supplies. Little wrote: "The following wholesale prices of provisions and groceries in St. Louis will show you that this western country is no longer a place for high wages and cheap provisions. Flour from $6 to $7 per barrel, bacon 12½ cents per pound, sugar from 10½ to 15 cents per pound . . . and other articles of consumption in proportion and on the rise at present."[2]

The Scandinavians faced that sellers' market with little money. The cost of going west had gone up. Yet, a magnificent spirit of mutual support existed among the *Westmoreland* company, and consequently a number who had the means to go by wagon elected to go by handcart so that their brethren would not be left behind.

At Clear Creek there was a change in the company's leadership for those who were to go west by handcart. From this point on, Matthias Cowley would lead a wagon train to the Valley of the Great Salt Lake. A number of those who had come on the *Westmoreland* would go west in Cowley's company of 198 people and 31 wagons. Surviving records seem to indicate Cowley was well-liked and his leadership appreciated.

Among those at Clear Creek was Peder Christensen who later assumed the surname, Klemgaard. Peder had been baptized 26 November 1854 in Denmark. He and other Scandinavians steamed from Copenhagen 29 November 1855 for Grimsby via Kiel, Germany. The trans-Atlantic crossing was made aboard the *John J. Boyd*. It was a long, tough voyage. Measles broke out. Peder lost his wife and two sons. Arriving in America's Midwest, he was placed in charge of Latter-day Saints in the Burlington, Iowa, area until he prepared to go west in 1857. He may well have received this assignment from Christian Christiansen. Klemgaard and his new 16-year-old wife, Line Kragschou, met her family at Iowa City. Soren Jensen Kragschou (Kragskov), his wife Maren, son Peter Christian and his wife, Christiana Maria, and their children, Maren Kristina and Joseph Severin Kragschou, had come to America on board the *Westmoreland*. This extended family went west with Matthias Cowley's wagon train. Kristine Marie Larsen, who had emigrated with the Kragschou family, would go west with the 7th Handcart Company. The wagon journey proved to be too much for 79-year-old Soren Kragschou. He died 29 June 1857 and was laid to rest in Iowa's prairie soil. Peder Christensen Klemgaard ultimately left the Latter-day Saints and affiliated himself with the Morrisites, and, in fact, became the leader of the Morrisite posse.[3]

The Nicholai Sorensen family went west with Matthias Cowley and faced their own unique pioneering challenges. The Cowley Company had to learn the art of managing oxen, many of whom had never been broken or trained to the yoke. At times, the oxen would pile up on each other despite the efforts of the teamsters working on each side of them. To facilitate the training and handling process, they left the yokes on each pair of oxen for the entire three weeks that it took the company to reach Florence, Nebraska. They encountered no buffalo stampedes while crossing Nebraska as had the Willie Company in 1856. Sometimes they were able to kill a buffalo for meat. They lost a number of oxen to "poison alkali," including the Sorensen's best ox, which necessitated the purchase of a yoke of young oxen. They also bought a cow for milk.[4]

Isaac Sorensen's observation concerning the loss of oxen to poison alkali is an indication these pioneers did not have, and probably could not carry, a sufficient supply of salt and other minerals for their cattle. Furthermore, heavy work results in an increase in appetite, so oxen would need to consume more forage to meet the daily dietary requirements for maintenance and work. When turned out to graze, salt and mineral-hungry livestock will attempt to satisfy that hunger by seeking out mineral licks and plants which have a salty taste. Plants which contain oxalate salts are an example of such a problem, for these oxalate salts can interfere with calcium levels in the blood, and proper blood calcium levels are critical for normal cardiac and skeletal muscle function. There are other toxic substances such as hydrocyanic acid; tremetol, an unsaturated alcohol; and alkaloids which are encountered in various poisonous plants.

While there are poisonous substances which produce acute symptoms, the effect of many toxic substances tends to be cumulative; that is, they gradually accumulate in the body as the physiological mechanisms for detoxification and elimination are inadequate to keep pace with ingestion. Then, over time they begin to progressively manifest symptoms such as a loss of flesh, an unsteady gait, erratic actions, general weakness, bloating, and finally prostration and death. Even though there were a number of farmers in the company, it was not always easy to identify the specific cause of death. The problem was further complicated by the fact that stock were grazed during the night time, which made accurate observation all the more difficult. Agricultural technology is highly location specific, and there are problems which are unique to different localities. It is entirely possible that they encountered both toxic mineral licks and poisonous plants such as Plains Larkspur, Arrowgrass, Silvery Lupine, and Lambert Crazyweed, for such are a part of the flora of the Great Plains.

Probably two others who had sailed on the *John J. Boyd* met the *Westmoreland* group at Iowa City or Clear Creek: Niels Christian Anderson, born 26 November 1835 at Lund, Malmo, Sweden, and Ingeborg Paulsen, born 9 April 1823 at Dyver, Christiania, Norway. After he reached St. Louis, Niels Anderson was called to serve a mission in Iowa. He went west with the Cowley wagon train. After Ingeborg Paulsen arrived in the Midwest, she went north to St. Paul, Minnesota. Undoubtedly, she was working to acquire the means to go west. Ingeborg went to Utah with the 7th Handcart Company. She and Niels Anderson married and settled at Ephraim, Utah. Their son, Andrew C. Anderson, born October 1, 1860, is the maternal grandfather of Elder Russell M. Nelson of the Quorum of the Twelve Apostles.[5]

Mads Christensen had owned his own land and home in Denmark. As a consequence, he was better prepared financially than many of the *Westmoreland* group. At Iowa City, Mads purchased a wagon and oxen with the intent of taking his family west with the Matthias Cowley Company. When it became apparent that some of their fellow saints could not afford even as much as a handcart and the necessary supplies to go by that means, Mads sold his ox-team outfit, purchased a handcart, and donated the difference so that others might make the journey. The grateful beneficiaries of his generosity promised to repay him as soon as possible after reaching Zion. His biographer wrote: "The Adolph Madsen family not only paid their debt, but every Christmas for many years afterward sent a monetary token of appreciation to the Christensen family."[6]

On June 13, some three miles west of Clear Creek, James A. Little, in his capacity as emigration agent, assisted by Henry Lunt and others, extended calls to James P. Park to serve as captain with David B. Dillie and Lorenzo D. Rudd as sub-captains of 200, Christian Christiansen as clerk, and Ola Liljenquist as interpreter. Henry Lunt noted in his journal that when leaving the camp he had stood up in a wagon, swung his hat, gave three cheers for the handcart company, and said, "God bless them," to which they responded with a tremendous and loud "Amen." Lunt said he had "very peculiar feelings in seeing them start and could scarcely refrain from shedding tears as well as laughing for it was certainly a peculiar sight" such as he had never before seen and "he felt like asking our Heavenly Father to bless them for they faced a journey of some 1,200 miles having to wade many rivers, and cross the plains which was inhabited by Indians, the buffalo, and wild beasts."[7] In their enthusiasm to get going, the Scandinavians had started west without the company leadership being formally in place.

James P. Park had been the presiding officer of the Latter-day Saint company on board the *George Washington*. David Dillie had served as one of his assistants.[8] Change can be difficult, and this one was. Park, a native of Scotland, did not understand their languages, nor did they understand him. They perceived his manner as unsympathetic toward them.[9] Park, who had been in a holding pattern for a month, was no doubt anxious to be on his way west. The *George Washington*, which sailed from Liverpool 28 March 1857, reached Boston on April 20, five days before the *Westmoreland* weighed anchor at Liverpool. Rested and ready to roll, Park must have been bursting with energy. Like all returning missionaries, he wanted to get home. The Scandinavians had been 53 days on the way since boarding the *L. N. Hvidt*. While enthusiastic about going west, physiologically their bodies would have been weary, their muscles out of tone. The nutritional adequacy of the diet aboard ship and train had been marginal at best.

The company's leadership understood that the cumulative effects of fatigue would build throughout the westward journey.

To minimize any unnecessary burden, the leaders directed that handcarts be loaded as lightly as possible, that only those supplies be taken which would maximize the probability of a successful plains crossing. The handcarts consisted of two wheels and a wood axle over which a shaft was fastened. In building the bottom of the handcart's box, strips of wood were laid over the axle and shaft. The bed of the box was made from canvas which covered the wood strips. During the journey west, bows were fashioned which were arched up and over the handcart's box. The bows were covered with canvas to protect the supplies from rain. Hickory seems to have been the wood of choice used in constructing handcarts—probably a matter of resource availability, for there are dense stands of hickory in the rolling hills near the Iowa City area today.

At Clear Creek, the Scandinavian saints faced some difficult choices. They had "brought with them some of their choicest household effects."[10] Now came a hard reality. To go west by handcart required that many treasured things be left behind. Extra clothing including their best suits, feather beds, books, and greatly cherished family heirlooms had to remain in Iowa. Anders Christian Christensen and his son, Peter, reluctantly gave up their violins. Anders, Peter, and his daughter, Christiania, had played violin trios together in Denmark. Christiania, the oldest child, had chosen not to emigrate when her family came to America. With the sacrifice of their violins, only Peter would eventually own and play another after coming to America.[11] It must have been an emotionally trying two days. In vain, the handcart pioneers hoped that friends who could not go on that season, would somehow hold and forward their possessions. Under camp conditions on the frontier, it was not easy to maintain an inventory of what belonged to whom. Additionally, the harsh privations suffered by those who came later made it necessary to use whatever resources were at hand. Those things left behind were, in a sense, consecrated to the common good, or as one said, "laid under contribution,"[12] to those who followed.

The weight allowance which was limited to 15 pounds per person, included the eating tinware, bedding, and any clothing the person wished to personally carry. In addition to those 15 pounds per individual, there were approximately 200 pounds of supplies. Generally, the small children rode in the handcart. C. C. A. Christensen remembered selling his best trousers to a passing ox driver for twenty-five cents. Others left valuable articles without compensation. Books were left in large numbers, to their owners' deep regret long years later. These saints had aspirations; they had come determined to make something of themselves. Their new homes, their towns, and their cities were to be places of refinement and culture.[13] They were uncommon common people, the "pick and flower" of Scandinavia.

Some things were discarded which should not have been. For example, much later in the journey, when the army had given them an injured ox for meat, a sub-captain wrote in reflection: "We didn't even have a decent ax in the whole company, for almost everything that was heavy was left in the campground at Iowa City."[14] That statement is indicative of the company's communication problems. These were first-time pioneers. Axes were absolutely essential tools. Given weight and space limitations, a cooperative approach as to what must be carried was needed. That probably did not happen. Occasionally, leaders mistakenly assume that because they have given instructions, those instructions have been clearly understood and carefully followed. In this case, instructions given in English had to be understood and implemented in Danish, Norwegian, and Swedish. Cowley spoke with an American accent, but Park's accent must have been heavily flavored by his native Scotland. Communication under those circumstances would have been a tall order for any leader and for any interpreter.

The company included four wagons pulled by mule teams which hauled the tents, cooking skillets, and heavy camping equipment. These mule-drawn wagons lightened somewhat the human burden and helped expedite the journey. But there were other difficulties. When they broke camp and started west the afternoon of June 12, they had been without heavy physical exercise for at least 55 days. Now they were confronted with day-long, physically strenuous exercise in the heat and humidity of America's Midwest. Eastern Iowa's wooded hills can be steep and its dales deep. There were streams and small rivers to ford. If they followed the "river-to-river road" west across Iowa as had the companies of 1856, they would have proceeded along Clear Creek toward Homestead, Iowa, crossing creeks and small streams which flowed toward the Iowa River drainage system. Walnut Creek, Little Bear Creek, and Big Bear Creek would have been among those smaller streams. They would have crossed the North Skunk River east of Newton, Iowa, and Indian Creek, and the South Skunk west of there, by which point they would have been moving west-southwest. That route would have required crossing the Des Moines—there was a long bridge (Flat Boat Bridge) over the Des Moines,[15] before they were half way to Council Bluffs. In picturesque language, one pioneer wrote there were "two middling good streams four miles west of Fort Des Moines."[16] (Perhaps those streams are Four Mile Creek and Beaver Creek. Many of Iowa's streams and rivers have forks or branches. Insofar as logistically reasonable, waterways tended to be crossed before the confluence of the branches or forks for stream flow or volume is smaller and consequently can be forded with less difficulty and risk.)

After crossing Four Mile Creek, they would have forded the Raccoon River near Adel. The route would indicate probable crossings of the Middle and South Raccoon rivers north of their confluence. Then came the Middle Des Moines River, Bear Station, the East Nishnabotna River, and Indian Town. The 7th Company did not mention seeing Indians before Florence, Nebraska. Indian Town referred to Big Foot's Village on Indian Creek, a short distance above its confluence with Nishnabotna River. Big Foot was a Pottawattamie chief whose band constituted about a third of the Pottawattamie tribe. They called their village Mi-au-mise. In 1846, twenty Mormon families made a settlement near that village which they called Indian Town.[17] Other travelers who used the Mormon Trail generally called it Indian Town as well. After the Pottawattamie had been dispossessed from their traditional homeland east of the Mississippi, they were given this area in southwestern Iowa in 1833. The Pottawattamie had compassionately accepted Nauvoo's Mormon exiles.[18] A subsequent treaty with the federal government resulted in their removal to Kansas during the 1847-48 period.

Big Foot's village had been deserted for nearly a decade when the handcart pioneers passed by. For a time this place was called Iranistan. It is just west of the present-day Iowa town of Lewis.[19] West of Lewis they would have crossed the East Nishnabotna, another Indian Creek, Jordan and Graybull creeks, the West Nishnabotna River, Silver and Middle Silver creeks, then the Keg and Mosquito creeks before arriving at Council Bluffs. Somewhere along their route, they may have passed over Pigeon Creek. Along creeks and streams in the counties of western Iowa which fronted the Missouri River, many Mormon settlements north and south of Kanesville had been built in the 1846-52 period. In fact, for a number of years this part of the Iowa road had been called the Pottawattamie Trail. Martin Hansen described the crossing of Iowa's streams in his handwritten memoir. He said they would unload their handcarts, carry their goods and supplies across the stream on their heads and shoulders to keep them dry, and then reload their possessions into handcarts. Fires would be built, around which they would dry their clothing and warm themselves.[20]

On the afternoon of Friday, June 12, the 7th Company rolled west from Clear Creek. Each handcart was assigned an average of five persons. After traveling two miles, they "camped for the night at an attractive place, where everything was green and beautiful." The large round tents with one pole in the center were pitched in two rows. Two or three families were assigned to each tent. People busied themselves with cooking and other work of the camp. Johan Dorius wrote that he felt glad to be enjoying the outdoors, that it was a pleasure to haul green branches, to listen to the hymns of thanks which came from the tents before the occupants retired for the evening.[21]

While the pioneers were focused on the trek to the valley of the Great Salt Lake, things of political consequence were unfolding which would impact their journey and the Church. Unknown to them, some 170 miles to the southeast on that very June 12, Senator Stephen A. Douglas, a former friend of the Prophet Joseph Smith, delivered a scathing political speech at Springfield, Illinois, in which he characterized "Mormonism as a loathsome ulcer on the body politic."[22] He charged that nine-tenths of Utah's inhabitants were alien and refused to take the oath of allegiance to the United States and that they were bound by horrible oaths to Brigham Young. He also declared that Brigham Young was in league with the Native Americans in prosecuting a system of robbery and murder against those American citizens who supported the authority of the United States and who denounced practices and institutions of the Mormon government.[23]

More than just the summer weather was heating up, for it was also an especially hot political period. James Buchanan faced civil unrest in Kansas. Passions ran high over the matter of popular sovereignty. Would the pro-slavery or free-soil elements ultimately prevail in Kansas' petition for statehood? Regional sectionalism was on the increase. The Dred Scott decision heaped fuel on an already rancorous antislavery debate.[24]

In a 26 September 2002 address at Brigham Young University, Justice Sandra Day O'Connor called the Dred Scott decision possibly the worst decision ever made by the United States Supreme Court. If one accepts that it is the primary responsibility of the court to defend the Bill of Rights and to protect the rights of the minority, she may well be correct in her assessment of court decisions made to this point in U.S. history, at least as we interpret the Constitution today.

America's Whig party was undergoing political demise and dismemberment. With the 1857 inauguration hardly over, posturing for the 1860 presidential campaign was vigorously underway, and there were a number of would-be presidents with serious cases of Potomac fever. If President Buchanan had enjoyed any sort of a political honeymoon, it had been very short indeed.

One of his chief rivals within the Democratic party was none other than Stephen A. Douglas. Highly ambitious, Douglas had caught the presidential bug. It had happened to others before him. For prominent senators, it remains a hazard to the formulation of sound policy even to this day. So it was that Douglas was busily exploring his options, for he was at the forefront of a parade of personalities who were weighing their prospects for a successful candidacy in the 1860 presidential election. While many in Washington were inflaming public passions against the Latter-days Saints, Senator Douglas had the opportunity to do much good, to set the record straight. He could have provided an opportunity for the public to hear a balanced case, for all sides in any dispute deserve their day in court. Sadly, Douglas abandoned objectivity. Expediency replaced principle. Rather than pour the conciliatory water of reason on the growing fire, he took the low road of perceived political advantage and fanned, with hot rhetoric, the simmering flames of resentment against a beleaguered minority. As an attorney and a statesman, he should have known better, for in fact, he had been forewarned.

Stephen A. Douglas had chosen to ignore the Prophet Joseph Smith's solemn declaration given toward the end of a lengthy 18 May 1843 conversation at Carthage, Illinois. According to the journal of William Clayton, who was present on that occasion, the 30-year-old Douglas had requested that Joseph Smith give him a history of the Missouri persecutions. Joseph Smith did so in minute detail for about three hours. Judge Douglas listened in rapt attention to the Prophet Joseph. The judge added his personal depreciation for the conduct of Governor Boggs and the authorities and mobs of Missouri, and stated they should be brought to judgment and the guilty punished. Then Joseph Smith, after prophesying that dire consequences would befall Missouri if the authorities did not redress the wrongs committed against the Latter-day Saints, said directly to Douglas: "Judge, you will aspire to the presidency of the United States; and if you ever turn your hand against me or the Latter-day Saints, you will feel the weight of the hand of the Almighty upon you; and you will live to see and know that I have testified the truth to you; for the conversation of this day will stick to you through life."[25]

That Stephen A. Douglas aspired to the presidency of the United States and was nominated 23 June 1860 by the Democratic Party, is a matter of historical record. His prospects of winning appeared bright for he was a charismatic politician, an eloquent and elegant orator. In an 1856 address, Abraham Lincoln, speaking by way of comparison concerning his political rivalry with Douglas, said: "With me, the race of ambition has been a flat failure; with him it has been one splendid success. His name fills the nation; and he is not unknown in foreign lands."[26]

The Democrats were the incumbent and dominant political party. However, when the electoral votes were counted, Abraham Lincoln had won 180, Breckinridge took 72, Bell 39, and Senator Douglas received but 12 electoral votes. Many historians ascribed his defeat to the issue of popular sovereignty regarding the matter of slavery in the territories. Douglas' espousal of that policy, which by nature was contradictory, enabled Abraham Lincoln to successfully corner him during the 1858 Lincoln-Douglas debates. Under the competing contradictions of that policy, that is, that the legislature of a territory by failing to pass laws to protect slavery could in fact exclude it, the Democratic party splintered into regional factions. While Douglas's short-term political gain was his 1858 reelection to the United States Senate, it had cost him the presidency, for in 1860 the South turned away from him. The failure to win the presidency must have resulted in extraordinarily deep disappointment. Coupled with the persistent memory of his conversation with Joseph Smith, his emotional state must have bordered on anguish and despair. It is said he was a heartbroken man when he died 3 June 1861. He was only 48.

By contrast, the lives of those going west as handcart pioneers were an eloquent testament to their acceptance of the divinity of the restoration of the Church of Jesus Christ. They knew Joseph Smith was a prophet of God. Even though the gathering to Zion placed their lives in peril, they were responding to the call of his prophetic successor, Brigham Young. Together with other Saints, in fulfillment of ancient and modern prophecy, they would build Zion and the Mountain of the Lord's House in the top of the mountains.

On Sunday, June 14, the 7th Company was divided into eight districts. The ability to organize a diverse group into a functioning and unified whole is a learned skill. Each district was given a captain. Johan Dorius and his brother, Carl, were appointed captains over nine handcarts each.

The company spent the remainder of that week moving forward, but not rapidly. Many were ill, so much so that their four wagons drawn by mules were often filled to capacity.[27] One day, an ailing mother, Bertha Marie Hansen, and other weary folks sat down to rest and wait for the wagons which were behind them. The wagons passed them by. They began walking to catch up to the camp. That night when Bertha Marie Hansen was found missing, her husband, Hans, and a mule team began the search. It was midnight before they had found her and were back in camp. It was a very hard ride for Bertha, as seemingly the drivers hurrying as rapidly as night conditions allowed, only "hit the high places" on the very rough road.[28] At this juncture, a Brother Christenson purchased a wagon and a yoke of oxen, for he determined that he would go west from Florence with the wagon company. Sister Hansen rode the remainder of the journey to Florence in the Christenson wagon. After that, during the remainder of the journey, special attention was taken to try to make certain no one was accidentally left behind.[29]

Going back at night to find those whose strength had failed during the day was a task given to the young men of the company. When an insufficient number of empty handcarts were taken on these recovery missions to carry to the campsite the exhausted pioneers found lying by the roadside, the search party members carried the other weary ones on their backs. One night 20-year-old Anna Margreta Christensen, suffering and ill with fever, was found and carried to camp and her family by her 18-year-old brother, Peter.[30]

A week later, Sunday June 21, Johan Dorius recorded "that an old sister died in camp and was buried in the woods."[31] They continued to push across Iowa although the sick of the company delayed them. The weather was a factor. They spent from two to three hours camped at midday because of the heat. The memory of Dorius' missionary friend was a little different. C. C. A. Christensen said they "suffered greatly for the first two or three hundred miles" while traveling through Iowa to the Missouri River. "The hot season of the year, frequent rainshowers, almost bottomless roads, exertion and the diet to which we were unaccustomed, and the inconsiderate course of action pursued by our leader, brought about much sickness and many deaths among us."[32] He paid high tribute to the Dorius brothers and their young wives, all of whom administered aid and encouragement to the ill, the despondent, and the exhausted.[33] The frontier roads of Iowa had come as a shock. These Scandinavians came from countries of stone-paved streets. Loving Christian concern for one another must have helped smooth the long, rugged road.

As they pushed across Iowa, a regular routine was developed. At evening, tents were pitched in a circle. Campfires lighted outside the circle were used for cooking. The smoke helped keep away the hungry mosquitoes. At 5:00 A.M. a whistle was blown to announce all should arise and get breakfast. Immediately afterward everyone assembled for a hymn, prayer, and instruction.[34] Frederick Hansen, the oldest child of Hans and Bertha Marie, described how his family managed their handcart. He wrote: "Father worked on the left side of the cart, my brother John on the right, I worked in the middle, pulling a rope about four feet long, one end of which was tied to the cart, to the other end of the rope was a small stick which had been fastened for use as a handle. We made what some called a spike team. I always thought I had the easiest part, as I did not have to hold back going down hill."[35]

Thursday, July 3, the handcart pioneers reached Council Bluffs. As they approached the town, officers of Council Bluffs refused them entrance to the city, alleging the company was infected with smallpox, a charge the immigrants denied.[36] Latter-day Saint preeminence in western Iowa and especially at Kanesville effectively ceased in the spring of 1852. At that time,

Elder Orson Hyde of the Twelve, at the instruction of President Brigham Young, issued the call for all to go west and most did. Some, wearied by the persecution and sacrifices attendant to the exodus from Nauvoo, were reluctant to leave the new farms and homes which they had begun on the rich prairies of Iowa. They were among those who tarried.[37]

The remaining residents were largely non-LDS people. An act of the Iowa Legislature changed the name of Kanesville to Council Bluffs effective 9 February 1853.[38] Prior to the 1852 exodus, Kanesville had LDS leadership and LDS newspapers, *The Frontier Guardian* (Whig) and *The Weekly Bugle* (Democrat). The Latter-day Saints enjoyed excellent relationships with the local Native American tribes from the beginning of their sojourn in western Iowa. New and continuing residents of Council Bluffs had undoubtedly laid claim to lands and shops formerly owned by early Latter-day Saints. That historical fact could have made them nervous about a company who might have grounds to lodge a counterclaim. Out of a desire to avoid difficulties, the handcart pioneers bypassed Council Bluffs to the east and south. These Scandinavians were the Master's disciples. Compelled to go out of the way, they went the extra mile. There was a steamboat landing south-southwest of the town.[39] They camped along the Missouri River that night.[40]

The crossing of Iowa had been a hard journey. Acclimatizing to hot and humid weather proved difficult for these pioneer saints, for Scandinavia was a land of pleasant summers and good roads. Driving high-powered, air-conditioned automobiles on today's controlled-access freeways, with their cuts and fills to grade, their concrete and steel bridges, their easy on-and-off eating places, we frequently miss the fact that in 1857 the road west through Iowa was an enlarged trail, with streams and rivers to be forded and waded, an up-and-down dirt road, a hard pull made all the more difficult when the soil was wet. Years later, Niels Christensen told a grandson they had aimed to make 25 miles a day, their camping places influenced by a suitable source of water.[41] Their exuberance led them to attempt to go faster than their strength allowed.

The crossing of some 275 miles[42] from Iowa City to Council Bluffs had taken 21 days. Assuming they remained in camp on Sundays, they had averaged 15.3 miles per day, a hard pace given the ill among them and other challenges faced. Once during the journey across Iowa, the company had to turn off the road to allow the U. S. mail to pass.[43]

In 1850, a stagecoach and mail service had been established across Iowa to Kanesville, and from Kanesville south to St. Joseph, Missouri. It was a fast coach, pulled by four horses handled by a skilled driver, and probably accompanied by a shotgun rider, who sounded a big horn to warn others of their approach. The handcart pioneers were at the foot of a large hill when they heard the warning sound come from over the hilltop. An eyewitness said the mail coach came down the road "at breakneck speed."[44] It was a taste of America's appetite for speed. "The mail's got to go through and quickly boy," was an expression which would find its ultimate manifestation with the advent of the Pony Express three years later. The mail stage did not delay the company long. It was the contrast of the mail carrier's speed compared to their plodding pace in the stifling heat and humidity of that June which caught their attention and remained a bright memory for many years to come.

NOTES

1. C. C. A. Christensen, *By Handcart to Utah...*, p. 338.

2. J. A. Little to Orson Pratt, *Millennial Star*, XIX:377-79.

3. Don H. Smith, "Peder C. Klemgaard, Leader of the Morrisite Posse." Paper given at the 1999 Ogden, Utah Mormon History Association meeting. E-mail copy in possession of the author courtesy of Dr. Smith of Pullman, Washington. Dr. Smith had ancestry in the James Willie Handcart Company. He is presently writing a comprehensive account of that company. See also the Mormon Immigration Index's *Westmoreland* roster for the names of the Kragschou or Kragskov family members.

4. Isaac Sorensen, "History of Isaac Sorensen," *Utah Historical Quarterly*, Vol. XXIV (1956) p. 53.

5. Russell M. Nelson, *From Heart to Heart: An Autobiography*, in Chapter 2 "From Europe to Ephraim," p. 8. Also see the Mormon

Immigration Index passenger list. Niels is listed as Nils Anderson, born 1836, and Ingeborg is given as Ingeborg Poulsen, born 1823. Niels must have been serving his mission under the direction of Christian Christiansen who is known from the Dorius account to have met the *Westmoreland* company at Iowa City. No doubt Niels and Ingeborg had become acquainted on the voyage of the *John J. Boyd*. The Cowley Company and the Christian Christiansen Company seemingly crossed paths at least three times on the journey across the plains.

6. Phyllis Christensen, *Mads Christensen 1825-1914*, Op cit., p. 6. [No Adolph Madsen is listed on the *Westmoreland's* roster as it presently exists. One Madsen family was given. It is the Peter Madsen family. Whether Adolph was also a name by which Peter became known afterward, or whether the Adolph Madsen family represents a family not recorded on the passenger manifest, is not known. What is clear is there was a Madsen family which went west with the 7th Handcart Company.]

7. Henry Lunt Journal..., p. 17.

8. The Mormon Immigration Index listed several of the elders on board the *George Washington* as company bishops. Dillie was one so designated.

9. J. M. Tanner, "Biography of James Jensen," *Journal History of the Church*, p. 14.

10. J. M. Tanner, Biography of James Jensen..., p. 14.

11. *A Sketch of the Lives of Anders Christian Christensen and His Wife, Sophie Marie Christensen*, p. 6. Which granddaughter of Anders Christian Christensen wrote this account of his life is unknown to the author. Hereafter it will be identified as *Anders Christian Christensen*. See also Carter, *Treasures of Pioneer History*, v, p. 283. Quoted by Hafen and Hafen, *Handcarts to Zion: The Story of a Unique Western Migration, 1856-1860*, University of Nebraska Press, 1960, p. 158, footnote 36.

12. Anders Christian Christensen, *A Sketch of the Lives of Anders Christian Christensen...*, p. 6.

13. C. C. A. Christensen, "By Handcart to Utah: The Account of C. C. A. Christensen," translated from Danish by Richard L. Jensen. Nebraska History 66: (4) Winter 1985, pp. 337-38.

14. C. C. A. Christensen, "By Handcart to Utah: The Account of C. C. A. Christensen," translated from Danish by Richard L. Jensen. Nebraska History 66: (4) Winter 1985, p. 343.

15. Frederick Hansen, "The Great Handcart Trek from Iowa City to Salt Lake City," Journal of History, 1916, IX:408-16. Published by the Board of Publication of the Reorganized Church of Jesus Christ of Latter Day Saints, Lamoni, Iowa. The RLDS Church will provide copies of this paper upon request through their offices in Independence, MO. [see a

copy in LDS Church Archives, Ms 2230, pp. 43-49, Acc. #27522]

16. Hafen and Hafen, Handcarts to Zion..., p. 210.

17. Floyd E, Pearce, "Cass County," in *The Iowa Mormon Trail*, Susan Easton Black and William G. Hartley, Editors; Helix Publishing, Orem, Utah, 1997, p. 251.

18. Howard R. Driggs, *The Old West Speaks*, Prentice-Hall, Englewood Cliffs, N. J., 1956, pp. 96-97.

19. Charles H. Babbitt, *Early Days at Council Bluffs*, Press of Byron S. Adams, Washington, D. C. 1916, reprinted in 1990 by the Historical Society of Pottawattmie County, p. 35. Babbitt gives the 1916 name as Iranistan and tells of Big Foot. Floyd E. Pearce in "Cass County" in *The Iowa Mormon Trail*, Susan Easton Black and William G. Hartley, Editors, Helix Publishing, Orem, Utah, 1997, pp. 247, 251 confirms Indian Town as Big Foot's village or Mi-au-mise, and identifies its location as just west of present-day Lewis, Iowa. He also tells that 20 Mormon families built a settlement near the Indian village. Pearce states that all seven handcart companies of 1856 and 1857 passed through Cass County. Shortly after passing Indian Town they would have entered present-day Pottawattamie County along a route known as the Pottawattamie Trail. In 1853 non-Mormon settlers platted the Indian Town area and it soon became a part of Lewis, the county seat. Pearce also indicates this route was the stagecoach route between Des Moines and Council Bluffs.

20. Martin Hansen, *A Synopsis or Short Sketch....*, p. 3.

21. Journal of F. F. Dorius..., p. 23. What was the purpose of green branches? One possibility was that it was an attempt to create a degree of privacy for such activities as nursing babies, and bodily elimination functions. These were sensitive, dignified people with a high degree of decorum.

22. Andrew Jenson, *Church Chronology or A Record of Important Events Connected with The Church of Jesus Christ of Latter-day Saints*, and the Territory of Utah. Salt Lake City, Utah, 1886, p. 54.

23. For a more complete account see Joseph Smith, History of the Church, Volume V, pp. 395-98.

24. In a September 26, 2002 address at Brigham Young University, Justice Sandra Day O'Connor called the Dred Scott decision possibly the worst decision ever made by the United States Supreme Court. If one accepts that it is the primary responsibility of the Court to defend the Bill of Rights and to protect the rights of the minority, she may well be correct in her assessment of court decisions made to this point in U.S. history, at least as we interpret the Constitution today.

25. Joseph Smith, History of the Church, Volume V, pp. 393-94.

26. Abraham Lincoln, 1989. *Speeches and Writings* 1832-1856. New York: Library of America, p. 384.

27. Journal of Johan F. F. Dorious..., p. 23.

28. Frederick Hansen, *The Great Handcart Train...*, pp. 413-414.

29. Frederick Hansen, The great Handcart Train...,pp. 413-414. Even though the Hansen family ultimately left the LDS Church, Frederick Hansen wrote of Brother Christenson that "Father's family and all those who Brother Christenson took with him felt we could never thank him enough for his kindness. I have often wondered what became of him. He joined the cattle train at Florence and started westward." This Christenson may have been Jacob Christenson.

30. Anders Christian Christensen, *A Short Sketch of the Lives of...*, p.3.

31. Anders Christian Christensen, *A Short Sketch of the Lives of...*, p.3.

32. C. C. A. Christensen, *By Handcart to Utah...*, p. 338. See endnote 10 of his paper for additional explanation as to why Christensen was critical of James P. Park.

33. C. C. A. Christensen, By Handcart to Utah..., p. 338.

34. Frederick Hansen, "The Great Handcart Train from Iowa City to Salt Lake City," *Journal of History*, IX:408-416. 1916.

35. Frederick Hansen, *The Great Handcart Train...*, p. 411.

36. Hafen and Hafen, *Handcarts to Zion*, p. 159. Langley Allgood Bailey was a member of the Martin Handcart Company. He records in his journal that as they passed through the towns and villages of Iowa, there were some people who came out of their homes and jeered them as they went west. *The Journal of Langley Allgood Bailey*, edited by Allen C. Christensen, p. 5. A copy is in the LDS Archives which is also the repository for the original journal. During the Mormon Pioneer Sesquicentennial celebration of 1996-97, the people of Iowa were highly enthusiastic about the history of the Mormon trails across their state, and highly supportive of the pioneer trek re-enactment.

37. Ed. Note: In the author's own extended collateral ancestral family were some who tarried. Lorenzo Dow Driggs and his wife, Melinda White, remained in Iowa. His younger brother, Starling Graves Driggs, had been a member of Brigham Young's 1847 1st Company and was a part of the San Bernardino Colony. His older brother, Shadrack Ford Driggs, an important wagon maker in Nauvoo, and his wife, Eliza White, Melinda's sister, came west with their family in 1852. Eliza and Melinda's brother, Samuel S. White, had served in the Mormon Battalion. Shadrack and Lorenzo had buried their father, Uriel, in a grave marked by a walnut tree in Lee County, Iowa, and their mother, Hannah, at Pigeon Creek. Rebecca Smith White, the mother of the White sisters, went west to the valleys of the mountains with Shadrack and Eliza, who are the author's ancestors. They made their Utah home in Pleasant Grove.

38. Charles H. Babbitt's *Early Days at Council Bluffs*, first published in 1916 by Press of Byron S. Adams, Washington, DC and republished in

1990 by the Historical Society of Pottawattamie County provides an interesting treatise on Council Bluffs and Kanesville.

39. Hafen and Hafen, Handcarts to Zion., p. 159. Charles H. Babbitt, *Early Days at Council Bluffs*, p. 7. Babbitt provides a map of the vicinity of Council Bluffs.

40. Frederick Hansen, The Great Handcart Train..., p. 415.

41. Clare B. Christensen, History of Niels Christensen, p. 2.

42. Hafen and Hafen, *Handcarts to Zion...*, p. 65. They give a range of 275 to 300 miles. The lower figure is assumed to be more realistic.

43. Frederick Hansen, *The Great Handcart Train...*, p. 412.

44. Frederick Hansen, *The Great Handcart Train...*, p. 412. Hansen wrote in reflection that this event occurred after June 21, about the same time as they crossed the Des Moines River. He did not remember whether they had crossed the river "above or below Des Moines."

Gail Geo. Holmes, President, Kanesville Restoration, Inc., Pottawattamie County: The Mormon Trail and Ferry System in Southwestern Iowa; Chapter 11 in *The Iowa Mormon Trail: Legacy of Faith and Courage*, Susan Easton Black and William G. Hartley, editors. Helix Publishing, Orem, Utah, 1997, p. 174. Lana Pals, a former president of the Iowa Mormon Trails Association notes there was a stagecoach stop located along Highway 25 about 2 miles west of present-day Orient, Iowa. (*The Iowa Mormon Trail*, Op cit., p. 245.) The Mormon Trail from Nauvoo crossed the property, but it seems likely the handcart pioneers passed north of this stage stop.

<u>Chapter 8</u>

BEYOND THE MISSOURI

On Friday morning, July 3, a steam boat ferried the 7th Company over the Missouri River to Omaha, Nebraska territory. During the crossing, the wagon carrying the trunks which contained the Garff family's clothing, bedding, and supplies of all kinds tipped over in midstream and their prized possessions were swept away.[1] The company did not stop at Omaha, but went north seven miles to Florence, arriving about noon.[2] The Florence town site had been known as Winter Quarters during the period of the Mormon exodus from Nauvoo. Waiting at Florence[3] were Latter-day Saints who earlier had emigrated from Scandinavia. Existent records indicate the Jens Gottfredson, Peder Jensen, Anders Larsen, Samuel Lublin, and Didrick Mortensen families were planning to go on to the Salt Lake Valley with the 7th Company. The Gottfredsons and Larsens had come to America on board the *John J. Boyd*, the Lublins were on board the *Charles Buck*. The Mortensens had sailed on the *James Nesmith* in January 1855 under the leadership of Peter O. Hansen, one of the four original missionaries to Scandinavia. They were part of a group of 150 who remained in the Weston, Missouri vicinity until they could earn sufficient funds to go west. The Jensens had come on board the *Thornton*, the ship which had brought most of the James G. Willie Handcart Company to America in 1856. They warmly welcomed the 1857 arrivals.

Many of those who sailed from Liverpool on board the *James Nesmith* had come to England from Denmark on board the steamship, *Cimbria*. Encountering high southwest winds and heavy seas on 27 November 1854, the captain of the

Cimbria, an experienced and safety-conscious seaman, turned about and put into Mandal, an excellent natural harbor partially enclosed by high granite cliffs on the southern coast of Norway. While waiting for the fury of the storm to abate, some of the Latter-day Saints lodged ashore. The residents of Mandal were curious about the new religion espoused by these Danish Latter-day Saints. They requested that someone preach to them. As a consequence of those meetings, some of Mandal's inhabitants embraced the restored gospel. The weather seemed favorable on the morning of 7 December and the *Cimbria* again steamed for England. However, they discovered the lull in the weather was simply a brief calm before an even more violent storm, which struck with increasing fury until it shattered the ship's bulwarks and broke a number of boxes. The initial

It was from this vicinity now on the University of Iowa campus in Coralville that the handcart companies of 1856-57 started west. The Univeristy of Iowa is attempting to keep the flora of this area much as it would have been then. Clear Creek is a little to the north of this site. Pictured left to right are Ann C. Anderson, her daughter, Elizabeth, the author, and Eric Christensen. Photograph by Kathleen A. Christensen.

thought was to return to Mandal. However, high winds and waves and a strong contrary current rendered that a very dangerous route, so the *Cimbria* returned all the way back to Frederikshavn, near the upper end of Jutland's east coast,

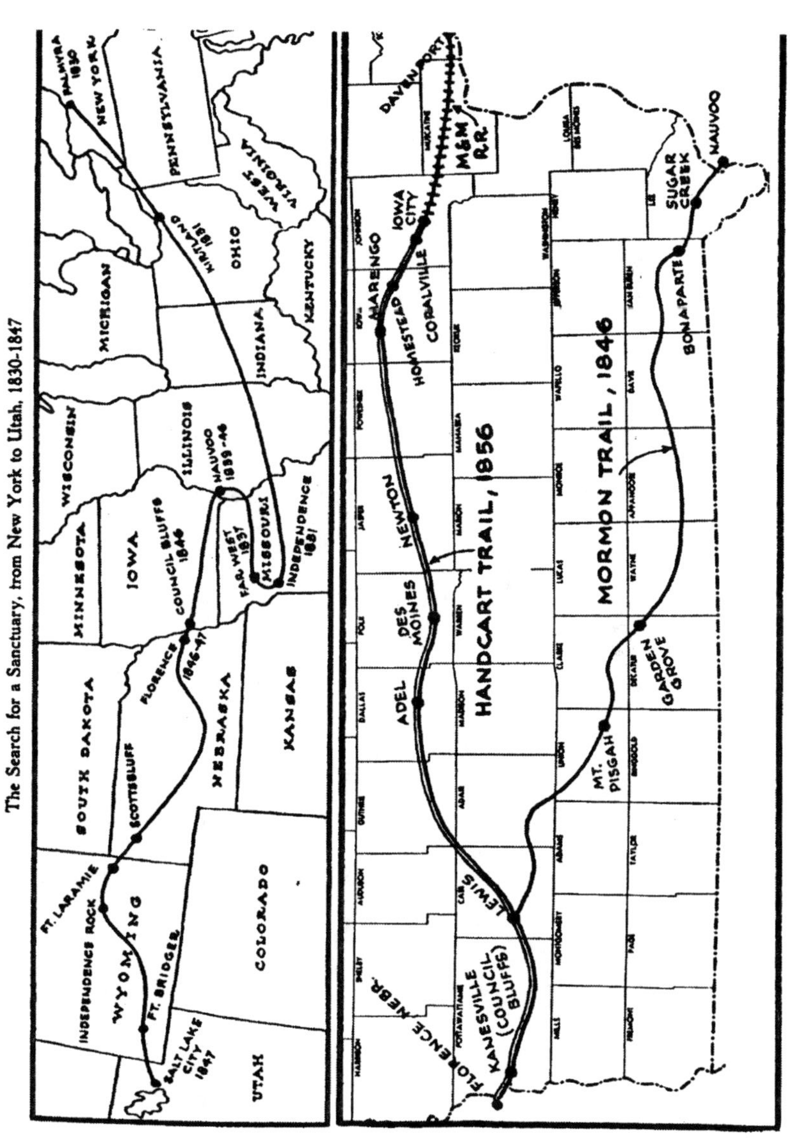

Courtesy of Iowa Historical Society

arriving there at 4 P.M. December 9. A number of meetings were held in Frederikshavn with residents of that seaport town who had previously been unwilling to listen to their preaching. On December 20, the *Cimbria* again put to sea. During the night of December 21, a storm arose more fierce than the two which had preceded it. The ship and all on board were threatened with destruction. For the third time, the *Cimbria*'s captain directed that they turn back. The captain and the crew were becoming discouraged. However, the Latter-day Saints prayerfully thanked the Lord for the preservation of their lives. About 2 P.M. December 22, the wind suddenly changed and blew from the north. The captain turned about and set the course for Hull. Amid rejoicing Mormon passengers, the *Cimbria* landed at Hull on noon December 24. On Christmas Day they took the train for Liverpool where they joined with smaller groups of

Clear Creek Iowa. Scandinavian handcart pioneers camped here June 9-12, 1857. Photograph by Carlyn Christensen-Szalanski.

Latter-day Saints who had left Copenhagen about the same time as the *Cimbria* had first departed Denmark.

It was at Florence where the *Westmoreland* group first saw Native Americans. Their description of them was short: "They were nearly naked." In the evening they were visited by brethren from Zion. Among those men was one of Brigham

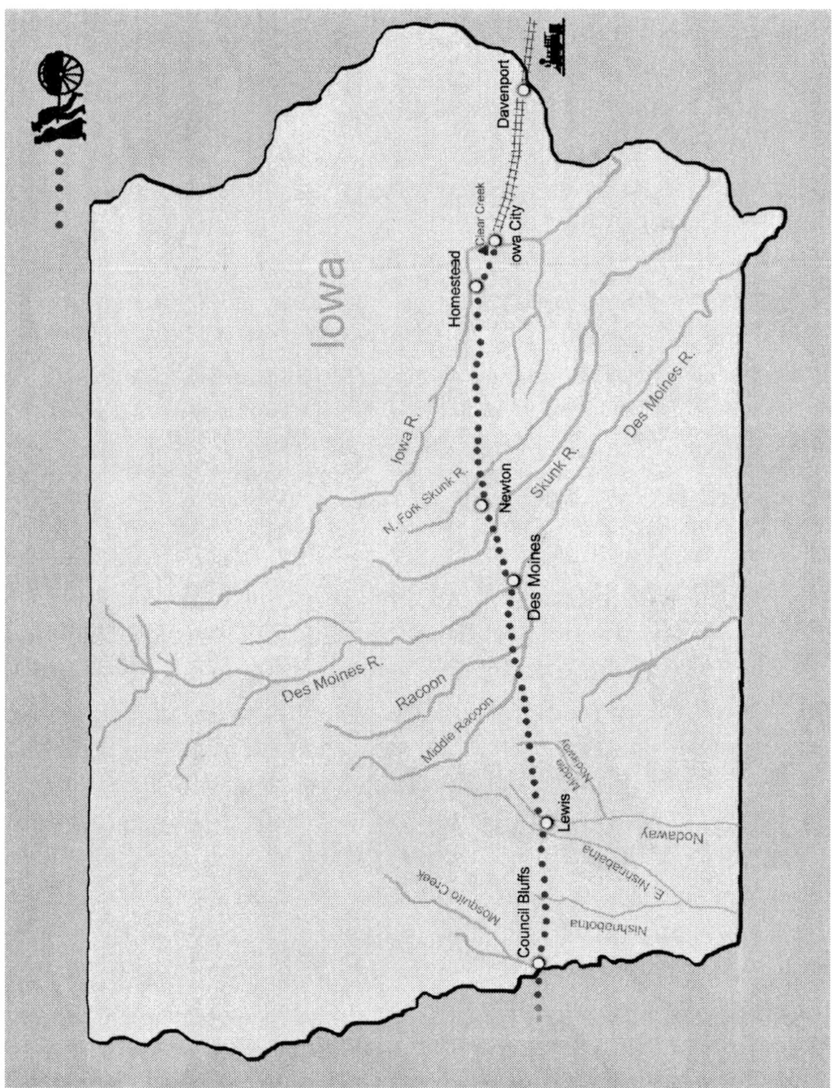

Map by Jeremy Munns

Young's sons[4] who spoke encouragingly to them. They were also visited by the Indians, and the pioneers gave them some of their food and drink. Perhaps the Brethren had given practical instruction regarding improving White-Indian relationships. They may have echoed President Young's classic declaration on the management of White-Indian relationships: "It is far cheaper to feed and clothe the Indians than to fight them."[5]

Later in 1857, Brigham Young, who was the Indian Agent as well as Governor of Utah Territory, expressed that sentiment to James W. Denver, U.S. Commissioner of Indian Affairs. His good intentions were seriously misread. In a November 11, 1857 communique, Denver accused the Mormon leader of attempting to set the Indians against the government. In part, Denver wrote: "This department has information from reliable sources, that, so far from encouraging amicable relations between Indians and the people of the United States, outside your own immediate community, you have studiously endeavored to impress upon the minds of the Indians that there was a difference between your own sect, usually known as Mormons, and the Government and the other citizens of the United States–that the former were their friends, and the latter their enemies."[6] Brigham Young had written Denver to express concern over government reimbursement delays and disallowance of voucher payments requests. The Commissioner concluded with a strongly worded rebuke: "It could have never been intended by Congress, that the money should be used in arousing savages to war against our own citizens."[7] Denver, if he had ever known of it, had forgotten the sage advice that you cannot pat a tortilla so thin that it will not have two sides and perhaps some uneven edges. Nasty letters also have a habit of surviving and making the writer look less than clever.

At Omaha and Florence were former Church members who attempted to dissuade the new emigrants from going west. Frederick Hansen said they had been counseled to avoid them.[8] One of them may have been Johan August Ahmanson, the brilliant missionary who had served with distinction in Denmark and Norway. He had been the sub-captain for the

Scandinavians in the James G. Willie Company the year before. Upon arriving in Salt Lake City he became critical of the leadership of the Church. In his anger, he left Utah in April 1857 and returned to Omaha. Ultimately, Ahmanson was elected to the Nebraska legislature. He became a man of some means and social prominence. Perhaps his service as a missionary and as a sub-captain of the Scandinavian unit in the Willie Company had helped him develop abilities which accounted for much of his later success.

Dissidents could argue that the rich, rain-fed prairies of Illinois and Iowa, with their longer growing season, provided a much greater possibility for improving the immigrants' financial circumstances than the high mountain valleys of semi-arid Utah. Those of Europe's poor who came to Utah expecting an economic Eden were deeply disappointed to discover that making the desert blossom as a rose would be a stretching, demanding, trying work. Brigham Young saw more than just economic advantages for newly arrived Latter-day Saints. Utah was a refuge from persecution.

Claiming they had been deceived, a few of the Scan-dinavians became virulent critics. Testing times come, and devoted persistence to any cause is a personal decision. Honoring covenants is an individual responsibility. Historically, in matters of religious faith, there have always been dropouts. It was that way during the mortal ministry of Jesus. After one particularly demanding doctrinal lesson, *many of His disciples went back, and walked no more with Him. Then said Jesus unto the twelve, Will ye also go away? Then Simon Peter answered Him, Lord, to whom shall we go? Thou hast the words of eternal life.*[9] Perhaps those arrivals in America who now ceased their discipleship and went away had forgotten, or had not heard, that on 6 August 1842, the Prophet Joseph Smith "prophesied that the Saints would continue to suffer much affliction and would be driven to the Rocky Mountains, many would apostatize, others would be put to death by their persecutors, or lose their lives in consequence of exposure and disease, and some [would] live to go and assist in making settlements and building cities and see the Saints become a mighty people in the midst of the Rocky Mountains."[10] Defection does not permanently deflect a righteous cause, which ultimately succeeds despite its detractors.

On Saturday July 4, America's Independence Day, "celebrations were held everywhere."[11] A substantive leadership council was also held. One matter carefully considered was emigrant health. The change of diet,[12] the hard pull across Iowa, the exertion, and the heat of the season combined with the sea voyage and rail journey had left a number ailing. No doubt the lessons learned from the experience of the Willie and Martin companies were a bright recollection. According to James A. Little, the council unanimously determined that it was wisdom for the 7th Company to go on, but all that were unable to walk should remain at Florence, so as to not burden the company. As a part of his journey home to Utah, Little had been asked to remain in the Midwest and serve as superintendent of immigration for that season, and in particular to assist with the immigration of the Scandinavian Saints.[13] Prior to that call, he had served for two years and eight months as a missionary in Great Britain where, among other responsibilities, he had been a counselor to Orson Pratt. Little's letter of July 12 regarding the council's actions was published in the *Millennial Star* of 22 August 1857.[14]

In light of that counsel, Kersten Erickson's parents, Marcus and Kirsten Erickson, and Mette Kirsten Nielsen, her 73-year-old grandmother, determined to remain at Florence and come west when health and energy permitted.[15] This family had previously undergone separation in the quest for Zion. Under the leadership of John E. Forsgren, the oldest daughter, Christine Ericksen Bensen, and her husband, Jeppe Bensen, had come to America on board the *Forest Monarch* in 1853. The youngest daughter, Anna Elizabeth Ericksen, had come with the company led by Peter O. Hansen on board the *James Nesmith* in 1855.[16] Christian Christiansen urged Kersten to go on, promising the Lord would bless her and her family.[17] Trusting the counsel of her priesthood leader, she went west.

Anders Jensen thought he and his family should remain in the Midwest. His wife and his daughter, Mariane, had not been well while crossing Iowa. However, his daughter, Christiane, was determined to go. She said if they didn't go then and there, they would never go west.[18]

Hans Hansen, the father of the Hansen family mentioned earlier, whose oldest sons were Frederick and John, determined not to go on that season, because of the health of the mother, Bertha Marie. They sold their company share to three young men who wanted to go west.[19] The name of Frederick, but not John Hansen, is given on the *Westmoreland's* passenger manifest. It may have been that young Hans changed his name to John.[20] Some who remained ultimately went west in a wagon train. However, the Hans Hansen family, of whom Frederick was the oldest son, never went west. They later associated themselves with the Reorganized Church of Jesus Christ of Latter Day Saints.[21]

Ole Petersen, also given as Ola Pettersen, and his family were not strong enough to go on. Ole and his family remained in the Council Bluffs, Iowa, area until the spring of 1861 when they went on to Utah by wagon train.[22]

The Hans Kofoed (Kofod) family remained in the Omaha area. They had walked barefoot across Iowa for their shoes were worn out.[23] Else Kirstina, Hans' blind mother and some of his children were ill. Cecelia was now nearly six-months pregnant. They were among those counseled to remain for a time. They would go west from Florence 3 July 1860 under the leadership of John P. Taylor's "Iowa Wagon Company." During the 1857-60 interim, Else Kirstina Kofoed died. David Omar, the son born to Cecelia 23 October 1857 at Florence, died 19 November 1857. Another son, 14-year-old Hans Peter, died during their Nebraska sojourn. Often they had little or nothing to eat. Once when they had nothing to eat, a kindly man by the name of Hire gave them five dollars to purchase a sack of flour. Given the prolonged period on a scanty diet, the heavy-dough bread did not agree with their digestive systems.

The problem of inadequate nutrition was exacerbated by

the fact that Florence was not an especially healthy place to live. The Kofoed family became ill with chills and fever. Local folk assumed the illness was the dreaded smallpox and drove them out of the community. On the outskirts of town, a man was sufficiently kind to allow them to live in an old shack. It provided meager shelter, but the weather was terribly cold. The competition for work was intense. There were many immigrants on the frontier attempting to earn enough money to finance the remainder of the journey west to Utah, Oregon, or California. Hans' broken English was a challenge, but he was resourceful and found work. Hans and Cecelia's oldest daughter, Mesella Christena, married George Stevens who belonged to another faith. Mesella Christena never came west.[24]

Jens Eskildsen (Jens Weaver Eskelson) and his family remained in Nebraska for a time. Two additional children were born ten miles west of Nemaha, Nebraska: Oscar in 1858, and Elnora Ellen in 1860. An additional three children were born to them in Utah: Ephraim in 1863, James in 1865, and David in 1867.[25]

Only the weakest and most seriously ill of the handcart pioneers were left behind.[26] Many who were terribly weary pushed west.[27] If 400 had departed Iowa City, as the appointment of two sub-captains of 200 would suggest, and some 30 others joined the company at Florence, then approximately 100 members of the initial 7th Handcart Company would have remained in Nebraska. Whether the plains crossing was undertaken by handcart or ox-drawn wagon, the pioneer trek was unquestionably a winnowing process. Seemingly parallel metaphorical images of those treks can be found in images described by Jesus in the parable of the sower.

From the events which transpired on Sunday July 5, the July 4 council meeting clearly had devoted attention to another pressing matter, the issue of company leadership. Church councils historically have been highly circumspect about such matters. The deliberations of the July 4 council are in harmony with that pattern. Decisions are announced. The process by which those decisions have been reached are not discussed, except in a general manner. In his 12 July 1857 report to Orson Pratt, James A. Little wrote that "H. S. Eldridge, P. H. Young, A. M. Musser, J. P. Park, D. B. Dillie, M. Cowley, G. W. Thurston, C. Christianson [sic], L. D. Rudd, J. [sic] Liljenquist and J. A. Little" had been a part of that council. At the council's request, P. H. Young had presided.[28] How were the councilmembers chosen? Who brought the issue of Park's leadership to the council? Was it Park himself? Surely he must have been somewhat aware of their dissatisfactions. David Dillie, Lorenzo Rudd, and Christian Christiansen had also been involved in the conduct of affairs during the Iowa crossing. What counsel might they have given? It is entirely possible that Ola N. Liljenquist, the assistant interpreter, was asked for a recommendation. He had been a principal bridge between the captain and the company. While tough questions must have been asked and various alternatives considered, it was a priesthood council in which brotherhood was affirmed and harmony emerged.

On Sunday July 5, it was announced that Christian Christiansen would captain the 7th Company and that his assistants would be Elder James P. Park and Elder Lorenzo D. Rudd. Sub-captains over 16 handcarts each were Elders C. C. A. Christensen, Johan F. F. Dorius, Carl C. N. Dorius, and Ole C. Olsen. If five individuals had been assigned per handcart, each sub-captain would have been responsible for about 80 people. That would account for 64 handcarts and 320 people out of the total of 68 handcarts and 330 people usually given as the membership of the company.[29] From this point on there were to be three wagons drawn by ten mules. They were probably using a three-mule hitch per wagon with a different mule being rested each day, or at least so the weakest of the ten might be spared. Perhaps the extra mule was used to scout the trail ahead.

Christian Christiansen had been presiding over Scandinavian saints in the Midwest during the 1856-1857 period. He had intended to return to Utah by wagon. Given his previous plans, it was a magnanimous, selfless gesture on his part to consent to lead the company, and then walk all of the way west so that he could properly gauge the strength of his people.[30] Captain Christiansen was a seasoned leader. An early Danish convert, he had been ordained an elder on 1 January 1851, the first recipient of the Melchizedek Priesthood in Denmark. Two years later he came to America on board the *Forest Monarch* which sailed 16 January 1853, from Liverpool bound for New Orleans where they landed 16 March 1853. That company had come up the Mississippi to Keokuk, Iowa, from which place they went west by wagon company. On that occasion, Christiansen served as a counselor to company leader, John E. Forsgren, one of the four initial missionaries to Scandinavia, and he was one of the seven missionaries assigned by John Taylor to design the original handcarts first used by the 1856 handcart companies.

The intervening four years had provided Christiansen a great deal of leadership experience. He understood that Danes and Americans had different ways. For example, in the 1853 wagon journey of which he had been a part, some of the Scandinavian emigrants rejected the American way of driving oxen in yokes. Rather than yoke them, they made ox harnesses following the Danish pattern. To their astonishment, the oxen refused to be guided by lines in the hands of the teamsters. Animals have to be trained. Changes in handling methods must be made carefully, as abrupt shifts on the part of human handlers make animals highly nervous and uncooperative. The switch from yoke to harness was just such a change. The oxen were frightened by the new technology. They crossed ditches and gulches in a frenzy. Pieces of wagons were strewn by the way. Finally, the terrorized critters were stopped by men who knew the ox responded to the yoke and the whip.[31] The Danes now understood that oxen technology was location specific. They adopted the new approach. Not infrequently with ox-team companies, cattle had been purchased that had to be trained to the yoke. An 1855 pioneer, Hans Peter Larsen, wrote, "We were not familiar with driving cattle and had a terrible time for a few days. It took four men to a yoke of cattle." He wryly added, "The cattle did not understand the Danish language."[32] Captain Christiansen appreciated the strengths of both cultures and understood the challenges posed in crossing the plains. Not only did he bring the 1857 Scandinavians through, he won their love and admiration in the process. He proved to be a splendid choice in a sensitive situation.[33]

With Danish-speaking Christian Christiansen now captaining the company, Liljenquist's language skills and leadership influence were not so urgently needed. The Cowley wagon train rolled west from Florence on July 6. Ola N. Liljenquist, the interpreter for the handcart pioneers from Liverpool to Florence, was allowed to rejoin his wife and family who were traveling west with the Cowley Company. In later years, Liljenquist served as mayor of Hyrum, Utah. Johan Dorius called Ola N. Liljenquist a "truly lovable man."[34] Unquestionably, Liljenquist had the ability to win and retain the confidence of people. It is assumed the Christenson who had bought the wagon and yoke of oxen during the crossing of Iowa went west with Cowley, although there were two other small wagon trains which departed Florence in mid July. (The Cowley wagon company of Scandinavian saints had departed Clear Creek on June 15. They arrived in Florence July 2.[35] They had probably caught up with the handcart company no later than Indian Town.)

The handcart company must have spent Monday, July 6, getting ready for the big push west. The three and one-half day layover would have given the mules an opportunity to feed and regain their strength. At Florence, a limited replenishing of food stores occurred, for it was cheaper to ship supplies up river from St. Louis than to freight them across Iowa. Part of James A. Little's stewardship as immigration agent was to purchase supplies and send them up the Missouri to Florence. The Niels Christensen account suggests that it was from Winter Quarters the pioneers felt they had really started west.[36] Ahead of them lay 1,000 miles of arduous pull and push, with only a few army posts and Mormon way stations to break the monotony of the routine, or so they thought.

NOTES

1. Peter Niels Garff, *A Biographical Account...*, p. 2.

2. Frederick Hansen, *The Great Handcart Train...*, p. 415.

3. While the name of the town or city remains Florence, The Church of Jesus Christ of Latter-day Saints has revived, in a formal way, the use of the name Winter Quarters; on 22 April 2001 a new temple was dedicated just south of the Mormon Pioneer Cemetery which is named the Winter Quarters Nebraska Temple.

4. This report may have been incorrectly remembered for it appears that it was Phineas Howe Young, a brother of Brigham Young, who was the prominent Young in camp.

5. *Journal of Johann F. F. Dorius...*, p. 24.

6 The James W. Denver letter is quoted, in part, in J. Cecil Alter's *Jim Bridger*, 1925, University of Oklahoma Press, Norman and London, p.168.

7. J. Cecil Alter, Jim Bridger, p. 168.

8. Frederick Hansen, *The Great Handcart Train...*, p. 410.

9. John 6:66-68.

10. Joseph Smith, *History of the Church*, Vol V, p. 85. Saturday 6 August 1842.

11. Frederick Hansen, *The Great Handcart Train...*, p. 415.

12. Scandinavians have historically eaten a diet rich in dairy products: milk, butter, cheese, and buttermilk, as well as eggs and meat including fish. Heavy work tends to increase both energy and protein requirements, especially as the body attempts to grow muscle tissue in response to work. Furthermore, the heat and heavy labor in the hot humid climate would have resulted in profuse sweating at times. The company may well have been short of dietary salt or other minerals. Vitamin A, B-12, C, E, and Riboflavin levels would have been marginal at best. The dietary stress was severe. It would become even more perilous as they crossed Nebraska.

13. *Autobiography of James Amasa Little*, 1822-1908, pp. 81-85. Microfilm, #MS 4518 Item 3, LDS Church Archives, Salt Lake City, Utah.

14. J. A. Little to Orson Pratt from Florence, Nebraska Territory, 12 July 1857, *Millennial Star* XIX:541.

15. Marcus and Kersten Christensen Ericksen and her mother, Mette Kirsten Nielsen, came later to Utah, apparently with a wagon company in either 1858 or 1859, for Mette Nielsen died in Lehi, Utah in 1859.

16. See the passenger lists for the *Forest Monarch* and the *James Nesmith*, Mormon Immigration Index.

17. *Autobiography of Kersten Erickson Benson*, LDS Church Archives,

Ms12065, pp. 1-3; Acc. #200259 and Ms8237, reel 3, item #26; Acc #209198. Name is spelled Ericksen on the *Westmoreland* passenger manifest.

18. Ethel S. Lowe, "Christiana Jensen Thomson." Ethel S. Lowe was a granddaughter of Christiana Jensen Thomsen. Manuscript copy courtesy of a descendant, Val Andersen, Brigham Young University, Provo, Utah. Copy in possession of the author.

19. Frederick Hansen, *The Great Handcart Train...*, pp. 415-16.

20. This information comes from the *Westmoreland's* passenger manifest published in the Mormon Immigration Index. Neither is listed on the passenger manifest as it is given in the *Journal History of the Church*.

21. Frederick Hansen's reminiscence, "The Great Handcart Train from Iowa City to Salt Lake City," was published by the Board of Education of the Reorganized Church of Jesus Christ of Latter Day Saints, Lamoni, Iowa in October 1916. On 6 April 2001 the Reorganized Church formally and officially changed the name of the RLDS Church to the Community of Christ. However, for the purposes of this account the RLDS designation will be used.

22. Martin Hansen, *A Short Synopsis or Sketch...*, pp.4, 20-22.

23. Jimmy B. Parker, *The Life Story of Hans Ancher Kofoed*, Privately Published, 1982, p. 52.

24 Jimmy B. Parker, *The Life Story of Hans Ancher Kofoed...*pp. 55-56. Telephone communication with Jimmy Parker, 25 April 2001. Parker stated Else Kirstina was not listed in the 1860 census while other family members were, thus the assumption was made that she had died prior to the census date. Parker states that Kofoed was the way Hans preferred to spell his name rather than Kofod, as it is listed in the *Westmoreland* passenger complement.

25. The year and place of birth for the children of the Jens Eskildsen or Jens Weaver Eskelson family were given in the LDS Ancestral File.

26. Given the health situation and the counsel that those who were ill should wait until they gained sufficient strength before attempting to come west, it seems likely the Petersen, Kofoed and Eskildsen families were all a part of the 7th Handcart Company from Clear Creek, Iowa, to Florence, Nebraska.

27. C. C. A. Christensen, *By Handcart to Utah...*, p. 338, tells they took a number of emigrants with them who were half-exhausted, only the very weakest were left behind.

28. J. A. Little to Orson Pratt, 12 July 1857, Florence, Nebraska Territory, *Millennial Star* XIX:541. P. H. Young was probably Phineas Howe Young, Brigham Young's brother.

29. C. C. A. Christensen, *By Handcart to Utah...*, p. 338 gives the number of handcarts as 30 to 40. He had not remembered the handcart number accurately. The Mads Christensen history written by Phyllis

Christensen identifies that Mads' family and their handcart were assigned to C. C. A. Christensen's sub-company. In the individual records discovered in the process of writing this account, only Mads Christensen identified the sub-captain to whom they had been assigned. As an aside, the wife of Richard L. Jensen, the translator of the C. C. A. Christensen Nebraska History article entitled "By Handcart to Utah," is a second great-granddaughter of Mads Christensen and Karen Marie Hansen Christensen.

30. C. C. A. Christensen was particularly glowing in his praise of Christian Christiansen. "He began with short daily travel and walked the entire way . . . rather than riding horseback as other captains. His gentle, fatherly treatment will never be forgotten by those whom he led . . ." *By Handcart to Utah...*, p. 338.

31. Mormon Immigration Index–Personal Accounts, *Forest Monarch* (January 1853), "A Compilation of General Voyage Notes."

32. *Autobiography of Hans Peter Larsen, James Nesmith* Personal Accounts, Mormon Immigration Index.

33. Richard L. Jensen, the translator of the C. C. A. Christensen account in p. 347, endnote 11, comments on the unusual occurrence of Christiansen replacing Park among a people known for their submission to officially appointed leadership. He believes the change resulted from Scandinavian complaints to the Latter-day Saint authorities at Florence, although he acknowledges the process is not well documented.

34. Journal of Johann F. F. Dorius, *Westmoreland* (April 1857), Mormon Immigration Index–Personal Accounts.

35. Don H. Smith, *Peder. C. Klemgaard...*, p. 3 of 7.

36. Clare B. Christensen, *History of Niels Christensen*, p. 2.

Chapter 9

POLITICS AND THE UTAH EXPEDITION

It seems likely the Scandinavians were largely unaware that when James Buchanan was inaugurated President of the United States, his administration was besieged by disgruntled people actively lobbying the new administration to protect the rights of Utah's non-Mormon community to the point of suppressing the rights of the Latter-day Saints. Critics were after Brigham Young's political scalp, thinking that if they removed him from the governor's chair, they would forever alter the future of Utah Territory. His political adversaries miscalculated the depth of his resolve and his capacity to command. Brigham Young was no "paper reed by the brook"[1] who could be shaken and driven away. The tempering fires of Zion's Camp, the expulsion from Missouri, his brilliant and courageous leadership during the exodus from Nauvoo, and the epic migration to the Great Basin, had steeled his soul and made him more than equal to the newly emerging challenge.

During the seven years Brigham Young served as governor, non-Mormon federal appointees frequently found themselves playing a faint second fiddle to the highly capable territorial governor;[2] they were extremely jealous. Foolishly, some had flaunted their prejudices against the Mormon faith and impugned the morality of Mormon women. Those appointees who departed Utah Territory under considerable local pressure filed spurious reports critical of the Mormons and their theocratic system.

In 1853, Captain John W. Gunnison returned to Utah with a survey party sent to determine the feasibility of a rail line from Missouri through the Southern Rockies into the Great

Basin. Thomas H. Benton and St. Louis merchants wanted a rail line west originating in Missouri, for such offered tremendous financial possibilities. It was an expedition with risk for the Walker War was on. Though warned by the Mormon bishop of Fillmore that a Pavant Indian war party was on the loose, Gunnison thought he would be safe, given his friendship formed with the Pavants during his time with Stansbury. Unaware of whom they were attacking, Moshoquop, the Pavant chief, and his warriors killed Gunnison and others October 25, 1853, near Sevier Lake. The captain's brother, Andrew Gunnison, was among those who blamed the tragedy on the Latter-day Saints, even though a Mormon guide was among those slain.

There was also the matter of money. The Mormon businessmen along the Oregon-California-Mormon Trail had more than proven their mettle in winning the ferry and supply business. They had the choice spot for crossing the North Platte in present-day Casper, Wyoming. Brigham Young had stationed stone engravers at Independence Rock. For a fee of one to five dollars, these stone engravers would cut travelers' names into the "Register of the Desert."[3] People want to be remembered. Why not let the travel industry help support the cause of Zion.

Another source of anti-Mormon criticism in the 1850s came from some on their way to California. Given the distance from the Missouri River to the Sacramento Valley, California-bound immigrants might spend the colder half of the year in the Salt Lake Valley. While in Utah, these in-transit immigrants competed with local people for jobs and foodstuffs. They were the beneficiaries of an orderly society, but resented paying taxes[4] to support a community they considered only a temporary home. This complaint about legitimate yet minimal local taxes was spurious and should have been dismissed by the Federal Government.

There are intimations that much of the Gentile-Mormon strife was at the instigation of the criminal element who had been a part of the California gold rush.[5] Why should men who robbed fellow immigrants and abused the Native Americans on the way west be expected to behave differently during their sojourn among the Utah Mormons? Regarding such wanton disregard for the life of Native Americans, Wilford Woodruff, in a September 12, 1857 letter to the editor of the *Millennial Star* stated: "Many companies of emigrants have passed through our city this season. The Indians north . . . robbed and killed many of the emigrants, in consequence of the cruelty of one company from California, who, it is reported, shot every Indian they could see on the route. This party was journeying from California to the States."[6] It is improbable that White-Indian atrocities during the summer of 1857 had much to do with the decision to send federal troops to Utah. However, Elder Woodruff's report supports the notion that depravation perpetrated by a cruel, corrupt element brought havoc and death to unsuspecting and innocent people traveling the pioneer trails.

In early 1857, opportunistic anti-Mormon critics saw a window through which they believed they could swing political and economic control of the Utah Territory their way. A new presidential administration had begun. Patronage appointments would be on the docket. New political initiatives would be considered. Disgruntled and angry Mormon enemies called in their political IOUs. Opposition had been building since 1855. As Buchanan struggled to grasp the scope of his complex responsibilities, those who bitterly opposed the Latter-day Saints brought the kettle to a boil.

The Buchanan administration faced a plethora of problems. The divide between North and South was widening. Sectionalism was again on the rise. It was a time of division and intrigue, where feelings of goodwill and national unity had begun diminishing across the nation. Balancing divided interests and sectional loyalties were challenges of no small dimension. In the hallways and cloakrooms of government, rumors of Southern secession began creeping back into the political dialogue. The decision of an activist U.S. Supreme Court in the matter of the slave, Dred Scott, angered northern Republicans, for that decision effectively reopened the possibility of slavery in territories previously determined to be free-soil by the Compromise of 1850. The debate over popular sovereignty was particularly intense between pro-slavery and free-soil elements in Kansas Territory. The debate was not confined to that territory alone, for it became a national issue which ultimately split the Democratic party.

Mississippian Robert J. Walker's appointment as territorial governor of Kansas proved to be a disappointment to the South, for Walker was insistent that the proposed Kansas constitution be submitted to a territory-wide plebiscite. Faced with a growing and potentially violent quarrel, Governor Walker successfully persuaded the administration that federal troops must be placed at his disposal to enable him to maintain order in Kansas. Colonel William Stephen Harney, who had been waging a vigorous campaign against Billy Bowlegs and his elusive Seminole Indians in Florida, was transferred and given command of federal troops in Kansas Territory. There is some indication that Buchanan and Walker thought Harney's reputation for brutality (he was ignominiously called "Squaw Killer"[7]) would be helpful in keeping in line the radical elements on both sides of the pro-slavery versus free-soil issue.

Lucrative military contracts, political kickbacks, and secessionist plots all must have played a part in the deepening divide. However, among all of the acrimonious political disagreement, there was one issue upon which North and South almost unanimously agreed, namely the need to bring the Mormons and the governor of the Territory of Utah into line on the matter of marriage law and the perceived indifference to federal authority. Those issues had been further agitated by hot rumors over alleged alien sedition which arose as a consequence of the large numbers of Europeans who had converted to Mormonism and immigrated to Utah. By contrast, many Utah citizens considered previously appointed federal officials as frequently morally corrupt and insensitive to, if not outright biased against, the Mormons, and so, indignant local citizens sent the discredited federal appointees packing in "fear for their lives." At least, those were the stories the appointees fed the national press. And such lurid tales sold newspapers, even then. *The Chicago Times*, which had initially defended the right to practice plural marriage on the dual grounds of religious freedom and popular sovereignty, turned against the Latter-day Saints.[8]

The June 1 edition of the *New York Times* recommended, tongue-in-cheek, that William Walker, an American adventurer and insurrectionist, who in 1855 had set himself up as president of Nicaragua and had been recently deposed, be appointed Governor of Utah. Walker, while popular with pro-slavery elements in the South, was considered to be a diplomatic embarrassment, especially in the matter of U.S. relations with Great Britain. In a June 12 interview with President Buchanan, Walker contended that he alone could restore order and safety to Nicaragua and revive its economy.[9] If Walker actually sought Utah's territorial governorship, he was unsuccessful in obtaining it, for in mid-June Buchanan appointed Alfred Cumming of Georgia governor of Utah Territory. Cumming was a fair-minded man of nerve and ability. To ensure that Cumming would be properly received in the territory, Buchanan placed Colonel Harney in command of 2,500 troops with orders to accompany the governor-designate west. However, Kansas Governor Robert Walker did not want Harney going west. He needed his own recognized military authority in Kansas.

As the 7th Handcart Company was leaving Florence, the first detachment of what would ultimately become known as the army of Colonel Albert Sidney Johnston was preparing to depart Fort Leavenworth. Fortunately for the Latter-day Saints, indecision, incompetence, and competition for the lucrative contracts for supplying the army interfered with the expedition's preparations. John B. Floyd, the initial Secretary of War in the Buchanan cabinet was eventually asked to resign his office as a result of the scandal associated with his handling of various U.S. Army contracts. Some have suggested that Floyd, governor of Virginia from 1849 to 1852, was acting collaboratively with southern senators and may have pressed for the expedition as a means of reducing federal pressure on the South over the slavery issue. Others have argued that Buchanan wanted to send the South the message that he had both the ability and resolve to react quickly and forcefully against secession.[10]

Whatever underlying political motives were driving the expedition, its military efficiency was further compromised by confusion at the top over the matter of field command. Secretary Floyd was a Harney advocate, whereas General-in-Chief Winfield Scott did not like Harney, and Scott had, in fact, argued against mounting the expedition in 1857. He contended that it was too late in the year, that neither soldiers nor supplies could safely reach Utah before winter. Indecisiveness may have reached beyond the War Department and included even Buchanan himself. Governor Robert Walker's uncompromising position that he required federal troops to keep the peace in Kansas undoubtedly contributed to administrative wrangling. Foul spring weather set the army back. Then Harney apparently came to believe that it was too late in the season to take a large force west. Despite all the machinations, it was not until August 28 that Colonel Harney was recalled. In an environment where political maneuvering successfully outflanked and stalled the military mission, Harney never formally joined his men. The outcome of these competing complications resulted in a very late start, for it was not until July 18 that first elements of the army marched west from Leavenworth.[11]

The political quarrels within the Buchanan Administration had provided vital breathing space to the Mormons. It was a case of their adversaries being so busy fighting among themselves for position and profit (ego and greed are fierce enemies to unified action) that the government and its military leadership had little available time for subduing the supposed rebellion in Utah Territory. Walker resigned the governorship December 15, and Buchanan subsequently appointed Harney governor of the Territory of Kansas.[12]

S. W. Richards and other missionaries bound for Great Britain discovered on reaching Fort Kearney August 28, that desertion among the troops and teamsters of the Utah Expedition had become an increasing problem for the army, that officers had been required to hold out inducements and adopt rigid regulations, including the withholding of pay for one year in order to suppress the spirit of desertion. There was concern that the problem of desertion would increase as they encountered the severity of mountain storms. Among the false inducements noised about were that attractive Mormon women who were "as thick as blackberries . . . would jump into their arms," and they would spend the winter dining sumptuously in Utah.[13] This was a definite case of faulty intelligence among the ranks.

The government contract to freight the quartermaster's supplies by "bull-train" or "bull-outfit" to the valley of the Great Salt Lake had been awarded to the firm of Russell, Majors, and Waddell. That contract was sufficiently lucrative that high wages of $40 dollars per month in gold were offered for teamsters. The standard train consisted of 25 "J. Murphy wagons" which had been built in St. Louis specifically for the plains-freighting business. Stoutly made, each wagon could carry 7,000 pounds of freight. These 25-unit wagon trains were staffed by about 30 men. The wagon master was in command; his deputy was called the assistant wagon master. Next in line was the "extra hand" followed by the "night herder" and then the "cavallard." The cavallard[14] was responsible for driving and caring for the lame and loose cattle. Each wagon was pulled by several yoke of oxen, frequently six yoke of large oxen for wagons of this size. The men did their own cooking and were divided into messes of seven. One man cooked, another brought wood and water, another stood guard, etc. Each had a duty to perform during meal preparation. All men were heavily armed with Colt revolvers and Mississippi yagers.[15]

One "bull-train" was led by Lewis Simpson, a tough, seasoned, reliable wagon master. Simpson's "extra hand" was an eleven-year-old youth named William F. Cody. Cody said his mother was decidedly opposed to his going on this trip. She was frankly worried over the uncertainty of whether he would ever come back, given the Mormon difficulties, and his recent narrow escape from death at the hands of plains Indians. Neither did his mother like the appearance of Mr. Simpson. Upon inquiry, she learned to her dismay "that on nearly every trip he had made across the plains he had killed someone."[16] After

Simpson and Russell made personal commitments to her regarding the boy's welfare, Mrs. Cody relented and allowed him to go. One of Simpson's 25 teamsters or "bull-whackers" was a "tall, handsome, magnificently built [21-year-old] who could out-run, out-jump, and out-fight any man in the train." His name was James B. Hickok who afterward became better known as Wild Bill Hickok. [17]

NOTES

1. Isaiah 19:7

2. For a celebrated and widely acclaimed historian's appraisal of Brigham Young's abilities as a political leader of extraordinary talent, see Stephen E. Ambrose's *Nothing Like It in the World: The Men Who Built the Transcontinental Railroad* 1863-1869, Simon & Schuster, New York, N. Y., 2000, pp. 278-79. In part, Ambrose wrote that Brigham Young was "noted for his firmness, intelligence, decisiveness, good looks, and the ability to put long-term interests of those in his charge ahead of their short-term gain. Like the top politicians, he had a remarkable memory for facts and figures, geography, who owed what favors or money to whom, the names of his competitors, and his followers and their wives. He knew who had taken what position on this or that issue and when, and what his own position had been. Had it not been for his generally feared or despised religion, he quite possibly might have been a president of the United States, and, depending on the time, a good or even a great one."

3. The information about the fee structure charged by the Mormon stone-cutters who had been stationed there by Brigham Young was taken from historical markers at Independence Rock placed at the site by the state of Wyoming. See the 27 July 1992 entry in *Journal of Allen C. Christensen*, XIII:118. Microfilmed copy is in the LDS Church Archives.

4. A complaint about minimal local taxes should have been dismissed. Today, travelers think nothing of paying sales taxes, room taxes, toll fares, and airport taxes; tips for service rendered could be considered a voluntarily tax. Yet in the 1850s, America was not that far removed from the notion that taxation without representation had been a major factor leading to the war for Independence.

5. John D. Unruh, Jr. *The Plains Across*, University of Illinois Press, Urbana and Chicago, 1993, p. 330.

6. Wilford Woodruff to the Editor of the Millennial Star, 12 September 1857, *Millennial Star* XIX:766.

7. The name "Squaw Killer" probably had its origins in the massacre of the Brulé Sioux at the Blue Water in Nebraska in 1855 by Harney-led troops. However, according to Dee Brown in *Bury My Heart at Wounded Knee: An Indian History of the American West*, Bantam Books, 1972, p. 97, the Cheyenne called Harney "White Whiskers." Other accounts indicate Cheyenne also had been killed in this battle.

8. Kenneth M. Stampp, *America in 1857...*, p. 200.

9. Kenneth M. Stampp, *America in 1857...*, p. 192.

10. Ray B. West, Jr., *Kingdom of the Saints: The Story of Brigham Young and the Mormons*, The Viking Press, New York, 1957, pp. 255-56.

11. Leonard J. Arrington and Davis Bitton, *The Mormon Experience*, Alfred A. Knopf, New York, 1979, p. 166. Andrew Jenson, Church Chronology, Op cit., p. 54.

12. Ray B. West, Jr., *Kingdom of the Saints...*, p. 258.

13. S. W. Richards to Orson Pratt, 4 October 1857, *Millennial Star* XIX:670.

14. The term *cavallard* may have been a colloquial adaptation of the Spanish word, cabálléro, which refers to skill in horsemanship, which skill would have been required for simultaneously managing both lame and sound, loose cattle.

15. The Mississippi "yager" was a percussion-lock shoulder rifle of either .544 or .58 caliber. Its name came as a result of its performance in the hands of a Mississippi Regiment commanded by Jefferson Davis during the Mexican War. (See Civil War Talk.Com—Weapons of the Civil War) Yager is an American spelling of the German "jägen" or "jaeger" Originally it referred to a rifleman in a regiment of light infantry from certain German states. In German it meant huntsman.

16. Buffalo Bill [William F.] Cody, "Robbed by Danites," in *The Great West,* edited by Charles Neider, Coward-McCann, Inc., New York, 1958, pp. 221-22.

17. William F. Cody, *Robbed by Danites...*, p. 223. On this page in the Neider edition, Cody gives the army's trail-routing as northwest through Kansas crossing the Blue River, then over the Big and Little Sandy. They entered Nebraska near the Big Sandy. They proceeded along the Little Blue for some 60 miles, crossing a range of Sand Hills and striking the Platte some 10 miles below [south of] Old Fort Kearney. Up the South Platte to the Ash Hollow crossing, then 18 miles to the mouth of the Blue Water where Harney had his great battle with the Sioux and Cheyenne in 1855. From that point, they followed the North Platte past Court House Rock, Chimney Rock and Scott's Bluff to Fort Laramie where they crossed the Laramie River. They followed the North Platte for some considerable distance to the point where the trail crossed the river at old Richard's Bridge. They followed the Platte to Red Buttes, crossed Willow creeks to the Sweetwater, where they

passed Independence Rock, Devil's Gate and the Three Crossings of the Sweetwater. Cody states that they passed "Cold Springs, where, three feet under the sod, on the hottest day of the summer, ice can be found." The trail then passed Hot Springs and Rocky Ridge, through the Rocky Mountains and Echo Canyon and into the Great Salt Lake valley. Of course, the army was halted for the winter at what had been Fort Bridger.

Chapter 10

PIONEERS BEYOND THE ELK HORN

While young Bill Cody anticipated that the plains crossing would be an exciting and well-paying adventure, those who pulled handcarts were fully cognizant by this point that the way west was a test of physical and spiritual stamina. Determined to persevere in their quest for Zion, the 7th Company started west from Florence on Tuesday, July 7. The first night an inspection was made to determine whether any were unfit to go on. An emigrant from Sweden, Christopher Hultberg (Hulberg)[1], was advised to turn back because of his wife's ill health. However, Hultberg had his heart set on going to Zion. He dropped back and trailed a little behind the company for about 50 miles. When he was too far from the base camp at Florence to go back alone, he rejoined the company. Much of the way west he pulled his wife and children on the cart. He was described as one of superior strength and an unquenchable desire to go west.[2]

A reasonable estimate of the date when Hultberg and his family rejoined the company would be the evening of Friday, July 10. At that point, the company would have already crossed the Elk Horn River and would have been moving alongside the Platte. Water dictated the road west. They would have forded Shell and Looking Glass creeks and the Beaver River (creek) on the way to the Loup Fork ford. The Latter-day Saints were building a way station at the Beaver River in 1857. It seems likely they came through the Beaver station for they were undoubtedly using William Clayton's *Emigrants' Guide*. This "twenty-four-page, pocket-size paperback booklet of 1848 was simply the first practical and best emigrant guide of its day."[3]

Samuel Lublin and family joined the 7th Company at either

Florence or Clear Creek. Samuel was the son of Magnus Lublin and Ketta Heiman. Ketta was born in Middleford, Denmark, in 1790. Magnus's parents were Jews from Poland. The family name in Poland had been Samuel. They assumed the name Lublin, apparently after the Polish city from which they had come. Among Magnus and Ketta's ten children were Esther, Abraham, Hanna, Rebekka, and Saul, given names which reflect their Old Testament heritage. Samuel was born 13 October 1816 (possibly 1813). Samuel married Johanna Christena Larsen, the daughter of Christian Larsen and Bertha Benson. Johanna was born 1 June 1820 at Musse, Aalhelm, Denmark. Samuel heard the message of the restoration and was baptized 13 September 1852. Johanna was baptized 1 November 1852. Disowned by family and friends, the couple determined to go to Zion. In 1854, they sailed from Copenhagen with their family of three daughters and one son. There was a wait of several weeks in Liverpool before they sailed 17 January 1855 on board the *Charles Buck*

William Henry Jackson's **Westport Landing**, at the Big Bend of the Missouri River.

with a Latter-day Saint company of 403. Seventy of those 403 passengers were Scandinavian saints.[4]

When Samuel and Johanna went west with the 7th Company they took their daughter Johanna Sophie B. (11), son Herman Magnus (9), and six-month-old son, Hyrum, who had been born at Alton, Illinois, or Omaha, Nebraska, on 31 December 1856. They left their five-year-old daughter, Anna Kristine. She was to come later by wagon train. No mention was made of three-year-old Josephine. She is not listed among those who died at sea or came up river from New Orleans. Perhaps the rigors of life on the frontier resulted in her death. If that were the case, it would explain why the Lublins sought to minimize the risk of losing another little girl. A wagon train journey was less stressful than a handcart crossing. Additionally, Johanna would have needed all of her strength to nurse and care for baby Hyrum. The Apostle Matthew records a demanding test of discipleship: *He that loveth father or mother more than me is not worthy of me: and he that loveth son or daughter more than me is not worthy of me. And he that taketh not his cross, and followeth after me, is not worthy of me.*[5] Even understanding the precious price of discipleship, most pens cannot capture or adequately portray the depth of a mother's emotions under such wrenching circumstances. Love and conversion enable people to do great things. Spiritual and physical stamina were absolutely mandatory for it would have been so easy to fall by the wayside and surrender to the cares of the world.

In the 7th Company, only two handcarts were pushed and pulled entirely by women. One of the two belonged to the three Olsen sisters, Karen Marie, Christina, and Nicoline. A fourth young woman had been assigned to their cart to ease their burden. She became ill with fever. For a time, Christina and Nicoline pulled the handcart alone, for Karen Marie developed a bad leg which necessitated that for a time she ride in one of the wagons.[6]

The company reached the Loup Fork, a large Platte tributary, on Thursday, July 16. No arrival time is given, as the crossing may have occupied the entire day. C. C. A. Christensen called the Loup "one of the most difficult streams they had to ford."[7] The river was "running wide" at the time of their crossing. The Clayton *Guide* gives it as "about 300 yards wide." Treacherous quicksand bars in the Loup's riverbed made fording it risky. The handcart pioneers hired Native Americans familiar with Loup's hazards to assist them in the crossing. Provisions were hauled across by wagons pulled with double teams. Each handcart would have had to have been unloaded and then reloaded on the other side. The strongest men pulled

"The Handcart Company" 1900 by C.C.A. Christensen, © by Intellectual Reserve, Inc. Courtesy of the Museum of Church History and Art, Salt Lake City, Utah. C.C.A. was a sub-captain in the 7th Handcart Company. This painting is illustrative of his written account: the gathering of buffalo chips, the building of a cooking fire, a mother nursing her baby, the approach of the Indians on horseback, the fording of a stream with handcarts with canvas tops, the boy helping to pull his family handcart with a rope attached to the drawbar. Note that none of the men seem to be bearing arms. The scene typifies the lanscape of present-day Nebraska.

the emptied carts across the Loup. Some women and young girls crossed by riding double, clinging to the backs of the "nearly naked Indians" or "half-naked Indians" who guided their horses through the river.[8] The crossing went well. Nothing was lost, and no one was hurt.[9]

Those Indians were most likely the Pawnee. By 1857, the U.S. government had settled them along the Loup area of the Platte. The pioneer record tells that the Indians were encamped in a village at the site of the ford. If they were Pawnee, the village was probably one of earthen lodges, for such housing typified their tribal culture. These earth lodges were large enough to hold up to 40 people. They were built over an evacuation dug several feet into the soil and featured a fireplace in the center of the lodge with an opening in the roof which allowed the smoke to escape. Firewood was stored in the lodge. Pits dug in the floor were used to store dried foods.[10] The Pawnee earthen lodges seemingly would have provided much better protection against the winds and bitter cold of the Plains' winter than would have been furnished by the buffalo-hide tipi. According to current maps, the ford would have been made just to the west of the Loup's confluence with the Cedar.

NOTES

1. The *Westmoreland* passenger manifest lists a Christopher and Karna Hultberg. They are undoubtedly the same people, so one surname is a misspelling. The names of the two children are Anna Catrina, born 1850, and Anders, born 1854.

   Mormon Immigration Index's *Westmoreland* passenger manifest. The Journal History of the Church lists Christopher and K. Hultberg, but the children are not given in the latter record.

2. The source for this vignette is the J. M. Tanner account, *Biography of James Jensen...*, pp. 26-27 which is also cited by Hafen and Hafen, *Handcarts to Zion...*, p. 161.

3. *The Latter-day Saints' Emigrants' Guide* by W. Clayton, St. Louis, 1848 edited by Stanley B. Kimball with an introduction by James B. Allen, the Patrice Press, 1983, p. 13. Kimball, citing Allen, states that Clayton left Winter Quarters 10 February 1848 by steamboat for Saint

Louis where he had 5,000 copies of the Emigrants' Guide printed. (Op cit., p. 160)

4. *Biography of Kate Lublin Alexander* by George Alexander (her son). A copy of this biographical sketch is in the possession of her descendant, Dale Zabriskie. Also see the Mormon Immigration Index, *Charles Buck* Personal Accounts. There is a difference in the birth year for Samuel Lublin between the two accounts. The route of this voyage was south through the Irish Channel to the Bay of Biscay which was reached January 20. They passed between Spain and the Azores January 21. Inasmuch as they had not found the desired northeast trade winds, they continued south-south-west to Cape Verde which was reached February 10. February 26 they were at Guadeloupe Islands, the next day at Antigua, and Monteserrat. They reached Puerto Rico February 28 and Santa Domingo March 3, arriving in New Orleans March 14. A Danish sister, Sarah Autosen, 57, died March 14 and was buried at Balize at the mouth of the Mississippi.

5. Matthew 10:37-38.

6. Rebecca Wright Snow Payne, *A Resume of the Life of My Grandmother...*, pp. 8-9.

7. C. C. A. Christensen, *By Handcart to Utah...*, p. 339.

8. C. C. A. Christensen, *By Handcart to Utah...*,p. 339, and Hafen and Hafen, *Handcarts to Zion...*, pp. 160-161. C. C. A. Christensen said the Indians were half-naked. This must mean the more fully clothed wore buckskin leggings and loin cloths, the others only loin cloths. All of the Pawnee braves were undoubtedly naked from the waist up; it was hot July weather. They saved their clothing for the bitter winters of the Great Plains. For Victorian-age Europeans, the mode of Native American undress came as a major cultural shock. Their records which survived don't seem to tell of much else about the Indians.

9. The observation by C. C. A. Christensen that no one was hurt or nothing was lost overlooks the premature birth and death of Karen Gottfredson's baby girl, Platine.

10. Nancy Bonvillain, 2001. *Native Nations: Cultures and Histories of Native North America*, Prentice Hall, Inc., Upper Saddle, New Jersey, p. 183.

Chapter 11

THE WAY STATION AT GENOA

Due to illness, two families from the 7th Company remained at Genoa, a new way station or in-transit settlement being built by the Latter-day Saints in 1857 at the Beaver Creek, Loup Fork site.[1] The family of Jens and Karen Gottfredson (Gotfredsen) was one of the two families. Their oldest son, Peter, had been born in Jutland, Denmark, near the North Sea coast. The missionaries found them in 1851 and they were baptized. Shortly thereafter they moved to Aalborg. They left Denmark in 1855 and sailed from Liverpool 12 December 1855, on board the *John J. Boyd*.[2] Landing in New York on 15 February 1856, they did not have sufficient means to go west. For a time, the family resided in Alton, Illinois, where Jens worked in a brick kiln until June. On 4 July 1856, Karen Pederson Gottfredson died from "Weaver's Consumption." (Brown lung disease.) Karen had woven on a handloom for most of her life. The fine lint from the material being woven found its way into her lungs and ultimately was a causative factor in her death. Before leaving Denmark, Karen had a rather vivid dream concerning the journey to America. While she did not have names for places the family would encounter during the Atlantic crossing and journey to Illinois, they were as she described them. She had not dreamed of reaching Utah.

Shortly after Karen's death, Jens moved his family across the river to St. Louis, Missouri, where he married Karen Marie Pederson[3] on 12 August 1856. Jens needed a wife to care for his young family. Karen had sailed on the *John J. Boyd* and had stayed for a time at Keokuk, Iowa. In the spring of 1857, the Jens Gottfredson family took a riverboat up the Missouri to

Florence, Nebraska, where they joined the 7th Company.

Peter described the Loup crossing: "When we had traveled about 120 miles, we came to the Loup Fork River. We crossed over and camped in a cottonwood grove. If we stopped in the river, the handcarts began to sink and were hard to pull loose."[4] Sadly, the strenuous crossing proved to be too much for Jens's pregnant wife. That night Karen gave birth prematurely to a baby girl. The baby daughter was blessed and given the name of Platine in remembrance of the Platte River. The tiny baby died and was buried there. The 7th Company went on without them; there was no stopping.

The family placed the new mother in the handcart and pulled her back across the Loup Fork. They went north to Genoa, the small way station settlement, located near the point where the Beaver empties into the Loup Fork. Jens staked a quarter section of buffalo grass prairie near Genoa, and built and covered a dugout in a hillside as a home for his family. He left his family there and went back to Omaha to find work. For a time he was unable to send food to his family. Settlers in Genoa raised some corn, which was hit by an early frost, and some buckwheat, which matured. The Gottfredsons ground the buckwheat with a coffee mill and mixed it with the wild plums and sour grapes which grew abundantly on the lands bordering the Beaver and Loup Fork streams.[5] For over a month, the Gottfredson family was without any bread. Later, Jens was able to send them a sack of flour and some bacon which sustained them. In November, Karen hired a man with a yoke of oxen to take them back to Omaha. In the spring of 1858, a small company of Utah-bound Danish immigrants arrived in Omaha. Among them were Rasmus Olson, Karen's sister, Maren Pederson Meilhede, and brother, Peder Pederson Meilhede and his wife. Rasmus was engaged to be married to Maren. He was more financially secure than many. He bought four yoke of oxen and a new Schutler wagon and took the Gottfredson family with him to Salt Lake City.[6]

In 1905, Peter's grandson, Floyd, was born in the railway station at Kaysville, Utah to his son, Albert, and daughter-in-law, Amelia. Albert raised his family in Siggurd, Utah. His family knew much of financial hardship and difficulty. Floyd's arm was seriously hurt in a hunting accident at age 11. Nine surgical operations were required to repair his arm. Because playing outdoors during this long period of recuperation was not possible, Floyd developed an interest in art. To finance the art correspondence courses, he went door-to-door selling copies of his grandfather's memoirs. He was unable to perform farm work because of the injury to his arm. The movement of his hand was limited. He had lost most of the normal flexibility. Consequently, he learned to draw using his entire arm. This technique gave his drawing a sweep and flare which few others seem to have acquired.

In early adulthood, he held several cartooning jobs with Utah periodicals. Floyd moved to Los Angeles, California, in search of better opportunities. His first job was as a theater projectionist. While working in that position, a movie poster caught his attention. In 1929, he went to work as an animator. His objective was to draw cartoons. Unexpectedly, in 1930, the man who drew the studio's principal cartoon character resigned in order to strike out on his own as a freelance cartoonist. Floyd accepted the studio's offer to replace him, but only "for two weeks" until another cartoonist could be found. The two weeks became 45 years. Floyd Gottfredson's Mormon upbringing and his unfailingly positive outlook made him an ideal keeper of the cartoon series. Uncomplaining about the poverty of his youth and the trauma of the hunting accident, Floyd brought the same values to the cartoon character he drew. His character was one of good cheer and courage who gave gentle lessons in morality and a sense of right to a nation caught in the wake of the Great Depression.

As time passed, Floyd became good friends with the owners of the studio. One evening one of them requested that Floyd give him a ride home as his car was in the repair shop. As they drove toward home, the studio owner told of his love for model railroads, that he'd even built one in his yard which he could sit in and drive. However, he lamented, his wife did not want him to expand it. Floyd suggested he get another parcel of land and build on it a railroad as big as he wanted. After due consideration, the studio executive determined he would build instead an amusement park with a theme based on the character which Gottfredson had been drawing for so many years. In 1955, Walt Disney opened the world-renowned park which bears his name. While Disney had created Mickey Mouse, it is said that Floyd Gottfredson Mormon's heritage helped developed the cartoon's character. The boy who came from the family which had known so much of soul-trying hardship on behalf of their faith became highly instrumental in bringing happiness to the children of the earth.

The other family who remained at Genoa was that of Christian and Inger Mortensen Hansen. They had been part of a group which had contributed money to acquire a wagon and a span of mules to haul the heavy items. Christian's heavy trunk was placed on the wagon's bed and covered with luggage. Initially things had gone well for them. However, 100 miles west of Florence, Christian became ill and was unable to help pull the handcart. Captain Christiansen assigned another man to help Inger, thinking that Christian's health would soon improve. Twenty miles farther west, Inger's strength was exhausted. Neither she nor Christian could go farther, so lacking any alternative, they remained at Genoa.

Martin Hansen recalled that Genoa was a small Latter-day Saint community except for a few cattlemen. A man who was living in the neighborhood traded 160 acres to the Hansens for their place in the 7th Company. As a great deal of labor would have been necessary to unload and reload the supply wagon, the heavy Hansen trunk which contained their best clothing went west without them.[7]

The Hansen home at Genoa was a dugout, a square hole dug into the hillside with a log front containing one window and a door which faced south. The roof was made of logs covered by willows and then earth. At the back of the dugout was a fireplace on which they cooked and heated their earthen home. The man from whom they had obtained the 160 acres had broken a few acres of prairie sod and had planted some potatoes and squash. Christian Hansen returned to Omaha to find work. For the three weeks he was away they ate "potatoes boiled in the jackets and squash."[8] There was no salt nor pepper, no bread nor money with which to buy flour. "It was hunt, work or starve, which we nearly did."[9] After a wait of three weeks, Christian was able to send his family 100 lbs of flour and a piece of bacon. When Inger opened the sack of flour, her hungry children put in their hands and ate dry flour until they nearly choked. Inger mixed some flour with water and cooked it on a skillet in the fireplace.

Martin was sent to a neighboring ranch to get some buttermilk. When he arrived, the rancher and family had just sat down to a chicken dinner. He had to wait until they finished their meal. He was so hungry he kept wishing they would offer him a crust of bread or a chicken bone to pick. Instead, the bones and crumbs all went under the table for the cats. After they finished their meal, Martin was given the promised buttermilk. As he crossed their yard he saw the severed feet and shanks of the chicken which had been eaten for dinner. He picked up the chicken feet and took them home where he thoroughly cleaned and scalded them. The chicken feet were then put into a sauce pan and boiled for soup. While they were boiling, he peeled potatoes. To his watching mother, Martin said, "Look Mother, there are beads on our soup." There were tears in her eyes as she said, "Yes, your dinner will soon be ready." His younger siblings were away playing at the neighbors, so Martin and his mother "ate the chicken dinner alone."[10]

The Genoa countryside was beautiful. In the spring of 1858, Martin and his sisters, Caroline and Hannah, went for a walk through the rolling hills which were covered with large bunches of wheatgrass. While tramping through the grass they discovered a baby fawn. Martin said: "I'm going to take this home and show it to Father." When the fawn was picked up it began to struggle and called in alarm. Shortly, the Hansen children saw a herd of deer coming their way. They dropped the fawn and ran for home. Christian had hunted in his younger days and had a gun. He grabbed it and Martin led him to the spot, but the deer were gone. They tracked them to a stream, but were unable to follow them farther.

Christian Hansen found game on other occasions. The family also picked grapes, black and red raspberries, and Pottawattamie plums, all of which grew in abundance in this area. They planted a crop of corn and potatoes and early garden vegetables. They cut and stacked the rich prairie grasses for hay as they had acquired some livestock. Martin became a good fisherman and once caught three large fish which he was able to sell for a dollar each to passing emigrants. Once, Martin caught a 20 pound fish which pulled him into the river up to chest level before he was able to land it. One day he hooked a large turtle. He dared not attempt removing the hook from the turtle's mouth, so he herded the creature toward home. A man Martin encountered en route home told him the turtle's meat was as good as that of a chicken. The turtle was dispatched, prepared, and eaten by the Hansen family. The meat was delicious. Christian took the turtle's colorful shell and made a cradle for his daughters' dolls.

Christian Hansen also built a log cabin for his family from the timber which grew along the Loup Fork and its tributary streams. They had not been living in the new log home long when two men with bedrolls on their backs asked if they could use the dugout for the night. The visitors made their beds in one of the dugout bunks and were soon fast asleep. The next morning one of them told the Hansens that when they awoke, one fellow asked the other, "What is the matter with your leg? It has been as cold as ice all night." As they began to move, they heard a hissing noise. They threw back the covers to discover that a large rattlesnake, intent on warming itself, had crawled between them while they slept. One man drew his pistol and shot dead the uninvited bed partner.

About this same time a new danger emerged for those at Genoa. Along the river, two tribes of Native Americans had engaged in a fierce battle over hunting rights. Some of the warriors approached the settlers at Genoa and asked for their support in helping to drive the other tribe across the river. The pioneers declined to be involved, saying they were unprepared. That ended the trouble temporarily. However, near harvest time in 1858, the Indians returned. Urged on by some cattlemen, they gave the Mormons just 48 hours to pack up and get out.

The Hansen family went east to Council Bluffs where they found Ole Petersen and family. The Petersens and others aided the Hansens. The Hansen children attended school in Council Bluffs where they learned to speak English. Work was plentiful, and the family prospered and prepared to go west. Fascinatingly, Christian Hansen had partly paid the way for Ole and his family in 1857. These families went west together in 1861. En route they met returning soldiers of what had been Johnston's Army, who were eastbound to fight in the bitter quarrel between the Northern and Southern states. After two days in Salt Lake City, the Hansens went south to Utah Valley. At the point of the mountain which divides the Salt Lake and Utah valleys, they met Bishop Edward Hunter, the Presiding Bishop of the Church. He asked their destination. They replied: "American Fork." "It was a good choice," he said, "for there was a lot of hay there."[11] (Bishop Hunter owned an American Fork farm which at that time was being operated on shares by 7th Handcart Company members, Hans and Ellen Christensen and their sons.) On 8 February 1862, Inger Mortensen Hansen died. Challenges and tests of faith were not confined to the time spent on the trail.

NOTES

1. James Jensen, [Reminiscences]. In J. M. Tanner, *A Biographical Sketch of James Jensen* (Salt Lake City, Deseret News, 1911) pp. 23-40.

2. The 509 Latter-day Saints in passenger company of the *John J. Boyd* consisted of 437 Scandinavians, 30 from Piedmont (an agricultural region of the upper Po Valley in northwest Italy) and 42 from Great Britain. The voyage of the *John J. Boyd*, described by one as an old bark, had been difficult. There was much sickness. An outbreak of

measles resulted in many deaths, especially among the Danish children. The Atlantic winter had been terrible.

High headwinds (gales and hurricanes in some accounts) and heavy seas resulted in the loss of a number of ships that season. It was the type of blowing weather "that would loosen the hair on a dog." Peter Gottfredson said when they were about a third of the way across they were driven back to the coast of Ireland by fierce winds. About midway across the Atlantic they came upon the wrecked clipper ship, *Louis Napoleon*. Its masts and spars had all been swept away, its leeward bulwarks crushed inward. Charles R. Savage wrote that the *Louis Napoleon* "had been laying eight days in a fearful condition . . . the rudder, mast, and railings were gone with the man at the helm and the cook washed overboard." Twenty-one people were rescued, including the captain who, according to Patience Loader Rosa Archer, had lost his 16-year-old son, his only child, in the disaster. The rescue of the crew from the wreck helped save the *John J. Boyd* as the *Louis Napoleon*'s crew and food supplies helped meet critical shortages. (Passengers had been substituting for disabled sailors.) As it was, they only had about a day's supply of water when they docked at New York after 65 days at sea. The *John J. Boyd*'s captain, a superstitious man, blamed the Latter-day Saints for the difficulties and forbade them to sing and pray. However, fasting and prayer was conducted in secret. The captain was a violent and disagreeable individual. Some reports state he did not want to rescue the men of the shipwreck. He killed one of his crew members by striking him in the head with a rope with a hook in it because the sailor was slow in carrying out an order. For a more comprehensive report, see the Personal Accounts of the Mormon Immigration Index, for the *John J. Boyd*, December 1855. Knud or Canute Petersen was the leader of the Latter-day Saints on board. He would ultimately serve as the first president of the Sanpete Stake. His son-in-law, Anthon H. Lund, a native of Aalborg, Jutland, Denmark, served in the First Presidency as first and second counselor to Joseph F. Smith and as first counselor to Heber J. Grant.

3. Her name is given as Karen Marie Pederson Neilhode in one account, whereas Meilhede is the surname used by her brother and sister on the *John Bright* passenger manifest.

4. Peter Gottfredson remembered 120 miles. *The Latter-day Saints' Emigrants Guide* by William Clayton (Edited by Stanley B. Kimball) said it was 127 miles to the Old Pawnee Village along the banks of the Loup Fork.

5. There is a Plumb Creek in this area. Looking Glass Creek, called *Quitooquataleri* by the Pawnee meaning "Water That Reflects Your Shadow," has also been called Grape Creek. *The Latter-day Saints' Emigrant Guide* by W. Clayton, St. Louis, 1848 edited by Stanley B. Kimball, p. 45.

6. *Our Pioneer Heritage*, Vol. 2, pp. 43-44. The Mormon Immigration

Index–Personal Accounts, General Voyage Notes, tell that Rasmus Olsen and the Meihede family group had come on the *John Bright* which sailed from Liverpool 22 March 1858 and landed at New York 23 April 1858. Of the 90 Latter-day Saints on board, 75 were from Denmark. Iver N. Iversen was the Church leader. They had intended to come from Korser, Sjælland, Denmark, via Kiel and Hamburg, Germany, but ice in the Elbe River interfered with steamship travel. Instead, they took passage across Storebælt, the strait between Sjælland and Fyn, then across the Lillebælt to Jutland and then to Flensburg, Germany. At Flensburg, an unscrupulous innkeeper charged them 65 Crigsdaler (about 35 U.S. dollars) to provide each individual with a cup of coffee, a few cakes, and a mild beer. Many in this company made the plains crossing with the returning Scandinavia Mission president, Hector C. Haight. President Young had called home all missionaries in response to the emergency conditions created by the Utah War.

7. Martin Hansen, *A Short Synopsis of...*, pp. 3-7.

8. Martin Hansen, *A Short Synopsis of...*, p. 7.

9. Martin Hansen, *A Short Synopsis of...*, p. 7.

10. Martin Hansen, *A Short Synopsis of...*, pp. 7-8.

11. Martin Hansen, *A Short Synopsis of...*, pp. 5-22. Much of Martin Hansen's account is devoted to his family's life at Genoa and Council Bluffs during the 1857-61 period.

Chapter 12

ONWARD FROM THE LOUP FORK

On July 18, about the same time the handcart pioneers were leaving the Loup Fork, the Tenth Infantry, the vanguard unit of the U.S. Army's Utah Expedition, under the command of Colonel E. B. Alexander, began moving out from Fort Leavenworth. The artillery and the Fifth Infantry followed a few days later. Logistical problems, unseasoned troops (tradition has it there were many teenaged fellows among the ranks) coupled with Governor Walker's continuing intransigence that Colonel Harney must remain in Kansas, had all combined to compromise the Expedition's start.[1] While the delay would prove costly for the army, it would seem heaven-sent to the Latter-day Saints.

On the way west, a happy event occurred at the Wood River. Anna Marie Sorensen, 31, the wife of Niels Sorensen, 33, gave birth to a baby girl who was named Julia Marie.[2] Reflecting on that birth, a sub-captain wrote: "I remember a certain sister who came up one morning when the tents were being packed up, with something in her apron. Upon inspection it proved to be a little person who had come into the world the previous evening. The mother had walked with her handcart all day the previous day, and thought she would walk as far that day as she could."[3] However, the leaders insisted she ride in one of the wagons for several days. Both Anna Marie and baby, Julia Marie, survived the trip. They were alive and well and living in Monroe, Sevier County, Utah, several years later. Recorded in the Gospel of Luke is an account which would have comforted Anna Marie. Centuries earlier, half a world away Jesus was born under circumstances which must have been difficult for His mother.

An arrival date can be estimated for the Wood River camp. Assuming a trail distance of 55 miles from the Loup Fork crossing to the Wood, an average daily travel distance of 18 miles, and the fact that they broke camp on Saturday July 18, the 7th Company probably reached the Wood River on July 20. According to James Jensen, they traveled all day June 19 without water,[4] which meant on that occasion they did not halt for the Sabbath, a decision no doubt influenced because of the time required to cross the Loup Fork.

The distance given from Florence, Nebraska to Salt Lake City is 1,031 miles according to the *Latter-day Saints' Emigrants Guide* by W. Clayton, St. Louis 1848, as edited by Stanley B. Kimball. The 7th Company reached Fort Laramie on August 9 according to Hafen and Hafen. In volume IV:236 of his *Comprehensive History of the Church*, B. H. Roberts states that it was 513 miles from Fort Laramie to Salt Lake City. However, if one adds the daily mileage given in the Edmund Ellsworth, Captain and A. Galloway, Secretary: First Company Journal as reproduced in Hafen and Hafen, it is 1074 miles From Florence to Salt Lake City rather than 1,031 miles. Either figure may imply a preciseness which one could question, given the nature of trails and the sidetracking undertaken by the 7th Company to avoid the great herds of buffalo on the plains that season. Using the Ellsworth/Galloway account, the distance from Florence to Fort Laramie was 539 miles. From Fort Laramie to Salt Lake City was 535 miles. Generally, Sundays were spent in Sabbath observance. Exempting Sundays, the company moved an average map distance of 18.0 miles per travel day between July 7 and August 9. That average does not provide an adjustment for time spent fording rivers or any detours or sidetracking to avoid the vast buffalo herds which Niels Christensen (History of Niels Christensen p. 2) said were a part of the journey west. They traveled the 535 miles from Fort Laramie to Salt Lake City during the period of August 10, to noon, September 13. Assuming that August 16, 23, 30 and September 6 had been spent in Sabbath observance, the handcart pioneers would have traveled approximately 18.4 miles for each travel day. The terrain from Fort Laramie is considerably rougher than the broad Platte River Valley, but they would not have faced the Sand Hills of Nebraska. It was cooler across central Wyoming, but they had abandoned much of what they could have used to be comfortable at nights. They were getting terribly weary. Exhaustion coupled with malnutrition must have been the cause of a number of the deaths.

Life on the plains was not easy for children. There were other heart-wrenching experiences. The Hans Jensen family lost their baby daughter, Maria Sophie, as they moved up the Platte. The ill baby girl rode on the handcart as her mother pushed and her father and James (Jens) acted as the wheel team. Her sister Karen and another brother, Jacob Hans, helped as a 7-year-old brother, Soren, walked beside. Maria Sophie died before the journey was through. A new grave was dug into which the sorrowing family placed her emaciated body. A "sieve was placed over her face"[5] and earth covered her mortal remains. Zion, like Gethsemane, was exacting a dreadful price. Bravely, the Jensen family went forward.

For a small moment, Kersten Erickson's courage failed her. Terribly lonely, she became despondent. She thought she might as well die there as to suffer longer. One day she purposefully stayed behind and laid in the grass expecting to die. However, Captain Christiansen found her. From that point on he helped her pull up the hills and through the sand. She had been assigned to pull a handcart teamed with an older couple and a sickly girl. The older couple died. Kersten was assigned to a handcart with six pullers. Her shoes wore out; she made new shoes from rawhide obtained from dead cattle found along the way. Crossing the creeks and rivers made the rawhide shoes soft. The hot sun and dry road made the leather hard. Her feet were nearly always sore and bleeding. Because she had to leave her bed clothes on the campground at Clear Creek, an old shawl served as her blanket at night.[6]

Before the end of July, the 7th Company's meager supply of dried beef, smoked pork, coffee, sugar, salt, and other seasonings had been exhausted.[7] After that, flour and its products sustained them. They baked bread, made hot cakes, porridge, gruel, soup, coffee, and other dishes from flour.[8] Whenever they found wild fruit or berries, they mixed them into the flour products to give a little variety.[9]

The 7th Company shot only one buffalo. It lagged behind the herd, and they were able to harvest it without exposing the company to a possible stampede.[10] At what point in the journey they took the buffalo is not specified. They would have been in buffalo country[11] even prior to reaching the Loup Fork until they were well into present-day Wyoming.

Why were these pioneers able to shoot only one buffalo when vast herds were spread across the plains that season? There were men in the company who had fought for Denmark against Germany.[11] They knew how to use firearms. The Danes manifested great bravery in the 1848-50 conflict over Schleswig-Holstein. They faced a German army equipped with superior weaponry, namely a breech-loading needle-gun. Although its effective range was shorter and it had other defects compared to muzzle-loading rifles which were developed later, the rate of fire was three times as fast—seven shots a minute rather than two. It could be loaded and fired while the soldier was lying flat on the ground, thereby making him a much smaller target.[12] Upon his return from that war, Hans Christensen told Ellen and her sons how they had implanted in the earth the stocks of their bayoneted muskets, which were then used to impale the horses of the German cavalry. Then, with swords they fought hand-to-hand with the unhorsed Germans. It was not a shortage of courage which resulted in the lack of hunting success.

Hans carried that sword to America, and it remained in his family for many years. Yet, there is no mention of him bringing a musket. Were muskets the property of the Danish crown? Were firearms seized as contraband at British or American ports? Peter Gottfredson said his father carried his Danish military uniform, sword, gun, and bayonet, all of which had been sewn up in a canvas. When the Gottfredsons landed in New York, those items could not be found. They had either been taken or lost.[13] Perhaps the immigrants' economic circumstances were such that they could not afford weaponry and ammunition. Immigrants would not have been advised to procure weapons in England. No handbook suggested the purchase of such equipment prior to their arrival in the United States.[14]

What other possible explanations might be given as to why there were no skilled hunters? Was it because by the 1850s hunting in Europe had been confined to the aristocracy and landed gentry? As a boy, Niels Christensen liked to tramp through the woods with the Royal Danish forester and watch him shoot foxes. Niels wanted to be a Royal gamekeeper when he became a man.[15] An unproven oral tradition in Hans Kofoed's family indicates he was a hunting companion of the prince on the Royal Hunting preserve on Bornholm. However, even if it were true, Hans Kofoed was unavailable, for he and his family remained at Florence at the direction of the leadership. These examples suggest there were only limited hunting opportunities for commoners in Denmark in the 1850s.

Britain's common lands had been enclosed by the late 18th century. By the 1850s, hunting had long been confined to the upper classes. Common folk could not have afforded the necessary firearms, ammunition, or time for hunting, had they been given permission to hunt on the estates of England's landed gentry and aristocracy.[16] Except for illegal hunting or poaching, meat would have been procured at the village and town butcher shops. Among Britain's commoners, hunting and harvesting skills would have been limited to catching rabbits, fish, and the like.[17] The hunting situation in southern Scandinavia must have been similar to that in England. Denmark's agricultural character would not have provided the space necessary for large game animals. The Danes were largely farmers, shopkeepers, fishermen, and artisans.

The 7th Handcart Company had an unusual vocational mix. Of those individuals who came on the *Westmoreland*, there are 105 whose vocations are known, if the six spinsters are included. That vocational census does not include homemaker, the usual occupation of married women. Vocations tend to be recorded only for heads of families. Only one woman, a tailor, Anna Muraitsen, listed a vocation other than spinster. Apparently, it was assumed that homemaking was the occupation of most women. For the other 99 people, their given occupational categories were as follows: farmers, 41; laborers, 15; tailors, 12; carpenters, 6; joiners, 4; shoemakers, 4; weavers, 3; and one of each of the following: brazier, brick-maker, butcher,[18] cabinetmaker, coachman, goldsmith, iron founder, mechanic, miller, musician, painter, potter, printer, stonecutter, stonemason, and one farmer who was also a wheelwright. A company of American pioneers may well have included frontiersmen, men with experience as a woodsman, hunter, gunsmith, and fisherman, as well as those of blacksmith, farrier, harness and saddle maker, wheelwright, wagon maker, and other trades associated with land transportation methods common to that time.

On the American frontier, boys learned to hunt early. In their teens, they were allowed to hunt antelope when the wagon trains came west from Kanesville in 1852, although buffalo hunting was confined to more seasoned men on horseback.[19] Taking game animals was necessary for survival for most pioneers. Perhaps that need had been the philosophical undergirding for the adoption of the 2nd Amendment in the Bill of Rights. Another factor may have been the egalitarian attitude that in America, hunting will not be a right confined to the privileged few.

For the most part in Europe, the largest game animal was the deer. By the 1850s and 1860s, existing populations of the moose, roe deer, and deer were scarce and almost extinct in some parts of southern Sweden and Norway. Hunters took the adult moose and left the calves. However, the calves did not survive without their mothers. Very few common people would have had an opportunity to develop the requisite big-game hunting skills, and the necessary meat-handling and preservation techniques which would have enabled them to utilize big game for food. Those skill deficiencies included the use of firearms. There were wild reindeer in remote parts of Norway's high mountains, but those animals were not easily accessible. Few attempted to track them. Even fewer were actually success- ful in harvesting a reindeer. Bear could be hunted, as there were many in Norway in the 1850s. However, most of the early con- verts in Norway came from urban areas. City dwellers had little opportunity to learn to hunt. The combination of those factors resulted in an absence of experienced hunters and frontiersmen among these Scandinavian Latter-day Saints.[20] There may have been the limited few, like Christian Hansen and Hans Kofoed, who had some hunting experience, but whose personal or fam- ily health difficulties prevented them from going on.[21] (Today there are polar bears and caribou or reindeer in northern Norway.)

The handcart company's situation may have been com- pounded by an overall shortage of both firearms and ammuni- tion. Four years later, when America's Civil War broke out in April 1861, neither the North nor the South was prepared to engage in a major war. Except for the Mexican War and the continuing skirmishes with Native Americans, there had been several decades of relative peace. The major conflicts with the Plains Indians were yet in the future. Consequently, there were limited stockpiles of small arms in the United States. Pre-Civil War firearms were rather rudimentary. Reflecting on his days as a lieutenant in the Mexican War, General Ulysses S. Grant observed that "at a distance of a few hundred yards a man might fire on you all day long without your finding out." The 1855 invention of the rifled barrel quickly made the smooth- bore rifle obsolete. It was a more complicated process to load and fire a muzzle-loading rifle than the hunting rifles of today. Ten specific movements were required. In order they were (1) lower the musket's stock to the ground, (2) handle the car- tridge, (3) tear the cartridge, (4) charge the cartridge, (5) draw the hammer, (6) ram the cartridge twice, (7) return the ham- mer, (8) cast about or return the gun to the firing position, (9) insert the primer cap, (10) cock the hammer and point the rifle. Trained soldiers were expected to complete the ten steps in 20 seconds, or to fire three shots per minute. Yet, even such slow firepower gave the army a decided technological advantage over arrow, axe, and spear.

The .44-caliber 1863 Military Henry Rifle, which became the forerunner of all Winchester lever-action rifles, saw only limited action during the Civil War. The 1863 Henry's magazine held a dozen rounds or bullets. A lever action simultaneously cocked the rifle's hammer, ejected the spent casing and inserted a fresh round in the firing chamber. The Confederate soldiers referred to the Henry as "that damn Yankee rifle that can be loaded on Sunday and fired all week." For that day, Henry rifles were expensive. The first 1,731 Henry rifles were delivered to the Army's Ordinance Department at a cost exceeding $36,000, or approximately $21 each.[22] (For comparison purposes, the cost per person to travel by handcart was $15; to purchase one wagon, with bows, yokes, four oxen, and a cow or two, was given as $275 in 1857.) While some people now look upon guns with abhorrence, they were absolutely necessary tools during the pioneering era. Even teenaged boys understood their value. After arriving in the Salt Lake Valley, 13-year-old Niels Christensen spent the first winter working for his board with a family in Cottonwood. The man of the family owned a muzzle-loading rifle which had a revolving chamber similar to that of a six-shooter pistol. Niels said: "I would have worked a whole year for that gun.[23]

Bison, elk, moose, and grizzly bears are part of the mystique of the American West. There were smaller animals such as antelope, deer, rabbits, and prairie chickens. There are intimations in the accounts which survive, that grave concerns existed that the vast buffalo herds moving across Nebraska's grasslands might be easily startled and the company annihilated in the resulting stampede. These great herds were described as "often just a gunshot away." Niels Christensen remembered the company sidetracking to avoid the great herds of buffalo. The need for skilled hunters may have been one thing which had been accidentally overlooked in the planning process. It may have been that there were those with hunting skills who went west with Cowley, or, in the case of Christian Hansen, remained in the Midwest because of health problems. Americans quite naturally would have assumed there would be plenty of men and boys who knew how to hunt. It is just something men did on the frontier.[24] Surviving accounts do not seem to indicate that saddle horses were a part of the company's livestock inventory. If that surmise is accurate, then anyone with even rudimentary big-game hunting skills, would not have been able to go out and harvest buffalo at a distance which would have provided safety to the handcart train. By contrast, the 1st Handcart Company harvested a number of buffalo on the journey west, as many as four in one day. They even halted to make jerky.[25]

C.C.A. Christensen ascribes their safety from the great herds of buffalo to "the angels of the Lord, though unseen, for we were walking defenseless in a long spread out row, in a land of wild Indians."[26] That observation is supported by east-bound missionary, S. W. Richards, who wrote, "The blessing of our Heavenly Father has been upon this mission, fully equal to the duties we have had to perform. We passed several bands of Indians upon the plains, together with the principal body of Sioux, but were not molested by any," except for the Indians attempting to swap for matches, bread, and other items. "Every evil eye towards us has seemingly been blind, and no angry heart has been suffered to do us any harm."[27]

NOTES

1. Andrew Jenson, Church Chronology, Historical Record, 1890, p. 54.

2. The *Westmoreland* passenger manifest gives their names as Nils and Anna M. Sorensen. The Swedish Nils is pronounced the same as the Danish Niels, and the surname spelling indicates they were Danish. The Journal History of the Church for 13 September 1857, p. 26 uses the Danish spelling.

3. C. C. A. Christensen, *By Handcart to Utah...*, p. 340. [One wonders why Christensen did not identify people by name. He obviously remembered them, for he knew of their whereabouts.]

4. James Jensen, Journal History of the Church, pp. 16-23, 13 September 1857, LDS Archives.

5. Hafen and Hafen, Handcarts to Zion..., p. 161.

6. Autobiography of Kersten Erickson Benson, pp. 1-3.

7. The 1st Company was harvesting buffalo 20 days after leaving Florence. It seems likely that immigration leaders at Florence would have assumed the 7th Company would be able to do the same thing, hence the three-week supply of dried meat rations.

8. C. C. A. Christensen, By Handcart to Utah..., p. 340.

9. Clare B. Christensen, History of Niels Christensen, Op cit., p 2.

10. C. C. A. Christensen, By Handcart to Utah..., p. 340.

11. Hans Jensen is another 7th Company member definitely identified as having served in the Danish army. His son, James (Jens), said his father had been taken into the Danish Army in 1848 and was away three years. The care of the home and family had been left to his "determined and industrious mother" (Journal History of the Church, 13 September 1857, p. 12, taken from the Biography of James Jensen by J. M. Tanner).

12. B. H. Liddell Hart, "Armed Forces and the Art of War: Armies, in The New Cambridge Modern History," X, The Zenith of European Power, 1830-70, 1960, pp. 304-05.

13. Taken from the Mormon Immigration Index—Personal Accounts, *Autobiography of Peter Gottfredson* [Gotfredsen] p. 2, notes from the voyage of the *John J. Boyd*, December 1855.

14. Nicholas J. Evans, Willerby, Hull, England, Personal Communication, Op cit., 23 December 2000. Evans is a research fellow at the National Maritime Museum, and a Ph.D. research student at the Maritime Historic Studies Centre, University of Hull.

15. Clare B. Christensen, *History of Niels Christensen*, Op cit., p. 1.

16. Bryan Skelton, Kingston upon Hull, England. Personal communication December 4, 2000.

17. Nicholas J. Evans, Willerby, Hull, England, Personal Communication, Op cit., December 23, 2000.

18. It is C. C. A. Christensen, *By Handcart to Utah...*, p. 343 who identifies that a butcher is a part of the 7th Company. However, Christensen does not give the man's name.

19. Howard R. Driggs, *Ben The Wagon Boy*, Stevens and Wallis, Salt Lake City, 1944, pp. 58-60, 69-72.

20. Petter Svanevik, Personal Communication, January 5, 2001 and by E-mail communique, 12 January 2001.

21. Martin Hansen's account states his father harvested wild game but it does not identify what types.

22. "Long Arms of the Civil War," Civil War Talk.Com-Weapons of the Civil War, pp. 1, 5.

23. Clare B. Christensen, *Christensen Family Treasures,* p. 11. This is an unpublished manuscript now held in the archives of the author. Clare B. Christensen heard this vignette from his grandfather, Niels Christensen. Those who have never experienced the perils of the pioneering era or who have not lived through the hazards of war, probably do not understand what it means to sleep on their sword at night. Niels Christensen, who lived through the pioneering period and spent his last 29 years as a widower before he died 18 May 1923 understood. As a 22-year-old cavalry soldier in the Black Hawk Indian War, he helped cut a flint-tipped arrow from the shoulder blade of one of his comrades in arms. Even during the later years of Niels' life, Clare said: "If you knocked at the door of his home late at night, Grandfather opened the door with one hand, his six shooter in the other." Clare described his grandfather as mild-mannered man, one who was difficult to provoke.

24. A contrasting example is Addison Pratt's journal account of 2 October 1849, to 12 January 1850. See *The Journals of Addison Pratt,* edited by S. George Ellsworth, University of Utah Press, Salt Lake City, 1990, pp. 375-412. Addison Pratt, an older brother of Parley P. Pratt and Orson Pratt, kept rather detailed journals at various times in his life. He was a part of the 1849 Jefferson Hunt Party, a wagon company which went to southern California and began the Mormon Colony at San Bernardino. He details the flora and fauna and tells of his hunting activities en route. The surviving records of the 7th Company contain little information about the nature of the country, and there would have been a great deal of variety between Philadelphia and Salt Lake City. It would seem the prairie's grasses and clovers would have been new to them, but apparently there were few written observations. The danger posed by the buffalo seems to have been the dominant concern.

25. Hafen and Hafen, *Handcarts to Zion...,* p. 207.

26. C. C. A. Christensen, *By Handcart to Utah...,* pp. 339-40.

27. S. W. Richards to Orson Pratt, 4 October 1857, *Millennial Star,* XIX:670.

Chapter 13

THE PLAINS: INDIANS, BISON, AND HUNGER

Did defenseless refer to the buffalo and Indians? Was it a poetic expression, or were they really without much weaponry and ammunition?[1] They had reason to be concerned. The Plains Indians were armed and mounted. Horses were the technological basis of the buffalo economy, and the acquisition of horses had turned the Sioux, Cheyenne, and Arapaho into the dominant Plains tribes. Horses made it possible to pull larger lodge poles than when dogs pulled the travois, so the horse economy meant the size of the tipi could be increased. These Native Americans moved in a seasonal migratory pattern from sheltered, wooded encampments along streams during the snowy moons to the prairies flush with summer grasses and buffalo. They moved frequently so as to provide forage for the horses in a pattern determined by grass and water. Food, shelter, and clothing were heavily dependent on success during the buffalo hunt. Wealth was measured in horses, for the horse was the outward symbol of prosperity. Brides were paid for with horses. A test of bravery was to steal horses from an enemy tribe. Such economic and cultural factors fueled a raider mentality and intertribal conflicts frequently involved quarrels over hunting grounds.

White traders located their posts at a spring or other water source long used by these nomadic plainsmen. Where the trader provided goods desired by the local tribesman, these intrusions were not a particular problem in White-Indian relations. However, these traders and trappers were but a harbinger of things to come: waves of pioneers and whole companies of families moving west, leading some Indians to conclude the white man was relocating his entire tribe.

While the 1850s were not so rife with conflict between white and Indian as the post Civil War period, troubles were increasing and there were nasty incidents where blood was shed. In

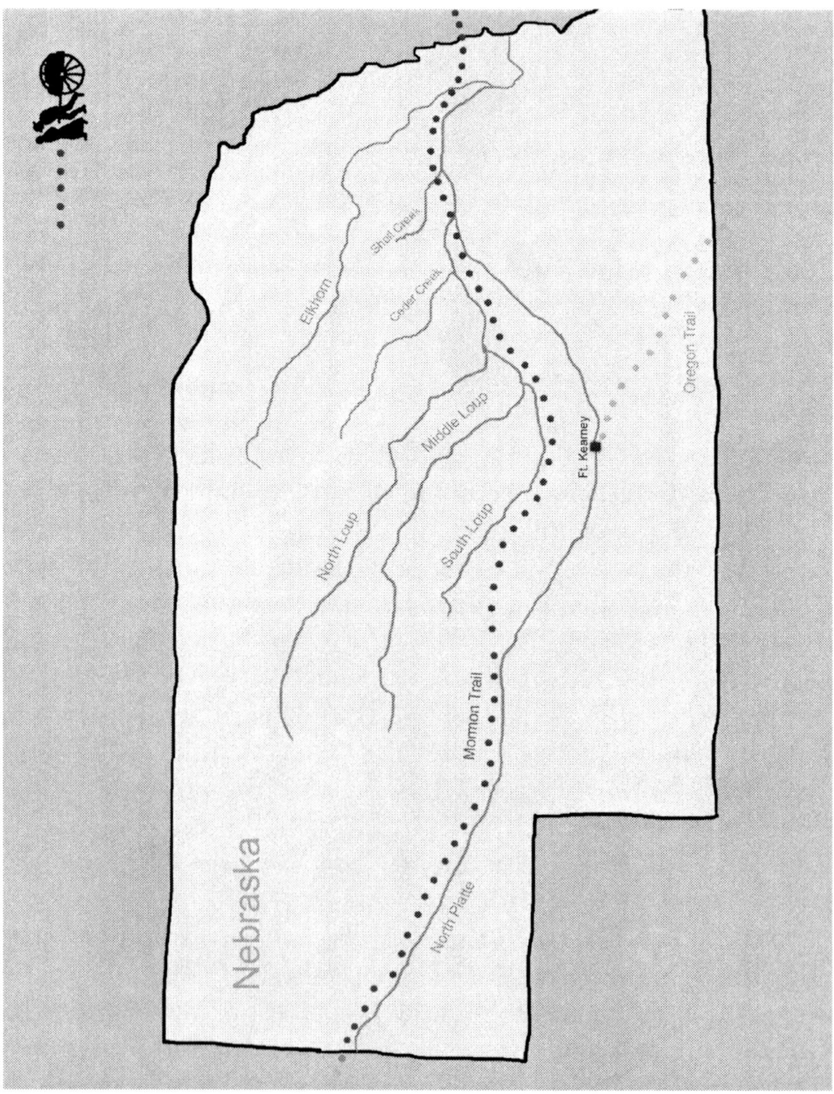

Map by Jeremy Munns

1854, near Fort Laramie, a westbound settler complained that Indians had killed his cow. Learning that one of his young men had killed the cow, Chief Conquering Bear went to Fort Laramie and offered to pay $10 to settle the matter, but the immigrant demanded $25. Reportedly, the cow was lame and not worth that much. A lame cow would not have survived the trek, so rightfully, the Sioux chief refused to pay the higher price, which he probably did not have anyway. A young army 2nd lieutenant, John L. Grattan, was assigned to investigate the matter. Lt. Grattan who, according to some reports was reckless and not especially clever, had apparently foolishly fortified his courage with whiskey. His detachment of 30 troops included a drunken interpreter and two cannons which were taken as a display of military superiority. Grattan and company rode into a large encampment of Brulé, Oglala, and some Miniconjou Sioux.[2]

The lieutenant apparently made little, if any, attempt at diplomacy, demanding immediate payment for the cow or the surrender of the young man who had killed her. An argument ensued and shooting broke out. Grattan opened fire with his cannon. Conquering Bear was mortally wounded and several other Sioux were killed. Only one of the thirty blue coats survived long enough to carry the story back to Fort Laramie. Realizing that retribution would be swift, the Sioux struck camp and moved northeast, so as to take their people out of harm's way. During their flight, Conquering Bear died and his body was placed on a scaffold after the manner in which the Plains tribes disposed of their dead.[3]

In reprisal, elements of the U.S. Army under the command of Colonel William Harney attacked the Brulé Sioux camp at Ash Hollow on Blue Water Creek, Nebraska, in 1855 and slaughtered 86 men, women, and children. Little Thunder led this band of Brulé Sioux, which band had had nothing to do with killing the emigrant's cow. However, the U.S. Army operated under the policy of "collective responsibility." It was a case of all Indians within reach of the army being guilty by association, for Native Americans were not accorded Constitutional protection of presumed innocence. Harney gathered up the wounded and other captives and drove them west toward Fort Laramie. He was so elated at his cruel victory that, Napoleon-like, he attempted to have his gunners shoot the top off of Chimney Rock.[4] The name "Squaw Killer Harney" is traceable to that blood-stained moment.

Andrew Jackson's policy of removing Native Americans when necessary to achieve Manifest Destiny still dominated the political mind-set of many in white officialdom. That period of social intolerance was seemingly encouraged by irresponsible journalism, for America's press published disparaging articles about the Indians. Yet, such editorial bigotry was not confined to Indians alone as Irish Catholics, the Jews of New York, the Chinese of California, and Blacks were all targets. In 1857, abolitionist writers were a precious few. Some journalists wrote: "European monarchies were systematically disposing of their paupers and criminals [in America.]"[5] It is stating the obvious to say that such blatantly negative editorial rhetoric toward any

Scott's Bluff in the Valley of the North Platte was an important landmark on the Mormon Trail. Photographed by the author, July 1992.

group is counterproductive to social harmony and the orderly incorporation of newcomers into the at-large community. Nonetheless, there was a singularly significant difference: the United States military did not hunt down and shoot white social groups as a matter of federal policy, although one could argue that such an initiative was what was expressly intended in the case of the Utah War. And it was a fact that charges of alien sedition and disloyalty had been an element in Senator Douglas' June 12 speech.

So, as had happened east of the Mississippi, white Americans and Europeans were once again crossing territory reserved by treaty to Native Americans, who must have viewed with alarm the ever-increasing numbers of settlers, cattle drovers, miners, and adventurers moving west along the Big Medicine Road. This was their home. It had been Indian land from time immemorial. Such had been the policy of Presidents James Monroe and John Quincy Adams. There had been tacit recognition of such in treaties negotiated by representatives of the United States. Yet, such treaties were not a white-man's deed, and they were conveniently ignored when new economic opportunities emerged for white Americans. Arrogant, cruel, and thoughtless acts perpetrated by whites crossing Indian lands had also bred resentment, creating conditions which ultimately resulted in reprisal. From the Indian's perspective, those crossing their lands along the Platte were intruders engaged in punching a major hole through the Teton Sioux, Cheyenne, and Arapaho frontier. The land was sacred. Trespassing was not taken lightly even among the tribes. For example, by 1860 the Sioux and Cheyenne had pushed the Kiowa south of the Kansas and Nebraska boundary.

The handcart pioneers were a part of that westward movement through the heart of Indian country. The trek was not without risk. Mormon worries about the possibility of an Indian attack were not just confined to the Sioux, for in 1856 the Cheyenne had twice struck Colonel Almon W. Babbit's wagon train of government property. On August 25, Babbit's westbound train was plundered by the Cheyenne near the Wood

River. A man named Nichols and two others were killed and a Mrs. Wilson was carried away captive. Then, in September, the Cheyenne hit them again just east of Fort Laramie. Colonel Babbit, Utah's Territorial Delegate to Congress, was killed, as were Thomas Margetts and child, James Cowdy and wife, and others. Mrs. Margetts was taken captive.[6] Those attacks set the stage for Colonel William S. Harney's and Colonel E. V. Sumner's punitive campaign against the Cheyenne in 1857.[7] That May, Colonel Sumner and his command were ordered into the field against the Northern Cheyenne, ostensibly to teach them to behave themselves. He trailed a large band of Cheyenne across western Nebraska and Kansas before he caught them at the Republican River in what is now northwest Kansas. Native Americans believed in the power of the Great Spirit. They had confidence in their Medicine Men to divine the situation and to tell them if the signs and omens were favorable for success in battle. On this occasion, the Medicine Man had informed the 300 Cheyenne warriors that if they washed in a particular lake, it would act as a shield against the soldiers bullets. However, for some strange reason, Sumner ordered his cavalry to unsheathe their sabers and charge. Their bullet-proofing magic in disarray, the Cheyenne turned and ran so fast that only four of their number were lost. Two troopers were killed and several were wounded. Sumner torched their village and continued his march of intimidation.[8]

It seems probable that such federal military activity may well have reduced the likelihood of Indian attack on emigrant companies, for Cheyenne and Sioux would have tended to move their camps to areas less frequented by the army. Those maneuvers may have interfered with preparations and delayed Harney's efforts to move the Utah Expedition west.

There were U.S.-Indian battles elsewhere in 1857. The Second Cavalry was aggressively pursuing the Comanche in Texas, while in New Mexico Colonel Benjamin L. E. Bonneville led the Gila Expedition, the decade's most successful campaign against the Apache.

There were equally legitimate reasons for the 7th

William Henry Jackson's painting of **Chimney Rock**, so named because of its appearance like an English chimney. Chimney Rock was considered the best-known landmark of the Mormon Trail. It is some distance to the south of the North Platte River

Company's concern over safety from the buffalo. One 7th Company participant reported that while they saw many buffalo, there were no thundering herds and that once the company had separated, so a small buffalo herd could pass through their line.[9] Henry Lunt, now going west with the William G. Young Company, recorded under the date of 31 July 1857, that "during the last five days we have seen an immense quantity of Buffaloes, the Platte Valley has been litterly [sic] black with them."[6] Lunt said that on a number of occasions they had been compelled to halt their train as they were fearful of their cattle becoming frightened and stampeded by the great herds of buffalo. He then wrote: "Once a very large bull Buffalo was alone behind the main herd of several thousand which had just crossed the south fork of the Platte and came on a loap [sic] going west after the herd and, but for me firing a shot at him in the head from my Revolver which turned him close by the hind

Chimney Rock, perhaps the most famous of the Mormon Trail landmarks. It is said that on a clear day it can be seen for more than 20 miles. Photograph by the author, July 1992.

end of the wagon, he would have bounded between my two yoke of oxen and, being the last wagon that day in the train, providently avoided serious results."[11]

A great herd of buffalo had gone through the Willie Company in 1856, splitting that company. As a result, the Willie Company lost a number of their draft oxen that pulled the wagons which carried the tents and heavy equipment.[12] The loss of those oxen seriously delayed them and caused much of their subsequent difficulty. Elder Franklin D. Richards instructed the men of the four wagons accompanying the Willie Company to wait at Fort Laramie for the Hodgetts Wagon Train, as they had a herd of cattle with them from which replacements could be found for the lost draft oxen.[13]

Living off of the land proved challenging in other ways. As previously indicated, James Jensen said that on July 19 they traveled all day without water. Many fell by the way and had to be helped into camp by the younger men.[14] It was the hottest time of the year. The company seems to have been in that stretch of the trail between the Cedar and Prairie creeks. The Mormon Trail took the north side of the Platte River Valley. An examination of the rivers of Nebraska, and the records which survived, tends to indicate they may not have run as close to the Platte as they did to some of its tributary streams while moving west. The tributaries would have been easier to ford some distance upstream from their confluence with the Platte. A reasonable estimate is that they were in the general proximity of the south side of the Loup for a number of miles. At the point where the Loup turned northwest they would have headed west for the Wood. The exact point where they crossed the Wood would have been dictated by a suitable ford. By July 20, the stream flow should have been somewhat diminished, thereby reducing the crossing difficultly. Furthermore, they were gaining experience. After fording the Wood, it appears they may have followed the Platte more closely. Consistent references to pulling the handcarts across the sand hills tend to support the notion that for a time they were closer to the Platte tributaries than the Platte itself. There are sandy and silt soils along much of the

North Platte, and for at least 25 miles prior to the confluence of the North with the South Platte.[15] (The Hafen and Hafen Route Map also supports the notion that the handcart pioneers had been in closer proximity to the tributaries while crossing central Nebraska.[16] For much of the way across Nebraska they appear to have been following the Platte River system rather than the Platte itself.)

It was somewhere along the North Platte system where they first saw the troops of the U.S. Army. Depending on the river's direction, the men of the infantry and artillery units were on the Platte or Sweetwater's south or western side. The handcart pioneers could see the sun's glint reflecting from the soldiers' weapons. The army's quartermaster corps and the freighting company of Russell, Majors, and Waddell were driving the large supply wagons and livestock which provided the army with fresh meat along the Platte's north or eastern side. One report said the quartermaster had 25 large wagons, each drawn by 12 powerful oxen in each bull train.[17] There were other immigrant trains going west. Some 50,000 head of cattle were being trailed to California over this route in 1857. The discovery of gold dramatically increased livestock prices in California. By 1849, sheep previously worth 75 cents to one dollar per head had risen to $12 to $15 per head. Severe drought in California in the 1828-30 and 1840-41 periods had markedly reduced its livestock numbers. Gold miners were heavy consumers of meat. The strength of the livestock market made trailing cattle and sheep to California a very profitable venture.[18]

Late summer and early autumn, known in the language of the Sioux as "Drying Grass Moon,"[19] figuratively came early in 1857. Coupled with the heavy traffic on the trail, by August, soil and plant materials were becoming very dry. The large cattle drives heavily grazed the native forages and kicked up clouds of dust along the trail. That combination of factors exacerbated the dry, dusty conditions for a people accustomed to the pleasant humidity of northern Europe. Their noses had pieces of skin hanging from them and almost every lower lip was covered with a cloth or piece of paper because they had become badly chapped. It made it difficult to speak, to smile, or to laugh.[20] Yet, the surviving accounts seem to indicate the prevalence of a generally cheery disposition throughout the company.

Generally, the company began moving forward at 6:30 A.M. Even though the buffalo, the other wild animals, and the Plains Indians gave them serious concern regarding the safety of the company's children, the situation required that all do their part. Those children who could walk were sent ahead, accompanied by older sisters. They were attempting to spare the children from breathing dusty air and to spare or lighten the load for those who pulled the handcarts for as long as possible. When heat and exhaustion overtook the children, they were placed on the handcarts. There were a few cows which had been purchased by those with more means. It was the responsibility of the small boys to drive the cows ahead of the company. There is a report that once tall, waving prairie grasses spooked the pioneers' cattle and horses. The resulting stampede caused a loss of some of their livestock. As a consequence of that loss, the leaders gave directions to lighten their load, to leave more of their goods by the wayside, to empty their feather beds and to fill them with grass.[21] Scandinavian feather beds were a duvet, a heavy blanket cover stuffed with feathers, or in the better quality with down feathers.

As the handcart pioneers pressed forward, their faith in Christ overcame anxiety and fear. From time to time reassurances came. One account records that once the company encountered a prairie fire which strangely subsided at their approach. It burned low over the trail as they crossed the hot earth. After they had passed by the fire again gained in momentum. The blaze again swept forward, its flames consuming the dry prairie grasses in its path.[22]

The hours were long. After stopping for the night, tents had to be pitched, fuel had to be gathered, cooking fires made, and bread mixed and baked in the camp skillets and Dutch ovens. The women worked late. Sometimes it was past midnight before the bread was done. Christiane Jensen said her mother and sister were ill the entire plains crossing, so she helped pull the handcart, gathered buffalo chips, handled the cooking, and, after supper, joined the camp for singing and dancing. Years later, she would tell her family, "Strange, but I never got tired!" At night, she would sleep on the ground with her little red cape for a covering.[23] Older boys and men took their turns at guard duty every fourth day for four to five hours at night. Men gathered firewood when it could be found. On the plains of Nebraska, women and children gathered dried buffalo chips for fuel, or "Ko-kasser" as dried bovine dung is called in Danish.[24] Then, early in the morning, they were moving again. Nightly and morning prayers were held regularly. Only scoffers would doubt they were being watched over.

One 60-year-old Norwegian sister was blind. She was accompanied by her daughter. When they would approach a stream, the daughter would call out a warning to her mother. The mother would ask: "How deep is the water?" Then, at a satisfactory answer, she would walk cheerfully into the stream. This blind sister was pushing on the handcart her daughter was helping to pull, and she walked all of the way to Utah. Another girl who walked on a wooden leg also completed the long trek west.[25]

Perhaps some saw in the travails of Anna Marie Sorensen, Karen Marie Gottfredson, and Maria Jacobsen Garff, in the blindness of the sister from Norway, and of Else Kirstina Kofoed of Bornholm, in the young woman who walked the entire way west on an artificial limb, and in the deaths of tiny Platine Gottfredson and little Marie Sophie Jensen, a partial fulfillment of the word of the Lord spoken by Jeremiah: *Behold, I will bring them from the north country, and gather them from the coasts of the earth, and with them the blind and the lame, the woman with child and her that travaileth with child together; a great company shall return thither. They shall come with weeping and with supplications, will I lead them: I will cause them to walk by the rivers of waters in a straight way, wherein they shall not stumble: for I am a father to Israel, and Ephraim is my firstborn.*[26] Then, given the fact that in Scandinavia the Bibles were largely in the hands of the clergy, it would seem more likely they were unaware of Jeremiah's prophetic utterance spoken two-and-one-half millennia earlier. What seems absolutely certain is all was well with their faith. Surely their names are held in cherished remembrance in the collective memories of their families. Like the humble shepherds of Bethlehem, they undoubtedly are lovingly remembered by a gracious and well-pleased Lord.

Behind the handcart company were the lead elements of the U.S. Army's Utah Expedition. On August 7 the Tenth Infantry and Phelps' Battery arrived at Fort Kearney.[27] Of necessity, accompanying quartermaster supply trains would have provided supplies for each of the army's several units, for an army marches on its stomach as much as it does its feet. The army had covered approximately 300 miles in their first 21 calendar days. Along the Platte they quickened their pace, for they aimed to winter in the valley of the Great Salt Lake.

NOTES

1. In 1862, a company of 264 Scandinavians who had come to America on board the *Franklin* went west in a wagon train under the leadership Christian A. Madsen. The inventory of supplies indicated 40 wagons,* 14 horses, 174 oxen, 99 cows, 37 heifers, 7 calves, 6 dogs, 10 chickens along with 22 tents, 32 cooking stoves, 5 revolvers, and 37 rifles. That is a ratio of 1 firearm to every 6.27 persons. The 7th Company does not provide as detailed an inventory, but Christensen's report could be taken to mean they were not well-armed. Other reports, Rebecca Wright Snow Payne's for example, say there were too few frontiersmen in the company. Pioneer times were difficult and the circumstances worrisome. Those conditions helped produce traits of caution, of preparation for meeting unanticipated, potentially life-threatening hazards. Even in his last years Niels Christensen, who died in 1923, continued to sleep with his cap-and-ball revolver under his pillow. (*The Pioneer Sesquicentennial Deseret News* 1997-98 Church, page 174, gives the number of wagons in this company as 45.)

2. The Teton Lakota, or Dakota as the Sioux are known among themselves, were an entity of seven distinct bands. The Oglala, meaning "they scatter their own," were the largest group. The Sicangu, meaning "burnt thighs," are the same as the Brulé, the name by which they are referred to in this treatise, which comes from the French word mean-

ing "burnt." The Miniconjou means "those who plant by the stream." See Nancy Bonvillain, *Native Nations...*, p. 207.

3. Ralph K. Andrist, *The Long Death: The Last Days of the Plains Indians*, University of Oklahoma Press, Norman 2001, pp. 23-24. Andrist states that the emigrant who lost his cow was a Mormon, whereas others who have written of this refer to the immigrant as a settler without any reference to the individual's faith. The hardline attitude of the immigrant is not in keeping with Brigham Young's policy of it being cheaper to feed the Indian than to fight him.

4. Ralph L. Andrist, *The Long Death...*, pp. 24-25.

5. Kenneth M. Stampp, *America in 1857...*, pp. 38-39.

6. Andrew Jenson, Church Chronology, Historical Record 1890, p. 52.

7. John D. Unruh, Jr., *The Plains Across*, Op cit., p. 216-17.

8. Ralph K. Andrist, *The Long Death...*, pp. 25-26.

9. Anders Christian Christensen, *A Short Sketch of the Lives of...*, p. 3.

10. *Henry Lunt Journal...*, p. 19.

11. *Henry Lunt Journal...*, p. 19.

12. One technique used to keep the oxen from drifting away at night was to yoke them in opposite directions. This would enable the oxen to graze, but would restrict them from moving very far afield.

13. Don Smith, Personal Communication 9 January 2001 and e-mail communique 10 January 2001. Don Smith, a Pullman, Washington, orthodontist, is a long-time researcher of the handcart companies and the routes they took west. Fresh cattle from the Hodgetts' herd likely meant the ox-team drivers would have had to have broken and trained new cattle to the yoke. Subsequently, these four wagons were probably among those of Hodgetts' train when it was stalled in the snow at Martin's Cove. Note: Don Smith said that one of the drivers of the four Willie company wagons was William Wilford Allen who was returning from an 1854-56 mission to Texas. W. W. Allen is the great-grandfather of the author.

14. James Jensen, *Journal History of the Church*, pp. 16-23, 13 September 1857, LDS Archives.

15. By the time the 1st Company reached Chimney Rock they had been pulling through heavy sandy soils for three or four days. See Hafen and Hafen, Op cit., p. 69, 207-08.

16. Hafen and Hafen, *Handcarts to Zion*, pp. 50-51.

17. Don H. Smith, Peder C. Klemgaard..., p. 3 of 7. This description of the Army's supply trains came from a sighting by the Matthias Cowley train. No doubt the handcart company saw this as well, for the two companies had been in sight of one another for a part of plains crossing. The size of these ox-teams and their wagons is confirmed by

William F. Cody's description.

18. Edward Norris Wentworth, *America's Sheep Trails*, The Iowa State College Press, Ames, Iowa, 1948, pp. 128-29, 134-35. It was famished gold miners who ruined Captain John Sutter. They stole and killed his cattle and sheep for meat, and then turned the sheep's skin inside out for use as a rough coat to protect them from the Sierra Nevada cold.

19. Dee Brown, *Bury My Heart at Wounded Knee: An Indian History of the American West*, Bantam Books published in arrangement with Holt, Rinehart and Winston, Inc. New York, New York, 1971, p. 97.

20. C. C. A. Christensen, *By Handcart to Utah...*, p. 342.

21. Anders Christian Christensen, *A Short Sketch of the Lives of...*, p. 3-4.

22. Anders Christian Christensen, *A Short Sketch of the Lives of...*, p. 3.

23. Ethel S. Lowe, "Christiana Jensen Thomson," p. 1.

24. C. C. A. Christensen, *By Handcart to Utah...*, p. 341. The Scandinavians had been accustomed to wood-fueled fires. The smoke from dung fires would have hung heavily over the campground. From the time they left Florence until they reached Fort Laramie, buffalo chips had been the chief source of fuel. In his classic painting "Handcart Pioneers," C. C. A. Christensen has shown the women and children gathering and starting buffalo-chip-fueled cooking fires as they prepare to camp. The experience with buffalo-chip fuel was never forgotten.

25. C. C. A. Christensen, *By Handcart to Utah...*, pp. 338-40. This would indicate that at least two women in the *Westmoreland's* passenger complement were blind, because Else Kirstina Kofoed who was also blind, was a Dane from Bornholm.

26. Jeremiah 31:8-9.

27. Andrew Jenson, Church Chronology, Historical Record 1890, p. 54.

Chapter 14

WEST FROM FORT LARAMIE

The handcart pioneers reached Fort Laramie on August 9. This outpost on the western edge of the great plains was originally called "Fort John." It had been built of adobe and located at the junction of the North Platte and Laramie rivers. By 1857 Fort Laramie had been a social and economic intersection for Native Americans, adventurers, explorers, mountain men, Oregon and Mormon pioneers, and California gold seekers for more than two decades. The fur trade had lost its financial punch. Those early adventurers had to look for other opportunities if they intended to remain a viable part of America's developing west.

Built initially as a trading post, the U.S. military acquired Fort Laramie in 1849 as a base to protect overland immigrants. During the years of the Sioux and Cheyenne wars, it became a major military post. Native Americans from the surrounding regions brought pelts, skins, and robes to Fort Laramie to trade for rifles and ammunition, knives, cooking kettles, bright cloth and beads, and a few food items such as sugar, coffee, and whiskey, which the tribes called "firewater." Whiskey was a bane to happy Indian family life. It was frequently at the core of misunderstandings which arose between Native Americans and those who had come into their tribal lands. Alcohol has been called the white man's worst assault on the integrity of Native Americans.[1] While cholera, smallpox, and measles riddled their ranks with deaths in epidemic proportions, whiskey destroyed their nobility of soul. The Indian Intercourse Act specifically prohibited the sale of alcoholic beverages to Indians. Yet the law keeps only the genuinely lawful honest. Liquor sales to

Indians brought black market premiums to unscrupulous traders. According to one report, a fine buffalo robe could be procured for a pint of whiskey. The tremendous profit margins which accrued from selling watered-down and peppered whiskey to a race with little physiological tolerance for alcohol, was an economic temptation of such magnitude that only the most highly principled traders complied with the law. In the long history of corrupt business practices, selling liquor to Indians is arguably the one which has been the most destructive to the noble manhood of both buyer and seller.

The wave of human immigration moving west saw Fort Laramie as a supply station. However, ready cash was a principal medium of barter for any gold seeker, pioneer, or traveler who planned to re-provision at Fort Laramic. The prices negotiated at trading posts historically have been weighted heavily in favor of the post ownership. They had a monopoly—not only had they cornered the market, they were the market. Given the

William Henry Jackson's painting *Fort Laramie,* the midpoint in the trail between Florence and Salt Lake City. Built initally as a trading post, the U.S. government took it over for use as a military outpost in 1849.

Three views of trail ruts along the Oregon-Mormon Trail near present-day Guernsey, Wyoming. The iron-tired wagon wheels cut the trail down in the rock. Eric and Kathleen Christensen are in the bottom photography. July 1992.

tight money situation of the handcart company, it is doubtful they were able to secure much by way of additional supplies at Fort Laramie. According to the Clayton Guide, they were 522 miles from Winter Quarters. They pushed on, for they had reached the halfway point.

Two days out of Fort Laramie, Josephine Patrina Garff, the two-year-old daughter of Niels Jorgen Garff and Marie Jacobsen Garff, died. It had been the second death in a matter of a very few days, for Niels J. Garff also had died and had been buried on the plains just prior to the death of his only surviving daughter. To the family's oldest son, 14-year-old Peter Niels, fell the sad duty of burying his little sister and his father. He dug the graves of each in the sand, fully cognizant that following their departure, wolves would probably dig up and devour the bodies of those he loved.[2] It was a justifiable fear. Henry Lunt noted that on August 12 we passed "the grave of one of our Danish brethren, the wolves having dug up the body which made it a frightful sight to behold."[3]

Niels Garff had known prior to leaving Denmark that his health would not allow him to reach Zion. Nevertheless, determined that his family should live among the Latter-day Saints, and with great faith in the cause, he was willing to pay that price. Before Niels died he called Elder Gudmundsen to his beside and asked the missionary who had taught them the gospel to care for his family.[4] It was Niels and Marie's youngest son, Decan, who had been born on the Atlantic. In a reminiscence, Louis (Lauritz) Garff wrote: "The rest of our family barely escaped death. The untold sufferings and hardships that we as a family and this company suffered during this long journey from Denmark would require more time and space [to tell] than will ever be taken in this life..."[5] Somehow, little Decan survived the trip. He was ill the entire journey, his head and face were "one mass of sores."[6] Even in the long after-years, Louis' hurt of a boyhood without his father and younger sister seems apparent.[7]

Niels J. Garff had been a free-holding farmer. He and Marie brought a nurse and midwife with them. Better fixed financially than many, he had sent money ahead to purchase a team and wagon. The individual entrusted as their agent failed them. Somehow Niels J. Garff found sufficient means to purchase a half share in another wagon. Existing Garff family records seem to indicate they were connected with both the Matthias Cowley and Christian Christiansen companies.

One morning their wagon was the last to leave the campsite. When the wagon train had moved on, the co-owner announced he was going back. He offered to take them with him. Marie Garff resolutely responded: "We will not turn back. We will go on!" The co-owner unloaded the Garff possessions and turned back. Marie and her surviving three children turned to the Eternal Source of help and prayed that someone would be sent to their rescue. When the Cowley Company discovered the

The North Platte River at the Mormon Ferry in present-day Casper, Wyoming. Eric Christensen is in the foreground. Photographed by the author, July 1992.

Garff family was missing, a wagon was sent back to help. A place was found in other wagons for Marie, Christen and infant son, Decan, while Peter was assigned to the 7th Handcart Company where he helped a 65-year-old woman pull her handcart to Zion.[8]

Once, when the wagon train paused to rest, Marie walked away with Decan in her arms. Sorrowing over the loss of husband and daughter, she sat down by a sagebrush, laid her baby on the ground, and wept. Lost in her thoughts, she looked up to discover the wagon train had moved on. She jumped up and started hurrying after the company. After going some distance she realized she had left little Decan lying by the sagebrush. She quickly retraced her steps to the spot where she had laid him. She was relieved and grateful to find the four-month-old boy where she had left him, still fast asleep. Gathering him into her arms, she hurriedly turned back to catch the company. She discovered the wagon company had crossed a large stream (probably the North Platte), and she was now left behind. The river was too deep for her to cross with her baby. She knew that when night fell they would be discovered and attacked by wolves. In that desperate situation she turned again to the Lord and pled for help. Soon she discovered a man standing beside her.

"What is it that you want?" he asked.

"I want to get across this stream," she replied.

The man said he knew a place where the Indians forded the river, and that he would take her across at the ford.

"Get on my back," he said. "Do not let your arms get around my throat. Keep them well down."

This she did, and taking little Decan they crossed the river. After straightening her clothing she turned to thank him, but he had disappeared.[9]

From those who willingly have sacrificed greatly, come descendants with similar traits. In 1937, Peter Niels Garff's grandson, Mark B. Garff, returned to Denmark as president of the LDS mission. He was presiding in Copenhagen on that fateful day, September 1, 1939, when Hitler's Germany treacherously struck Poland. With the Luftwaffe providing air cover and

Eric Christensen pictured with a raft at the old Mormon Ferry. The construction, which used logs and planking, tied together with wood pegs and rope cords, would have been typical of the period. Photograph by the author, July 1992.

strafing Polish infantry columns and horse drawn artillery, German armor moved swiftly east. It was mechanized war unlike anything ever before known in the long history of warfare. Poland fell in three weeks. President Garff and Elder Joseph Fielding Smith of the Quorum of the Twelve Apostles, who at the time was touring the Church's European missions, began the immediate evacuation of all American missionaries from Europe. The missionaries serving in the East German Mission arrived in Copenhagen the night before hostilities commenced. The First Presidency, knowing war was imminent, used the diplomatic privileges of President J. Reuben Clark, Jr., and sent a coded message via the pouch that all missionaries serving in Germany were "to perform immediately as they had done during the Czech crisis." The West German missionaries did not receive the coded message in sufficient time.[10] During that crisis, all Latter-day Saint missionaries serving in Germany and Czechoslovakia had been withdrawn from their proselyting areas and evacuated to either Copenhagen or Rotterdam.

It was necessary to use the pouch and send the message in code because the Nazis monitored the cable traffic. Had Hitler and his henchmen realized that prior knowledge of what was about to happen was known to Church leadership in America, all missionaries and German members would have been executed as spies. And so it was that as the Wehrmacht spearheads thrust deep into Poland, a number of the missionaries were caught in Germany. When Prime Minister Chamberlain signed the ill-fated 1938 Munich accord, war was temporarily avoided. However in 1939 the war clouds were not blown away, and the fury of the ensuing storm soon engulfed all of Europe.

The Copenhagen, Denmark, mission home became a temporary refuge for those fleeing Nazi Germany. President and Sister Garff and their assistants, Elders Phil D. Jensen, Rheim Jones, and Joseph D. Mortensen, worked diligently to find and book return passage, to enable all American missionaries to get safely home. Essentially all had to go on small ships. The large ocean passenger liners were no longer an option. The Dutch closed their border. Native Dutch missionaries who had been

William Henry Jackson's painting *Independence Rock* along the Sweetwater River. Devil's Gate can be seen in the distance.

Independence Rock, looking East. Kathleen Christensen in foreground. Photograph by the author.

serving in Germany could not get their American companions through immigration and into Holland. Denmark alone kept its frontier open to those endeavoring to get out of the Third Reich. Then, instruction came from the First Presidency that Sister Gertrude Garff was to take their 2 ½-year-old son, "little Mark," and return home. President Garff sent Elder Mortensen as an escort for his wife and boy. Sister Garff said: "We caught a small freighter, a German pilot took us through the mined waters of the sea to Bergen, Norway, at which point the German pilot left us." From Norway they sailed for the United States. It took the small freighter 18 days to make the crossing. "Never was the Statue of Liberty a more glorious sight," she said.

In response to the deteriorating political situation, President Wallace Toronto of the Czech Mission had earlier sent his family and missionaries out of Czechoslovakia, except for four who had been jailed on charges on exchanging dollars for crowns on the street. While strongly cautioned against changing money except at banks, such exchanges were financially tempting for the street value of the dollar was five to six times that of the official rate. One Czech missionary had been entrapped by a Gestapo agent who had proposed such an exchange. The Nazis demanded $10,000 U.S. be paid as a condition of releasing the missionaries. Given the economic conditions of the time (America was still struggling to emerge from the Great Depression) such a demand was almost a king's ransom.

While President Toronto worked to get them freed, his four jailed missionaries spent 44 days on a bread, water, and soup diet. Then one day a Herr Bomelburg, the very German official he had been trying to see, thinking that President Toronto was from the American Embassy, invited him into his office. They talked for a long time, the German saying, "You are a rich church, you can easily afford $10,000." President Toronto said to himself, "If you can bluff me, I will bluff you," so he explained how extensive the missionary program was, that 150 missionaries were serving in Germany who each spent $50 to $75 dollars a month. President Toronto then said: "Figure it out for yourself as to the amount of money the Church is bringing into Germany. If you don't release my men right now, I'll have every American missionary withdrawn from Germany, and look at the amount of money you will lose for your country."[11] Bomelburg did the calculations, picked up the phone, and called the German agent directly responsible for the case, and said that Mr. Toronto was coming to his office and for them to release the missionaries on Mr. Toronto's terms. The missionaries were released the next morning for a payment of $1,000.

As the clouds of war grew ever more ominous, a deeply concerned Sister Toronto, now at the Copenhagen, Denmark, Mission home, worried for the safety of her husband and their four detained elders. Elder Joseph Fielding Smith and his wife were also at the mission home. Sensing her increasing anxiety, Elder Smith took her aside and said: "Sister Toronto, this war will not start until Brother Toronto and his missionaries arrive in this land of Denmark."[12] As it happened, President Toronto and the elders caught the very last train and ferry connection out of Germany to Denmark. They had come out with the British legation. Upon landing in Denmark, they called the Copenhagen mission home to notify them they were safely out. In the interval between the time they landed on Danish soil and their arrival at the mission home, England and France declared war on Germany. It was September 3, 1939. It had been as Elder Smith said it would be, the war did not formally begin between Germany and France and England, until President Toronto and his elders were safely in Denmark. To President Garff and his assistants fell the responsibility for evacuating 350 missionaries. With unrelenting devotion, they ran the narrow pathway between freedom and internment as they successfully found passage for all. Every Latter-day Saint missionary from America was safely evacuated from Hitler's Europe. President Garff arrived home on Christmas Eve 1939. Mark B. Garff was the son of George Garff, who was the oldest son of Peter Niels Garff, the eldest child of Niels and Maria Jacobsen Garff.[13] It was Peter who had buried his father and sister on the plains near Fort Laramie.

William Henry Jackson's painting *Devil's Gate*. The Sweetwater River flowed through a gate-like gorge in the low mountainous rock outcroppings, while the trail swung to the south (or point) side of the mountain. Embert Hansen of the Seventh Handcart Company died at Devil's Gate.

Devil's Gate Wyoming. Looking toward the Northeast. Photograph by Eric Christensen.

Sixty-two years later, when asked about his feelings during those difficult days, Phil D. Jensen said that "while conditions were threatening, we had confidence we would get through." Escape through Holland or England was no longer an option. Missionaries leaving from Copenhagen all took freighters, none of which carried lifeboats. They were equipped only with rafts should an emergency require them to abandon ship at sea. "Most impressive to me," he said, "was that non-Latter-day Saints were willing to pay any price to go on ships with missionaries. Somehow they felt they would be safe with the 'Mormon missionaries.'" With all American Latter-day Saint missionaries safely away, and local Danish members organized to administer the Church during the war years, it was their time to leave. Their escape route by train took them north from Copenhagen

Devil's Gate. Looking north-northeast. The Mormon trail came around the low mountain outcropping to the right. Photograph by Eric Christensen.

to Helsingør, across the strait to Sweden, and then north to Oslo, where they were joined by President John A. Israelsen of the Norwegian Mission. At Oslo they boarded the *Oslo Fjord*, a new $5,000,000 ship, the pride of Norway's merchant fleet. The ship traffic in the fjord was so heavy "it looked like a freeway." While sailing down the fjord they watched a freighter sink. As they steamed up Norway's west coast, a British cruiser stopped them near Bergen. Great Britain's power had long been dependent on control of the seas. Now locked in deadly combat with Germany, the British were taking no chances of the enemy surreptitiously slipping through. They had been running the gauntlet between the warring powers of Europe for more than three months when they arrived safely in New York, their mission accomplished. Miraculously, not a single Latter-day Saint missionary from North America had been lost. However, not all went so well for other seafarers. Nearing England, on its return voyage to Europe, the *Oslo Fjord* struck a mine and sank.[14]

Phil D. Jensen's Scottish ancestors were a part of the Willie Handcart Company. Like his mission president before him, Phil D. Jensen ultimately served in a number of prominent Church assignments, including that of mission president in Scotland. Rheim Jones, who had many ancestors of Scandinavian origin, became a physician after his days as a missionary to Denmark. Perhaps such stretching calls in demanding times help us to understand the loving, tutoring hand of the Almighty, for one cannot have experience without having experience. Once again, when a dangerous situation called for marked bravery, the sterling attributes resident in the Garff family and their friends were remembered and used to bless others.

On the plains of the American West that summer of 1857, there remained an ongoing battle for survival for the Garff family and members of the 7th Company. Yet a war is not won until the enemy is subdued. The foe was hunger, which progressively becomes an increasingly cruel enemy. It sapped their strength and thinned their ranks. Physiologically, it was a struggle with both malnutrition and under-nutrition, which nutritional inadequacies were further compounded by the arduous daily exertion associated with pulling handcarts. The pioneer trail diet was seriously deficient in protein. It was also deficient in food oils.[15] In the dust and dryness of the trail, one very old man completely lost his sense of smell. Thinking to aid the company with their meat shortage, he discovered a small mammal he thought might be incorporated into some nourishing soup. Unaware of the animal's unique form of defense, he killed the creature with his cane and carried it into camp. He had harvested a skunk. There was no change of clothing available. The well-meaning man was kept at a distance until the company arrived at Deer Creek way station a few days later. He had a son who was serving there. He received a change of clothing and remained with his son that winter. He came on to Utah the following spring.[16]

On an occasion when the Garff family was without food, Peter went hunting and shot an owl. For hours he boiled the tough old bird to make some soup for his ill mother. He now

Valley of the Sweetwater River with Split Rock in the distance (center). Pioneers of the Seventh Handcart Company passed through this area in August 1857. Split Rock is west of Devil's Gate. Photograph by Eric Christensen.

had but one lead ball remaining for his rifle. When they were again without food, Peter went hunting. He shot a rabbit and was returning to camp with his prize when he saw another rabbit. He hurriedly went back and searched the hard dirt bank behind where he had shot the first rabbit. He located the lead ball and reloaded. The second shot dropped another rabbit. The rabbit dinner was the best meal the little family had eaten in months.[17]

Somewhere along the trail, the three Olsen sisters experienced an especially strenuous day. Twice they had forded the Platte successfully. During the third crossing, Christina waded into the swiftly moving stream with her emptied cart. When she encountered deep holes and quicksand, she lost control. Desperately, she summoned all of her strength to try to save herself and the cart, when she felt herself being pulled downstream by a powerful undercurrent. She was apparently at the point of drowning when Hans Christensen, 26, and captain of a subunit of ten handcarts of which the Olsens were a part, noticed Christina and came quickly to her rescue. Later, when Christina related the near-fatal incident, she said her thoughts were: "Now I will not have to push this heavy handcart anymore."[18]

After leaving Fort Laramie and entering the Black Hills of the Platte, they left the river and unknowingly passed the only watering place. That night they had to camp without water or tents, as the wagons had gone too far in front of them. Christian Folkman, 66, went in search of water and became lost. He had survived on a few wild berries and water. He was found a few days later by some trappers who brought him back to the handcart company.[19] One of the sub-captains reported that only once had they been without water at night. Some men had to backtrack to get water for their crying children. He thought there had been a mistake in following the guide book, but at daybreak they broke camp and found water a few miles ahead.[20]

Present-day Glenrock, Wyoming, is the site where Deer Creek station once stood, some 411 miles from Salt Lake City. The Mormons were growing crops including grain to help support the westward journey. The company probably received some food supplies at Deer Creek. Men had been called as missionaries to establish that station. One missionary was Stephen Chipman of American Fork, Utah, a pioneer of Abraham Smoot's 1847 wagon company. He was serving there when the 7th Company came through Deer Creek in 1857. In the 7th Company was the boy, Niels Christensen, who 15 ½ years later became Stephen Chipman's son-in-law. On Niels would fall the responsibility to care for Stephen Chipman's orphaned second family. For some days now the handcart pioneers had been moving up the North Platte. From dates given which pinpointed when they were at Fort Laramie and the Upper Platte crossing, they probably spent the night of August 16 at Deer Creek.

A letter to Orson Pratt from England-bound missionary, S. W. Richards, written after his arrival in Liverpool, tells that the

William Henry Jackson's painting *Handcart Pioneers*. The landscape is typical of present-day Western Wyoming.

missionaries met the Israel Evans Handcart Company August 18 about five miles east of Independence Rock. He said these pioneers had been making four miles per hour. They next encountered Elder Moody with a part of the Texas company about 10 miles east of Willow Springs, and, but few miles further encountered the first of the government wagon trains with stores for troops of the Utah Expedition. This train consisted of 26 wagons, each of which was drawn by 12 yoke of oxen. That night, at the crossing of the Upper Platte, there were more government trains and three companies of Saints including the Cowley Wagon and Christiansen Handcart companies camped in the same vicinity.[21] The Upper Platte ferry and ford was 382 ½ miles from Great Salt Lake City. It was at this point that the trail west left the gentle valley of the North Platte and struck southwest toward the Sweetwater.

Accounts tell that one morning after the 7th Company had been without meat for several weeks, they passed a large, fat ox which had been left behind by the army. A loaded wagon had crushed its foot. The army gave them the ox for meat.[22] Niels Christensen remembered the army gave them the ox with the understanding that the pioneers would butcher and dress it for half of the carcass, and that soldiers would pick up their half the next evening. During the night a heavy rain fell; the ground was so muddy that the supply wagons could move only slowly. The saints pulled their light-weight handcarts out onto the grass alongside the trail. That day, some Indians carried the women and children across a stream on the backs of their ponies. However, that night under the cover of darkness, the Indians drove off the horses which pulled the U.S. Army's supply wagons. By the next evening the pioneers were so far ahead of the army, the 7th Company did not see them again.[23] The hungry Scandinavian saints ate the whole carcass.

Descendants of Jacob Bastian remembered that Jacob and another company member had been sent to get the lame ox. Jacob was beginning to understand English at a level where he could get the gist of what was being said; he even spoke a little English by this point in the journey. Gertrude had learned

English in school. She interpreted for him and must have been his English tutor. While he and the other man were there, a rider came galloping in from the west carrying a wild tale of some alleged Mormon atrocity. Jacob's companion spoke no English. Jacob had the distinct impression that he should remain silent and act as though he did not understand. The conversation became agitated and nasty. There were those who wanted to kill Jacob and the other fellow on the spot, and then destroy all of those "wretched Mormons!" Among the U.S. soldiers was a Sergeant Anderson, a Swedish-American. He challenged his comrades in arms saying: "What is the matter with you men? You men are beginning to behave like bloodthirsty savages. These people could not have anything to do with that. They are immigrants. They don't speak English. They are even ignorant of their present danger. You know they have traveled peacefully ahead of us for miles. I will kill the first man who molests them."[24] So persuasively confronted, their passions cooled. The Scandinavians were given the lame ox and the pioneers went west.[25] The account as remembered by Jacob's family is tangentially supported by Niels Christensen who said of the soldiers, "the Handcart Company preferred to keep out of the army's way."[26]

While a skilled butcher was part of the company, they did not have a decent axe with which he could stun the poor beast. Heavy axes had been left at Clear Creek. When hit on the head with the light axe, the ox simply shook his head at the blow. A man thought to belong to the militia of the nearby town came and shot the ox for them, although he hit the poor animal in the nose on his first try.[27] This incident supports the report that the company lacked skilled hunters. Perhaps there were few rifles and little ammunition. The gift of the ox probably occurred in later part of August, perhaps after passing Devil's Gate, as they were moving along the Valley of the Sweetwater. The attention given to this incident, which under ordinary circumstances would have been of minor importance, is indicative of just how intensely protein-hungry these pioneers were.[28]

The Indians who helped them on this occasion were probably either Cheyenne or Shoshone. The Mormon Trail proceeded

William Henry Jackson's painting *The Three Crossings of the Sweetwater*. 31 miles west of Devil's Gate. William Clayton describes this area as "the road turns between the rocky ridges." It eventually became an important telegraph station.

through the midst of both their tribal lands. While the Cheyenne did not seem to trouble the Mormons in 1857, they remained a definite problem for the U.S. Army. Noted historian B. H. Roberts wrote that the army had 480 head of cattle stolen by the Cheyenne in August.[29] John R. Murdock places the number lost by the Expedition at 850 with another 2,000 head of cattle being returned to the states.[30] Long recognized as brave and adventuresome, the Cheyenne were not afraid to raid the white man's buffalo. While the Army saw Indian fighting as an opportunity to win ribbon and braid, the punitive campaign of Harney and his officers failed to tame the Cheyenne, whose raid-and-run tactics unquestionably slowed the advance of the quartermaster's supply trains.

The Shoshone had been horse breeders even prior to the days of Lewis and Clark. The Cheyenne and Arapaho acted as brokers for trading horses acquired from them with the tribes of the Missouri villages, whereas the Crow functioned as intermediaries with northern nations.[31] The Shoshone were decidedly friendly to the Latter-day Saints. During the 1850s, Washakie, the Shoshone nation's most illustrious chief, became a firm friend of Brigham Young. In a letter to Brigham Young dated August 17, 1856, Washakie stated that his 'heart felt bad' when he had to fight, and further lamented the longstanding hostilities between his people and the Utes.[32] Nick Wilson, a Mormon boy from the settlement of Grantsville, Utah, lived among the Shoshone as the adopted son of Washakie's mother for two years beginning in August 1854.[33] Washakie's feelings for the Latter-day Saints were deep, for he converted to Mormonism and was baptized September 25, 1880, on the Wind River Reservation.[34] If the gift-ox incident occurred in late August or early September, the company would have been within Shoshone land. The stream could have either been the western reaches of the Sweetwater or streams which feed the Green River west of South Pass.

Perhaps the local tribes were as amused with the 7th Company's mode of dress as the Scandinavians had been with the state of Indian undress. While the company had a number

William Henry Jackson' photograph of Shoshone Chief Washakie (center) with two of his men.

of tailors, they lacked the goods from which to create new clothing. Yet, they met the challenge of sewing replacement clothing on the trail in unusual ways. "Bedding was often altered to become everyday clothing, and a gentleman with trousers sewn from bed ticking was no curiosity in those days," wrote C. C. A. Christensen. "Nor were the ladies so particular about whether their skirts could hide their poor footwear, if indeed they were well enough off to own a pair of shoes, for there were many who had none; but the Scandinavians managed well with wooden shoes in those days."[35] Some who had no shoes wrapped their feet in rags. Paul and Niels Christensen (Pedersen) were among those who walked barefoot all of the way.[36]

Brigham Young had directed the establishment of a number of way stations. Another station farther along the trail was Fort Supply. The pioneers were probably able to obtain some supplies at Deer Creek. Even the daily ration of flour had become scanty. As they neared South Pass they were met by wagons carrying flour. By giving their promise, or handcart equipment as security, they were able to purchase sufficient for their needs. They were met by friends at Fort Bridger who brought fresh bread, cakes, and fruit.[37]

Given the 7th Company's food shortage, one wonders if an effort had been made to catch fish. Except for Martin Hansen's report of their life at Genoa, that activity does not seem to be mentioned in existing records. Did the pace of the westward march minimize time available for fishing? The vocational mix indicates there were no commercial fishermen in the company. That lack of skilled personnel may have hindered any effort to take fish in meaningful numbers. While the stream flow of the Platte and its tributaries dropped during the late summer months, these rivers were still a source of brook trout, bass and catfish.[38] Conditions change from year to year and a plentiful supply of game was not always available. In 1860, the 9th Company failed to find much by way of big game animals. (The survivability of the bison calf crop and even the vast herd as a whole, must have been severely reduced by the rugged winters of 1856-57 and 1857-58.) However, when the 9th Handcart

Allen and Kathleen Christensen at South Pass. Photograph by Eric Christensen.

Company arrived at the Sweetwater, they found its bottom covered with fish. They too were protein hungry. Salted pork or sides of bacon had been their main source of meat given their lack of hunting success. The fish were a "treat after having to eat salty bacon" from the beginning of the long walk west.[39]

There were other nutritional problems on the plains that year. Scurvy began to appear in the ranks of Lieutenant Colonel Sumner's troops during his 1857 summer campaign against the Cheyenne. The soldier's daily food allowance consisted of a ¾ pound of a beef and apparently not much else.[40] Animal products are poor sources of vitamin C. Furthermore, high environmental temperatures may increase the metabolic requirement for vitamin C, and additionally affect the endocrine systems responsible for retention and proper metabolic functioning of the vitamin.[41] By all reports, it was a hot, dusty summer. Cereals are also poor sources of Vitamin C, and the 7th Company was on a heavy flour diet, yet scurvy is not reported in existing company records. Why? How were they able to avoid that nutritional problem? The answer apparently lies in the fruit which the Scandinavians had been able to harvest along the trail, and then mixed with whatever foods they prepared from the flour. That fruit may have included black and red currants, strawberries, raspberries, gooseberries, cherries, plums, and grapes. Currants, strawberries, and raspberries are especially good sources of vitamin C. Given their lack of familiarity with edible greens, and the heavy traffic headed west that summer, the 50,000 head of cattle being driven along the Platte River road and the huge herds of buffalo grazing on the Nebraska prairies would have consumed tremendous amounts of forage, it is unlikely that greens provided much of the vitamin C requirement even though a seasoned leader such as Captain Christiansen may well have known what could be safely eaten. By late June, there was apparently sufficient ripe fruit along the streams and in the stands of trees to prevent scurvy, or blackleg, as this nutritional disease was called in pioneer times. In all probability, the bread, hot cakes, mush, and other foods prepared from flour had been cooked in iron skillets and Dutch

Sout Pass, looking east. Photograph by author.

ovens, (the C. C. A. Christensen painting of handcarts pioneers suggests as much, and a Dutch oven hanging from the bed of the handcart was a usual means of carrying such cookware) which would have acted to spare vitamin C, for copper cookware is highly destructive to vitamin C's potency.

Karen Marie Olsen related that one day at sundown they came along a cool stream. She removed her heavily worn brogans and dangled her tired feet in the bubbling creek. Her pleasure ended abruptly when she discovered dozens of little eels swimming about her feet. Given her aversion to snakes, rodents, insects, in fact, all wriggling and creeping creatures, she retreated quickly to the camp. (Perhaps these eels were too small to be useful as food.) Sleeping on the ground was a terrifying experience for Karen Marie. She had come from a refined home. One night she determined she would sleep in the handcart. She used a prop-stick under the pull bar to level the cart. With meager bedding she fell quickly asleep. In the middle of the night something dislodged the prop-stick and she was catapulted out of the cart and onto the hard ground.[42]

On July 24, 1857, Brigham Young received word about the approach of the federal army. He was acutely aware of the challenges posed by Buchanan's military adventurism. Getting the oncoming Latter-day Saint companies safely to Great Salt Lake Valley were pressing concerns for the Church leadership. On August 15, Colonel Richard T. Burton and James Willard Cummings of the Utah Militia started east from Salt Lake City with 70 men. Their orders were to protect the oncoming immigrants trains and to reconnoiter the approaching U.S. Army. This contingent of the Utah militia reached Ft. Bridger on August 21.[43]

At present day Casper, Wyoming, for years known as Mormon Ferry, the North Platte flow comes from the southwest. Farther upstream it runs pretty much due north from its headwaters in Colorado. Near the ferry, the trail left the Platte River entirely. Their next source of water was the Sweetwater River which they reached a little east of Independence Rock. From that point they went west past Devil's Gate, just west of which is the storied cove where the Edward Martin Company had suffered so greatly in 1856. Devil's Gate is six miles west of Independence Rock. It is a chasm through which the Sweetwater River flows. The trail does not pass through the Sweetwater's gate-like gorge, but swings south around the low mountainous rock outcropping. In the 1850s, buffalo, antelope, and deer could be found along the Sweetwater's meadows in summer. However, these migratory game animals moved to areas of lower elevation and more moderate temperatures during the cold, snowy months. Devil's Gate was 704 miles from Florence; there were 327 miles of hard pulling yet ahead.

Embreth (Engebret) Hansen became so ill along the way, that his wife, Margrette, took his place pulling the handcart so that he could ride. Even her devotion was insufficient—Embreth died at Devil's Gate. It was the second time in her life that Margrette Ohlsen Englestead Hansen had been widowed. Her first husband had been Lars Jacobsen. A daughter, Mary, had been born about 1850. Two years later Lars died from cholera. She married Embreth Hansen in 1854. To them were born a son and a daughter, both of who died in infancy. Six-year-old Mary walked most of the way west. Margrette Ohlsen Englestead Hansen was born October 8, 1819, in Aggershus, Norway. She and Embreth had joined the Church in the early days of the Scandinavian Mission.[45] Faced with such wrenching adversity, her resolve to press forward is remarkable.

The 7th Company reached Devil's Gate August 22.[46] Exhaustion and inadequate nutrition took their toll. They followed the Sweetwater west past Split Rock, the Three Crossings of the Sweetwater (elevation 6,390), to the little streams which constitute its headwaters on the east side of South Pass. Although the elevation at its summit is 7,550 feet, South Pass rises almost imperceptibly where it crosses the Continental Divide. It derives its name from the fact that it is the pass south of the Wind River Mountains. Reports written by earlier handcart companies mention such well-known landmarks as Chimney Rock, Scott's Bluff, Independence Rock, Devil's Gate and Split Rock. Yet, the 7th Company seemingly mentions only

Devil's Gate. Is that an indication of the language barrier, or is it symptomatic of the extraordinary weariness which all were experiencing? Some rivers such as the Loup and Wood are mentioned. Those were obstacles to be overcome—the landmarks were not. They had come to build Zion; they were pioneers, not tourists. It may well be an indication they had their priorities right.

After crossing South Pass the trail turned southwest. The vegetation changed as the trail passed through vast tracts of sagebrush. They crossed the Little and Big Sandy streams, where in October Major Lot Smith and his men would burn the wagons of three of Johnston's supply trains and halt his advance. There is a report that Smith's troops met the Cowley train in that area on August 27.[47] It seems likely the handcart company would have been in the same vicinity. It had been a hard, fast pull from the Upper Platte to the Big Sandy, for they had been averaging nearly 21 miles per day, Sunday included. This was probably the section of the trail where the Scandinavians left the U. S. Army behind. Smith and his raiders had been ordered to assist the oncoming emigrants and harass the army without taking life. A few weeks later, in a series of brilliantly executed surprises, Major Smith and his men began burning the quartermaster's supply trains. After Smith and company burned the third supply train, one of which was captained by Lewis Simpson, Brigham Young sent word to cease, that the Latter-day Saints did not want to be in the position of having to feed the U. S. Army. The handcart pioneers forded the Green River on their way to Fort Bridger.

NOTES

1. Ralph K. Andrist, *The Long Death...*, p. 13.

2. *Peter Niels Garff*, A Biographical Account..., p. 8.

3. Henry Lunt Journal...p.19. The name is not given. It may or may not be the Niels Garff grave. Whomever it was, enough remained that Lunt apparently recognized him, but compassion and propriety constrained further disclosure. The Young Company which arrived at Fort Laramie

August 21 was about ten days behind the 7th Handcart Company.

4. *Peter Niels Garff*, A Biographical Account..., p. 7.

5. *Reminiscences of Louis Garff, Westmoreland (April 1857)*, Mormon Immigration Index–Personal Accounts. On the passenger manifest, Louis is listed as Lauritz, born 1852, and his sister as Trine, born 1855. Lauritz obviously Americanized his name to Louis. That was not an uncommon thing, as these immigrants adopted their new country with seemingly few reservations. The manifest's recorder had not recorded the name Patrina correctly. The Garff family had been baptized 31 March 1855. Louis states he was born January 13, 1855, in Eskebjerg, Sjaelland, Empt., Denmark. It seems the year given on the passenger manifest is correct, that somehow an error has crept in. He spelled the name of his brother, Decan, "Dicken."

6. Louis Garff, *Reminiscences*, LDS Church Archives, Ms 1754, p. 58 (manuscript) and p. 1 typescript, Acc. #118379.

7. Relatively little seems to have been written about the suffering. It was not what they chose to remember. Rather, the accounts tell of the cheerfulness and a lack of complaints despite the severe hardships faced.

8. *Peter Niels Garff*, A Biographical Account..., p. 8.

9. *Peter Niels Garff*, A Biographical Account..., pp. 9-10.

10. The coded message was sent using J. Reuben Clark's diplomatic privileges. President Clark was the first counselor in the First Presidency. He had been U.S. Ambassador to Mexico when he was called to the First Presidency by Heber J. Grant. Clifford E. Young, Jr., a grandson of President Grant, was a missionary in the East German Mission at the outbreak of the war. For Young's eyewitness account of how the East German missionaries had been alerted and withdrawn from Germany and their evacuation to Copenhagen, see Allen C. Christensen, *The Christensen Family of Sorø, Denmark and American Fork, Utah, U.S.A*, Family History Publishers, Bountiful, Utah, 1994, pp. 280-81. A copy of the Christensen history is in the LDS Archives. There are some reports that missionaries serving in the West German Mission were to go immediately to Rotterdam, Holland. However, many of them did not get that message before the Dutch border was closed.

11. Martha Toronto Anderson, *A Cherry Tree Behind the Iron Curtain: The Autobiography of Martha Toronto Anderson*. Privately published, Salt Lake City, Utah, 1977, p.26. Martha Toronto Anderson was the wife of Wallace Toronto. Pages 21-32 give her eyewitness account.

12. Martha Toronto Anderson, *A Cherry Tree Behind...*, p. 32.

13. Personal communication by telephone, December 15, 2000 with Gertrude Ryberg Garff, the widow of Mark B. Garff. Sister Garff, now 90, was an eyewitness and participant in the evacuation. She remembers vividly and in great detail the story of the evacuation and escape

from Europe. She was also the source of the Garff genealogical information. Phil D. Jensen was also an important resource. Sister Garff said the First Presidency requested that her husband write the account of the evacuation, and it was done.

14. Phil D. Jensen, personal communication, March 24, 2002.

15. Ethel S. Lowe, "Christiana Jensen Thomson," p. 1 wrote that her grandmother was a good cook who caught and carefully conserved any drippings from the meager meat allowance. Once, when others saw her cooking scones, they asked where she had gotten the cooking grease, for there was no food-oil ration.

16. C. C. A. Christensen, *By Handcart to Utah...*, p. 342. *The Seventh Company*, a two-page history of the 7th Company which is a part of the September 13, 1857 record and the LDS Archives.

17. *Peter Niels Garff*, A Biographical Account..., p. 8.

18. Rebecca Wright Snow Payne, A Resume of the Life of My Grandmother..., p. 10.

19. James Jensen's report in the *Journal history of the Church*, Op cit., and the Journal of Lars Christian Christensen in Kate B. Carter's *Heart Throbs of the West,* Daughters' of the Utah Pioneers, 1945, Vol VI:401-2 both make mention of this incident.

20. C. C. A. Christensen, *By Handcart to Utah...*, p. 341.

21. S. W. Richards to Orson Pratt, Liverpool, October 4, 1857, *Millennial Star*, XIX:669.

22. C. C. A. Christensen, *By Handcart to Utah...*, p. 343.

23. Clare B. Christensen, *History of Niels Christensen*, Op cit., 2.

24. Arthur L. Crawford, *Jacob Bastian...*, p. 3.

25. Personal communication, July 26, 1997. See *Journal of Allen C. Christensen* XX:186-188. It was on the occasion of Elder David C. Castleberry reporting his mission to the Philippines San Fernando Mission. Jacob's descendant included David C. Castleberry, his mother, and his siblings. David's sister, Kristen, had spoken of Jacob's conversion which had been influenced by Gertrude Pedersen, and of her death three days after arriving in the Salt Lake Valley. Alone, and on the border of despair, Jacob built her coffin and buried her essentially by himself. In a discussion later that day, the Castleberry family told the account of Jacob and the other fellow being sent to get the ox. The Castleberry family assumed the atrocity had been the Mountain Meadows massacre. That would not have been possible, for that event occurred on September 11, 1857 in southern Utah, at which time the pioneers were only two days out of Salt Lake City. Whatever the rider was trumpeting was quite obviously a malicious rumor. But then, 1857 was a year of nasty rumors. Utah was in rebellion, or so the fabricated story went. It was this climate of rumors, innuendos, and distortion that made its way to the new President's ears in Washington, DC. The

situation was not adequately investigated and Buchanan sent the troops west. Any assistance given the saints by Native Americans along the way west may have fueled the rumor that the Mormons were in league with the Indians.

26. Clare B. Christensen, *History of Niels Christensen*, Op cit., p. 2.

27. C. C. A. Christensen, By Handcart to Utah..., 343.

28. In 1959, the author took a graduate nutrition/physiology class at the University of California, Davis, which dealt, in part, with specific hungers and the mechanisms by which they are mediated. It was taught by the eminent nutritional research scientist, Dr. Samuel Lepkovsky. Lepkovsky had conducted extensive research on specific hungers and aversions and the mechanisms by which they are mediated in the human body. He had studied the C rations and K rations which had been developed and used during World War II. Anecdotally, he reported that World War II prisoners of war developed gambling systems using food as items to be wagered. A system had been established whereby points were assigned to each food item. The point values assigned to the different foods were an accurate reflection of their nutritional/food value. Eggs were assigned the highest point total, chocolate the lowest. The specific hunger for protein on the part of 7th Company pioneers is reflected in a number of accounts, including that of Mads Christensen, whose account indicates they had been given the lame ox in present-day Wyoming.

29. B. H. Roberts, 1930. *A Comprehensive History of The Church of Jesus Christ of Latter-day Saints, Century I, Deseret News Press*, Salt Lake City, Utah. IV: 249.

30. B. H. Roberts, *A Comprehensive History of The Church...*, IV:249, footnote 16.

31 Nancy Bonvillain, *Native Nations: Cultures and Histories of Native North America*, Prentice-Hall, Inc., Upper Saddle River, New Jersey, 2001, p.184.

32. Jay G. Burrup, "Washakie, Chief," in *Encyclopedia of Latter-day Saint History*, edited by Arnold R. Garr, Donald O. Cannon and Richard C. Cowan, Deseret Book Company, Salt Lake City Utah, 2000, pp. 1311-12.

33. For a complete account see E. N. Wilson and Howard R. Driggs, *The White Indian Boy*, World Book Company, Yonkers-on-Hudson, New York, 1919. Wilson said he was 12 years old when he went to live with the Shoshone in August 1854. He did not see a "white man for two years." (p. 11.)

34. Jay G. Burrup, *Washakie, Chief...*, p. 1312.

35. C. C. A. Christensen, *By Handcart to Utah...*, p. 342.

36. Clare B. Christensen, *History of Niels Christensen...*, p. 2.

37. *The Seventh Company*, record of September 13, 1857, LDS Archives, p, 2.

38. Vernon Combs, personal communication, 29 December 2000. Vernon Combs, 75, is a life-long resident of North Platte, Nebraska. Combs said while the stream flows would have decreased during the course of the season, there would have been water to support the fish in those early days, and that Wilford Woodruff's account of the vanguard company in 1847 indicates he caught a number of fish. From 1980-1990, Vernon Combs served as Nebraska State Director of the Pony Express Trail. He was the third branch president of the LDS Church in North Platte.

39. Hafen and Hafen, *Handcarts to Zion...*, p. 183.

40. Durwood Ball, *Army Regulars...*p. 43.

41. M. L. Scott 1975. Environmental influences on ascorbic acid requirements in animals. *Annals of N. Y. Acad. Sci.* 258:151.

42. Rebecca Wright Snow Payne, A Short Resume of the Life of My Grandmother..., p. 10.

43. Andrew Jenson, *Church Chronology, Historical Record 1890*, pp. 54-55.

44. Hafen and Hafen, *Handcarts to Zion...*, p. 304.

45. *Our Pioneer Heritage* Vol. 1, p. 46.

46. James Jensen, *Journal History of the Church*, pp. 16-23.

47. Don H. Smith, Peder C. Klemgaard..., p. 3 of 7.

<u>Chapter 15</u>
JIM BRIDGER AND HIS FORT

The Green River derives its name from the border of trees and willows which line its banks. That border of green can be seen for miles. It is a vivid contrast to the purplish-gray sagebrush which stretches across the landscape west of South Pass. The Green River was in Utah Territory. In 1857 the uppermost or northeastern territorial boundary was the Wind River Mountains. This was the land of the Shoshone who called the Green the Seedskadee, or Prairie Hen River. (The Green River crossing of the Mormon Trail was still part of Utah territory in 1866.[1]) The Church, through its agent, Lewis Robison, had purchased Fort Bridger for $8,000. Fort Supply, which was 12 miles to the south on Willow Creek, had been built by the Church at a cost of $50,000, and the lush grasslands around them would be torched before winter as a part of Brigham Young's scorched earth strategy. President Young had determined the Latter-day Saints would not be driven from their homes again.

During the winter of 1842-43, Jim Bridger established a trading post, a private frontier fort which bore his name.[2] Bridger was aware that the profitability of his trapping business was not what it had once been. Trapping beaver that winter had been difficult and was described as being as hard as catching bank notes fluttering in the wind.[3] Complicating the problems of a lowered catch were declining prices for skins—European fashion styles were changing from beaver hats to silk hats. One after another, the old rugged band of trappers had given up their quest for fur. Called shrewd by some, Bridger seemed to possess keen economic foresight. He sensed that the oncoming,

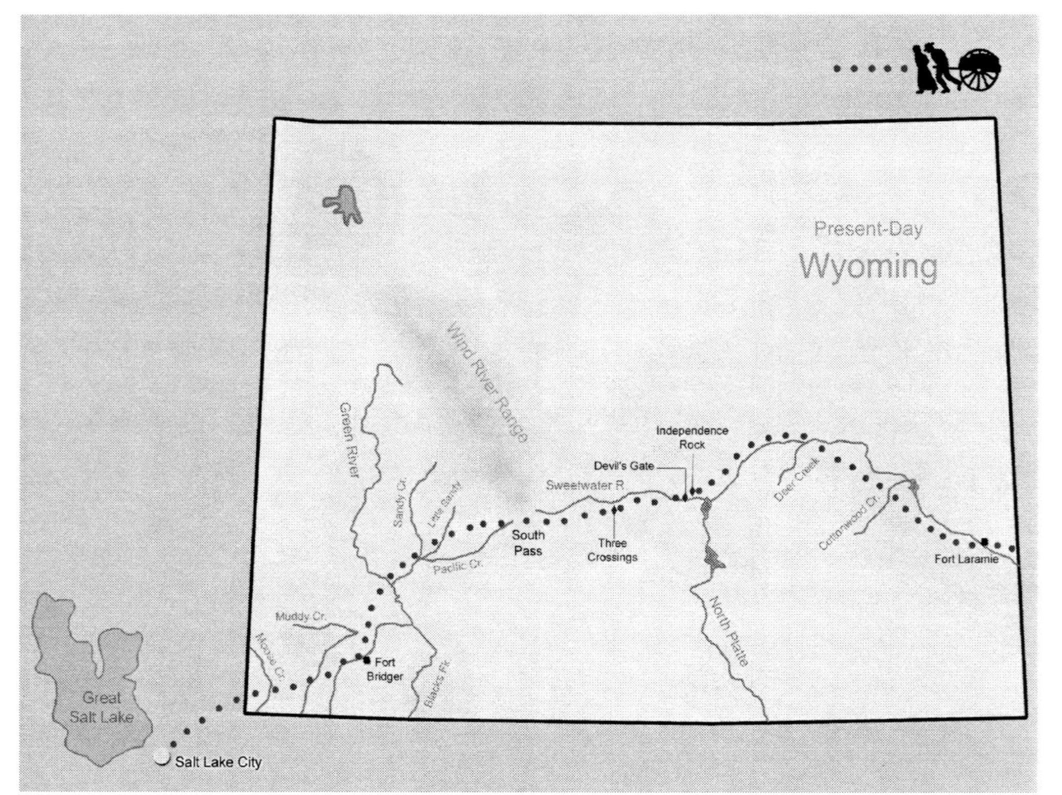

Map by Jeremy Munns.

somewhat scattered, small trains of covered wagons would become a great stream of migration to the Rocky Mountains and beyond. Bridger and his partner, Louis Vasquez, built their trading post on Black's Fork, a tributary of the Green River. It was in the vicinity where the Oregon-California and Mormon trails would ultimately diverge. The Black's Fork passed the trading post in several channels. The streams of its grassy meadows were alive with spotted mountain trout. There were sage hens in the surrounding hills. Deer, elk, and antelope were also available. The water was cold and clear; there were willows and cottonwood trees. Other mountain men and their native wives also lived nearby and prospered from the trade. Shoshone, Bannock, and Ute tribes frequented the fort.

As a part of his establishment, Bridger had a blacksmith shop and a supply of iron. As a young fellow in St. Louis, Missouri, he had been an apprentice blacksmith and had gained some experience in gun smithing as well.[4] Horses, mules, and oxen would need to be re-shod and wagons repaired. With the good grass provided by the meadows, he could trade fresh, well-fleshed animals to immigrants whose stock were worn and thin at a trading ratio to his advantage. The swap for a fresh horse might involve the worn animal plus $25 to $50 in cash.[5] Every transaction was separately negotiated, the deal influenced by such factors as the animal's quality, overall customer demand, and an individual's ability and willingness to meet the price. It was an effective way to market the meadowland's grass crop. Wilford Woodruff's journal entry for 7 July 1847 indicates that in the afternoon he had gone to "Bridger's house and traded off my flintlock rifle for four buffalo robes, which were large, nice, and well-dressed. I found things generally at least one-third higher than I had ever known them at any other trading post I ever saw in America."[6] The legendary mountain man became a successful merchant and livestock broker, apparently finding to his financial satisfaction that immigrants, unlike the beaver, could be caught and skinned while he kept warm by the fire.

Jim Bridger's initial relationships with the Latter-day Saints had been excellent, but that changed dramatically in

William Henry Jackson's painting *Fort Bridger*. Bridger built his trading post in 1843. In 1855, the Church's agent, Lewis Robison, purchased the fort for $8,000. At Brigham Young's direction, Lewis Robison set the torch to it in the fall of 1857, thereby depriving the U.S. Army of the shelter it would have afforded.

1853. Profit margins at his post had become an economic arrowhead in the flesh of the Mormon community and invited competition, and competition came in several forms. W. A. Hickman, a Utah attorney, left Salt Lake City with a good supply of merchandise in the early spring of 1853. He determined to establish a trading post east of Fort Bridger with the intent of intercepting the westbound trail traffic. Hickman claimed to have netted $9,000 in three months. Bridger, no doubt, was painfully aware of his own drop in revenue. The Utah territorial legislature granted a charter to McDonald, Thompson, and Hawley of Salt Lake City to operate immigrant ferries on the Green River. The expanded business community proved sufficiently annoying to Bridger and his mountaineer friends that they attempted to enforce their previous market monopoly with guns. With the coming of fall and the close of immigration for the season, the Mormon traders returned to Utah. They carried to Salt Lake City reports that Bridger was selling powder and lead to the Ute nation and inciting them to fight the Latter-day Saint settlers. It was during 1853 that Chief Walker led his Ute warriors into a war with the Mormons. Even during this period of wide-open economic innovation, gun running to hostile tribes was not allowed.

When Jim Bridger came to this wild country he was subject only to the laws of survival and any rules imposed by his employer. For a decade, he had done things his way, governed only by the economics of the moment. Now he and his fort were geographically a part of Green River County and within the political jurisdiction of Utah Territory, and as such became subject to Utah territorial law as administered by its no-nonsense governor, Brigham Young. The Governor dispatched the sheriff and a posse to investigate the matter, perhaps with instructions to arrest Bridger. The wary scout got word and seemingly vanished, apparently hidden by friends for a time. The posse, unable to apprehend the old scout, did not return to Salt Lake City empty-handed for they gathered up several hundred head of livestock and the mountaineer's whiskey stores. During the hunt for Bridger, they engaged in a gunfight with mountaineer ferry operators during which two or three of the latter were killed. The posse and livestock gone, Jim Bridger reappeared and engaged a government surveyor, John M. Hockaday, to do a survey of his land claim. The survey was completed on 6 November 1853 and filed 9 March 1854 in the General Land Office in Washington, DC. The plat of the Bridger land claim amounted to 3,898 acres. Realizing the Mormons were here to stay, Bridger moved east to a farm in Little Santa Fe, Missouri.

With the approach of the U.S. Army in the fall of 1857, the log houses, shops, and picket fence corrals were burned to the ground. While Governor Young had ordered the Utah Militia to avoid taking life, he had no intention of aiding the federal troops. Rather, it would be his strategy to take every advantage afforded by the terrain and climate, he would make the upper Green River's bitter winter his ally. From the Latter-day Saint perspective, this was an unjust struggle, forced upon them by various and sundry political foes in the eastern United States. Brigham Young, the Mormon prophet-general, determined this would not to be another Nauvoo or Far West. His followers, seasoned by the testing experiences of those difficult earlier years, backed him to the hilt.

The Latter-day Saints had built an additional immigrant support station of their own. They called it Fort Supply. It was located at an elevation of 7,200 feet above sea level and consisted of "one hundred or more good, hewed log houses, one sawmill, one gristmill, and one threshing machine . . . straw and grain stacks."[7] Unquestionably, if the U.S. Army had taken Fort Supply intact, it would have been a tremendous prize of war. Both the troops and their livestock would have fared much better during the oncoming winter. The Mormon settlers of Fort Supply, who, over a four-year period of labor and sacrifice had established the settlement and brought it to that level of productivity, now applied the torch at Governor Young's request.

At Fort Laramie on 16 July 1857, Lieutenant P. W. I. Plympton, quartermaster, engaged Jim Bridger as a scout, guide, and interpreter for Albert Sidney Johnston's 1857 Utah Expedition for the robust salary of five dollars a day. Not content with working for high wages, Bridger also leased to the army by formal written agreement, (the instrument of lease was signed by Captain Dickerson of Johnston's quartermaster corps), the Fort Bridger property for a fee of $600 dollars per year. That lease conveniently overlooked an earlier real estate transaction, for in 1855, the Church, through its agent, Lewis Robison,[8] negotiated with Bridger's partner, Louis Vasquez, the purchase of the Fort Bridger trading post and ranch for $8,000. Vasquez's stepson, Hiram, who was 12 years old when the fort was sold to the Church, spoke often in later years of the pile of gold placed on the table at Fort Bridger.[9] Vasquez may not have had Bridger's permission to sell, but that is exactly what he did.

That transaction muddied the fort's title when Bridger attempted to lease or sell it to the army in 1857. It apparently was either a case of Bridger believing he still owned the fort, or that given the instability of the political situation in consequence of pending U.S. military intervention in Utah Territory, he thought the Mormons were in no position to make their case regarding their purchase of the property. Was he bluffing? For years, he had pushed his luck in trapping and living among hostile tribes. The cagey beaver in those western mountain streams had been unable to escape his traps. Now, Bridger demonstrated new daring in the real estate business when he pushed a questionable land claim toward the edge of the cliff. The U.S. Government never paid him the rental fee, although thirty years later, it paid Bridger $6,000 for the improvements on the land but awarded nothing for the land itself.[10]

It was a savvy decision by the quartermaster to retain the services of Major Bridger,[11] as Jim Bridger came to be called. His knowledge of grasslands, more sheltered terrain, water, etc., probably spared the army even greater difficulty than the severe problems which they encountered. West Point training was still more along classical European lines at this stage in America's military development. Furthermore, the officer corps was dominated by well educated, middle-class Americans of Anglo-Saxon descent[12] who carried, in many instances, an air of personal superiority. Out West, however, things were very different from

Europe's "civilized wars," and the army's most effective officers learned from the Indians, from comrades seasoned by service in the field, and from other local talent—they adapted tactics and formulated strategy to fit frontier conditions. Fascinatingly, in the matter of combing the tactical elements of surprise, terrain, and climate, even though they had fewer horses and definitely inferior firepower, the Mormon militia outwitted their professional counterparts in 1857.

Back in the staging area, the U.S. Army continued to experience serious logistical difficulties. Governor Walker had been threatening to resign if Harney and his troops were not retained in Kansas. Harney had become increasingly apprehensive regarding the hazards of leading an army west so late in the season. Policy makers sweating out the oppressive summer heat and humidity in Washington, DC, apparently overlooked or discounted cold weather as posing much of a problem. With so much energy expended on the business and politics of the war, that is, in the getting of supply contracts and army commissions, in getting the signals straight between Washington and Fort Leavenwoth, in getting a firm decision at the top regarding command of the operation, meant, that in the final analysis, the army had trouble getting going. The leadership question was not settled until August 28 when the War Department recalled Harney and gave the command to Colonel Albert Sidney Johnston. Johnston's name would become the one ever after associated with the Utah Expedition.[13] Johnston had been serving as commanding officer of the U.S. Second Cavalry, which unit had been involved in a punishing and lethal campaign against Comanche raiders in Texas. He had made the Second Cavalry a crack military outfit. With Johnston's departure, Lieutenant Colonel Robert E. Lee was given command of the Second Cavalry. Less than four years later Abraham Lincoln would offer Colonel Lee command of the Union Army.

A gifted warrior, Albert Sidney Johnston fought under three different flags during the course of his career. An 1826 West Point graduate, he resigned his commission in 1834. He went to Texas in 1836 where, in the course of a year, he rose from private to senior brigadier general in the army of Texas. He became Texas' Secretary of War and operated a plantation. During America's war with Mexico, Johnston led a regiment of Texas volunteers against the Mexicans.[14] In 1849, he again reactivated his U.S. Army commission which he resigned in 1861 to fight under the Stars and Bars of the Confederate States. During the American Civil War, General Johnston became the South's commanding general in the western theater. Ironically, the man who in 1857 had ordered his men to treat every armed Mormon as a rebel enemy, who had survived the miserable winter in the Upper Green River, and the rigors of the Great Basin during the so-called Mormon rebellion, would himself die 6 April 1862 in the rebel uniform of the Confederacy. His mortal foe in that bitter battle was U.S. Grant and the Union Army at a place called Shiloh. It is said that after Shiloh, the South never smiled again.

Governor Walker resigned in December 1857, and Buchanan ultimately named Harney governor of Kansas. Colonel Johnston spent time that winter in political discussions with Governor Alfred E. Cumming, Thomas L. Kane, and others who had been seeking a negotiated rather than a battlefield settlement of the question. Some of the conversations must have involved who would determine the political agenda, the civil or the military authority, and there was a decided difference of opinion. Those seeking military honors and glory born of blood in deadly combat would be disappointed with the outcome, for cooler heads prevailed. Fascinatingly, while in Mormon literature the Utah Expedition continues to bear his name, for Albert Sidney Johnston there would be no Medal of Honor.

NOTES

1. *Map of the Territory of Utah.* To accompany the annual Report of the Commissioner of the General Land Office. Department of the Interior, General Land Office, October 2nd 1866.

2. Grenville M. Dodge, a Civil War general and famed chief construction engineer of the Union Pacific Railroad gave Fort Bridger's location "in latitude 41 degrees 18 minutes 12 seconds and in longitude 110 degrees

18 minutes 38 seconds, 1,070 miles west of the Missouri river by wagon road, and 886 miles by railroad." (Grenville M. Dodge, "James Bridger, Mountain Man" in *The Great West* edited by Charles Neider, Coward-McMann, New York, 1958, p. 159.) Dodge does not identify in this article from which place on the Missouri River he took his initial measurement, although one might surmise it was Omaha.

3. J. Cecil Alter, *Jim Bridger*. University of Oklahoma Press, Norman, 1962, p. 205. Alter uses the expression "greenbacks," rather than bank notes. However, greenbacks did not come into use until the Civil War. Therefore, such a literary figure of speech would not have been used in 1843 as this was two decades before greenbacks made an appearance in the U.S. monetary system.

4. J. Cecil Alter, *Jim Bridger*...p. 7.

5. Howard R. Driggs, *Westward America*, Somerset Books, Inc. New York, 1942, p. 128. According to John D. Unruh, Jr., in 1849 Vasquez and Bridger spent much of their time encamped near South Pass on the Sweetwater River trading livestock with California-bound gold seekers. Sales were frequent and brought high prices. Horses ranged from $65 to $150; mules from $75 to $125; and oxen brought up to $125 per yoke. (John D. Unruh, Jr. The Plains Across, p. 261.)

There is an old livestock-market saying that a horse or cow is worth what you can get for it. Bridger and Vasquez had been livestock brokers for economic, not humanitarian reasons. They must have used the meadow lands along the Sweetwater and around Fort Bridger to rejuvenate weary horses, mules, and oxen. Livestock prices fluctuate from season to season, influenced by supply and demand. The peak years of the California gold rush had been times of great demand and short supply. There had been little competition along the trail. Bridger and Vasquez were in position to drive hard bargains, and they no doubt did.

6. Matthias F. Cowley, *Wilford Woodruff: History of His Life and Labors as recorded in his daily journals*, Bookcraft, Salt Lake City, Utah, 1964, p. 309. Originally published in 1909.

7. Jesse W. Crosby, a Latter-day Saint who participated in the Utah Militia's campaign against Johnston's troops, as quoted by Milton R. Hunter, *Brigham Young the Colonizer*, 1945, Zion's Printing and Publishing Company, Independence, Missouri, 1945, pp. 288-89.

8. In 1857, Brigham Young sent Lewis Robison to Fort Bridger to put it to the torch. According to his 2nd great grandson, Laren Robison, Lewis said, "the old fort burned brightly." Personal Communication, Laren Robison, July 4, 2002.

9. J. Cecil Alter, *Jim Bridger*..., p. 278.

10. Grenville M. Dodge, "James Bridger, Mountain Man," *The Great West*..., p. 159-61. Dodge wrote that the land on which Jim Bridger located his fort had been obtained by Bridger from the Mexican Government before any of the country called Upper California had

been ceded by Mexico in 1848 to the United States. That seems highly unlikely given the lack of an official Mexican presence that far north. Furthermore, Fort Bridger was in a somewhat contested or ill-defined area near the point or junction of where Oregon Territory, the unorganized Indian Territory in the northwestern portion of the Louisiana Purchase and Upper California, all converged. Dodge states that in 1856 Bridger had trouble with the Mormons, that the Mormons had driven him off of his land by threatening him with death, and then had confiscated his property, livestock, and merchandise which Bridger claimed to be worth $100,000, an amount which also appears outlandish. By 1850, Bridger had moved his family to Santa Fe, Missouri, where his daughter Mary was born in 1853 and his son William was born in 1857. Bridger also served as Dodge's guide for the Union Pacific surveys and Indian campaigns in 1865-66.

In his lengthy tribute, "James Bridger, Mountain Man," Dodge seems to have accepted, without equivocation, Bridger's recounting and explanation of events, apparently so compromised by his open admiration for the legendary mountain man, that he forgot when discussing politics and contested business deals, there are at least two opinions accompanied by splinter groups.

John D. Unruh, Jr., wrote that in 1853 Bridger was believed to be aiding and abetting the Ute Indians in their war against the Latter-day Saint settlements. Bridger apparently failed to comply with Governor Brigham Young's order that no trade be conducted with the Utes during the Walker War. The sites of those Indian-Mormon battles were a considerable distance from the Fort Bridger area. In late August 1853, a large Mormon posse descended upon the fort intent on arresting Bridger. However, he had been forewarned and eluded arrest, but never again would he trade from the fort. In 1855, Bridger and his partner, Louis Vasquez, agreed to sell the outpost to the Mormons for $8,000. The allegation of gun running was not the first time Bridger had been accused of business dealings beyond propriety. Immigrants charged in Salt Lake City courts that Bridger and Vasquez had been selling horses without certifying that the animal's brand was the legitimate brand of the seller; that is, they had not guaranteed that the horse was not stolen property. John D. Unruh, Jr. *The Plains Across*, pp. 294, 314.

Perhaps the army's refusal to pay the rent agreed to by Captain Dickerson is indicative that they knew, or strongly suspected, that Fort Bridger was Mormon property rather than Jim Bridger's in 1857.

11. J. Cecil Alter, *Jim Bridger...*, p. 267.

12. Durwood Ball, *Army Regulars...*, p. 56.

13. Andrew Jenson, *Church Chronology, Historical Record 1890*, p. 55.

14. Durwood Ball, *Army Regulars...*, pp. 69-70.

Chapter 16

THE LAST LEG

In late August and September, the handcart pioneers were waging their own testing battle to survive, for the hardships of the trail had taken its toll of life and stamina. The 214 miles from Devil's Gate to Fort Bridger had been covered in 15 days. It was a hard pace. Paul Christensen (Poul Pedersen), Niels' year-older brother, took sick and nearly died on the way. "For three days his mother, Ellen, and another woman, half-led, half-carried him. There was no stopping. Paul was never strong enough to help pull the handcart again. For the last hundred miles Niels and his stepfather, Hans, pulled the handcart alone."[1] The other four assigned to the Christensen handcart were too worn out to help.

Lars and Britta Andersson Carlsen (Karlson) and son, Claus (Klaus) Herman, were from Sweden. Eight-year-old Claus was their only surviving child. They had buried two daughters, Clara Maria and Anna Sofia, and a son, Johannes Alfred, in Sweden, and their baby son, Joseph Adell, in Copenhagen, Denmark. Upon reaching Fort Bridger, Lars could go no farther. The exertion, the anxiety about his family's welfare, and the inadequate diet had exhausted his mortal energy. Somewhere near the banks of Black's Fork, Lars died 6 September 1857, just one week and 114 miles short of the valley. Britta and Claus never forgot that day. Sorrowing, they bravely pushed on.

Gertrude Bastian, Jacob's beautiful wife was in delicate health. The journey had been demanding, its hardships real and physically taxing. Jacob viewed with increasing alarm her deteriorating condition. Yet, she never complained and did her best to cheer and lighten the burdens of others.[2]

Echo Canyon as painted by William Henry Jackson. The canyon's ridgeline became a principal line of defense for the Utah Militia

Even the mules were worn out. When they came to the last steep hills of the mountainsides, men with ropes had to assist the mules up and over. Top-quality forage had been short on the trail in 1857. There had been heavy migration, in addition to the 50,000 head of cattle being trailed to California. Trail drovers tended to pause and graze their stock on the best forage. They aimed for their cattle to gain weight on the long drive.[3] When they could, teamsters stopped where the grass was best. There was another complicating factor—neither mules nor horses are as well adapted to use forage as is the ox. On the way west, the pioneers needed to make use of the natural resources found along the trail. Among those resources were the native forages including grasses, legumes, forbs,[4] and the leaves of some shrubs. The ox's digestive tract is so designed to make better use of those forages than is that of the mule or horse. The ox has a compound stomach. Its first two compartments, the rumen and the reticulum, actually constitute a microbial fermentation vat. Microorganisms live in the rumen and reticulum in a symbiotic relationship with the ox. The ox provides an environment in which they can survive and flourish. The microbes, in turn, digest the fibrous material of the various forages. The end products of that digestion can be used for work, growth, milk production, and to maintain the animal body. In turn, the microbial organisms become a source of quality protein for the ox. The ox or cow spends part of each day re-chewing the ingested feed. This provides another opportunity for the microbes to attack a fresh surface. Regurgitation and cud-chewing are perfectly normal processes.

Mules and horses are simple stomach animals, that is their stomach has a single compartment. They do not digest fiber in their stomach. Farther down the digestive tract, at the beginning of the large intestine, is a large, blind pouch called the caecum. It behaves similarly to the rumen-reticulum, although it has only about half the capacity of the rumen-reticulum. Once the ingested feed has undergone microbial fermentation in the caecum and has been returned to the large intestine, it is past the most efficient absorptive site, the small intestine.

Contrasted with oxen, mules and horses have another digestive difference. The equine intestine is quite susceptible to impaction and colic.

In the spring and early summer of the year, forages are higher in digestible protein and net energy. As the season progresses the grasses and other forages begin to mature. The fibrous material, cellulose, tends to be replaced, to a degree, by a woody-type substance called lignin, which is not digestible by the microbes. Key nutrient levels such as protein, energy and carotene drop and are less digestible. Said another way, during the crossing of the plains, the lush, easily digestible forages of springtime and early summer become the more difficult to digest forages of late July and August. When contrasted with the mule and horse, the ox has an even greater comparative advantage with mature forages and especially with browse. The mule and the horse require grain or concentrated feedstuffs to maintain themselves under conditions of heavy work. Oats are the grain of choice.[5] However, carrying sufficient oats in the wagons or the handcarts to supplement the mules' diet had not been an option.

During an 1851 campaign against the Navajo in New Mexico Territory, the U.S. Cavalry found it impossible to make long marches on grass alone. Furthermore, there was little grass in the desert Southwest. In 1852, Sergeant Frank Clarke reported that the trooper's weight and that of his rifle, a heavy single-barrel Dragoon pistol, one of Colt's six-shooter revolvers, a Dragoon saber, and his other equipment, amounted to 350 pounds. Given that workload, coupled with inadequate forage and grain rations, eastern-bred cavalry horses were generally so worn and nutritionally broken down that by the time they reached the point where the troopers intercepted the Indians, the cavalry could not overtake the Indians who were mounted on fresh horses. One trooper wrote that a daily feed allowance of 12 pounds of hay, and either 8 pounds of corn or 12 pounds of oats, was barely sufficient just to keep their horses alive, let alone be prepared for action. Even on the prairie grasses of the plains, horses grew weak.[6]

In short, oxen fare much better than either horses or mules when feedstuffs are limited to native forages. By the time the 7th Handcart Company pioneers reached Deer Creek and were proceeding across Wyoming through the latter half of August and early September, the feed would have been short and the protein and energy levels decidedly low. The mules were, by this point, malnourished and weak. The terrain was increasingly rugged. The men probably fixed pull ropes to the wagons and put ropes around the back side of the mules' thighs to help lift the worn-out animals up and over the steep places. The way west had also been marked with animal skeletons. The weary men of the company did not let their faithful mules perish. By aiding the mules in the rugged going, the mules continued to serve them.

The 7th Company was determined to stay well ahead of Johnston's Army. Relentlessly, they pushed on. The evening when they camped at the head of Echo Canyon, they were hit with a rain and hailstorm. The lightly clad Scandinavians suffered greatly from the cold. There was no extra clothing and many were without shoes; some used rags to cover their sore, bleeding feet.[7] Down through Echo Canyon came the weary pioneers. The aspen, scrub oak, and maple trees of Utah's mountains had changed into their autumn colors. The nights were crisp. The feel of fall was in the air that second week in September. When within 30 miles of Salt Lake Valley, they were met with teamsters driving wagons which brought them bread, cake, and fruit.[8]

About noon, on Sunday September 13, when people were just getting out of Church meetings, the ragged, hungry, sunburned, weary pioneers, with a Danish flag flying from the lead handcart, came into Salt Lake City.[9] They had walked 1,300 miles. It was the happiest day of their lives. A ragged blanket, a ragged shirt, and ragged overalls were all 13-year-old Niels Christensen had of this world's goods. His mother gave him a little bucket and told him to go ask for some milk. The first house had none, but a woman at the second home gave him some milk, and then asked if he had any bread. When he answered no, she gave him half of the loaf she had.[10]

A special welcome awaited the Dorius brothers. As they pulled their handcart through the streets of Salt Lake City, they saw their father, Nicolai, and his wife. Their father had immigrated earlier and had remarried after his arrival in the Salt Lake Valley. However, their little sister, Dorthea Nicoline, was not there for she had died February 26, 1855, and had been buried near a sugar plantation[11] as they steamed up the Mississippi, three days after they had reached New Orleans. The family walked together to the place where the handcart company would encamp. Then, Johan and his wife Karen, Carl and his wife Ellen, and her mother, Gjertrud Maria Rolfson, and sister Gjertrud, all went to the home of Father Dorius. It was a time of "inexpressible joy."[12]

In the future, significant missionary service would again be asked of the Dorius family. In the 1860s, Johan and Carl Dorius were called to serve second missions to Norway. Returning home in 1863, Carl Dorius was appointed leader of the Scandinavian immigrants on board the *Antarctic.* The old ship, whitewashed and covered with coal tar, leaked badly, and had to be pumped several hours each day to get the seawater out of her hold. Among the passenger company were Johan Andreas Jensen and his family. This is the same Captain Johan Jensen who had been one of the Norwegians that had been converted in Frederikstad Prison by Svend and Christian Larsen in the 1850s. Johan Dorius had been among the missionaries who had served with the Larsens. There were parallels with the 1857 journey. The train ride west was again in box cars. In the border states, especially in Missouri, the *Antarctic*'s Mormon passengers encountered the military. America was fighting a war between its northern and southern states. Additionally, on the Midwestern frontier, the U.S. Army was skirmishing with outlaws, jayhawkers, and bushwhackers. There were more than enough quarrels to create a shortage of men. The Army was on the lookout for trains carrying Mormon immigrants, as they were intent on forcibly enlisting the young men into the volunteer army. At Florence, these 1863 pioneers encountered RLDS members whose attempts to dissuade them from going west were unsuccessful. The Dorius brothers bought a yoke of oxen and a wagon. Carl said it seemed to be much better to be crossing the plains with oxen and wagon than with handcarts.[13] The Jensen family pulled a handcart west.[14]

For their close friend and missionary companion, C. C. A. Christensen, there would be no such joyful reunion with his mother. Before going to Norway, Christensen had arranged for his mother, Dorthea, and brother, Mads Frederik, to join the Saints in Utah. They had crossed the Atlantic on the 1854 voyage of the *Jesse Munn*. However, Dorthea died in Salt Lake City September 5, 1855.

In 1865, C. C. A. Christensen was called to serve another mission to Scandinavia. The eastbound journey was dangerous, for it was a season of Indian difficulties. Several whites had lost their lives that spring. One morning in present-day Wyoming, the missionaries discovered the scalped corpse of a young man who had been killed the previous night. Christensen and others spent two weeks at Omaha, Nebraska, where among other activities he held a lengthy conversation with Johan Ahmanson, the former Scandinavian missionary who had left the Church. Ahmanson's apostasy ultimately served to deepen Christensen's resolve. Utah's Black Hawk War broke while he was gone. Elise managed the farm and home and survived this Ute uprising. Still cooking over an open fireplace, Elise had been hopeful that her husband might borrow sufficient funds from her stepfather to buy a cook stove and bring it to Utah. The returning missionary brought more than that. Elise's parents immigrated with him. While her step-father never converted, he enjoyed cordial relationships with family and Mormon neighbors. There was another wonderful surprise. C. C. A.'s brother, August, who had earlier served as a Latter-day Saint missionary in Norway, had become disaffected from the Church and had joined the Norwegian army. In a marked turnabout, August was among those who accompanied his brother home to Utah.[15]

Apparently little had been written in the *Deseret News* concerning the 1857 arrival. Other things of significance had been happening. On September 4, Thomas B. Marsh, the original president of the Quorum of the Twelve who had been disaffected with the Church since the dark, difficult days in Missouri, arrived in Salt Lake City as a part of the William Walker wagon train.[16] The man to whom the Lord had declared: *Verily I say unto you, behold how great is your calling,*[17] must have been sobered and humbled when he looked on that which had been accomplished by his successor, Brigham Young, and the loyal members of the Church. Perhaps he could now see that defensive anger and foolish pride had cost him a remarkable place in American and Church history.

The war news had been the pressing concern. It, more than anything, had caught the attention of the *Deseret News* reporters. On September 8, Captain Stewart Van Vliet of General Harney's staff arrived in Salt Lake City. The next day, Captain Van Vliet had an interview with Brigham Young and spent several days observing the Latter-day Saints before he returned to his escort at Ham's Fork, from which place he proceeded east to Washington, DC. Captain Van Vliet's report to the government was very favorable toward the Latter-day Saints.[18]

Captain Christiansen's 7th Company reached the valley only one day after Israel Evans' 6th Handcart Company arrived, which company had departed Clear Creek three weeks earlier than the 7th Company. In large measure, the 7th Company arrived ahead of the Cowley wagon train, which entered Salt Lake City during the days of September 13-15. They had pressed forward at a hard pace. On September 15, Governor Brigham Young declared martial law throughout the Territory of Utah. The order forbid the entrance of federal troops into the Valley of the Great Salt Lake. Also that day, a heavy snow fell at Fort Bridger.[19] Winter was making another early appearance.

On September 17, Colonel Phillip St. George Cooke left Fort Leavenworth with the second division of the Utah Expedition.[20] Surely Cooke must have had mixed emotions when he thought of his former command, the loyal men of the Mormon Battalion. What would it be like to look down the barrel of your rifle at men who had proven their valor and patriotism in the

"Handcart Pioneers' First View of the Salt Lake Valley" by C.C.A. Christensen The scene may be the top of Little Mountain at the head of Emigration canyon, and would have been a vibrant memory of September 12 or 13, 1857. Courtesy of the Springville Museum of Art, Springville, Utah.

arduous 2,000-mile epic march from Fort Leavenworth to San Diego during the war with Mexico? There was nothing to compare with it in the annals of U.S. military history. He had been their commanding officer. When east-bound Captain Van Vliet met Colonel Johnston and his escort October 1, the Colonel and his men were 90 miles east of Fort Laramie.[21]

The *Buffalo Commercial Advertiser* reported there was no grass between Fort Laramie and Green River, a distance of 400 miles. The freight contractors, Messrs. Russell and Wadell, were losing large numbers of their cattle and the wagon trains had been making only 12 miles per day. Cooke's escort accompanying Governor Cumming had been making only 18 miles per day. An abundance of snow was forecast by the middle of October. The October 26 *St. Louis Democrat* reported that the cattle of the Government trains were dying fast, and it was believed the men of the trains would suffer greatly during the oncoming winter. Colonel Johnston, traveling with 19 light wagons, had been making 60 miles per day. Such speed had not been without cost. His mules were breaking down. Numbers of them were dropping by the way and had been rendered useless by his extraordinarily hard push.[21]

Not all who began the journey from Copenhagen lived to see the mountains of Ephraim. Three died at sea. Four died on the rail journey from Philadelphia to Iowa City. Six-month-old Franklin Jacobsen, the son of Jacob Christensen died in June 1857. Two-year-old Andrea Christensen died in August 1857. Other deaths have been noted, some have not been. A number of the 330 of the 7th Handcart Company died on the way west. James Jensen said, "one out of ten had died." Others had not strength nor health to immediately push on.

Gertrude Pedersen Bastian lived to see the Great Salt Lake Valley. Then, three days later, she died. Jacob built her coffin with his own hands, dug her grave, and laid her to rest. Married April 24 on board the *Westmoreland*, their time together in mortality had been only 145 days. It must have been a terribly lonely moment. Overlooked by others who faced their own difficulties, only Erastus Snow of the Twelve came to comfort him.

Jacob adored Gertrude. He had been attracted to the Church initially through her. He was stricken with grief, and sought Elder Snow's counsel. The Apostle advised him to marry again and try to overcome his sorrow through domestic life. Accordingly, he won the hand of Johanna Marie Sander (Sandersen), a Danish girl who also had been a part of the 7th Company. Jacob and Johanna were married 25 October 1857.[23] That fall, they moved to Tooele County where he worked as a carpenter in the construction of a flour mill.[24] Summer 1858 found them in Lehi. Jacob remained rock-solid in the Church and raised a large family.

When they arrived in Salt Lake City, the family of Niels Otto Mortensen was met by their daughter Anne Margrette. It was then they learned that Bodil had died in the bitter cold at Rock Creek Hollow. They were unprepared for such devastating news. Maren Kirstine's health, which was not good, never fully recovered from the emotional shock of her daughter's death; she died at Parowan in 1862.[25]

NOTES

1. Clare B. Christensen, *History of Niels Christensen*, Op cit., p.2.

2. Arthur L. Crawford, Jacob Bastian…, p. 3.

3. The calf-roping and steer-wrestling events of American rodeo are not an accurate reflection of how cattle were managed during a cattle drive. Neither are most western motion pictures. Cattle have been sold by weight and condition for many years. It made patently good sense to move the trail herd slowly and quietly to good feed and water.

4. The grasses would have included the Bluestem family, Indiangrass, Buffalograss, Switchgrass, Sideoats Grama, and others of the Grama family. Legumes would have included Catclaw Sensitivebrier, Blue Wildindigo, and Purple Prairieclover. Pitchers Sage, with its pale blue flowers, was one of the forbs. Given the rains of June 1857, the prairie must have been beautiful in early July. The Scandinavians would not have known the common names of the flora of the prairie had they had energy and inclination to record them. Furthermore, it was the worrisome presence of the buffalo, not the forage the buffalo grazed, which preoccupied their thinking. By 1955, the largest remaining unbroken tract of true prairie covered approximately 3.8 billion acres. It then

extended from near the Nebraska line south across Kansas and into Oklahoma where it is known as the Osage Hills.

5. Equine nutrition and practical feeding husbandry supports the statement found in D&C 89:16-17 which reads in part: "All grain is good for the food of man...nevertheless, wheat for man, corn for the ox, and oats for the horse..."

6. Durwood Ball, *Army Regulars...*, pp. 30-31.

7. Anders Christian Christensen, *A Short Sketch of the Lives...*, p. 4.

8. James Jensen, *Journal History of the Church*, September 13, 1857.

9. The lead handcart was apparently pulled by C. C. A. Christensen, for in "Beretning," *Morgenstjernen*, 3:205 (1884) he recorded he had a Danish flag flying from his handcart, and that his trousers were flapping about his legs in tatters. Given all else they had to leave behind at Iowa City, it is indicative of their feelings of love for their former homeland.

10. C. C. A. Christensen, "By Handcart to Utah," p. 344, tells that a Danish flag had been on the lead handcart. The other information is found in Clare B. Christensen's *History of Niels Christensen*, Op cit., p. 2. When a boy, Clare once complained that the gravy, which had been slightly burned, tasted nasty. His grandfather, Niels, said to him: "It is good, Clare. You eat it. You have no idea of what it is like to be hungry."

11. Peter O. Hansen, Personal Accounts, *James Nesmith, Mormon Immigration Index*.

12. Johann F. F. Dorius, *[Journal] in Church Emigration Book* (1855-1862) pp. 3-7. See Mormon Immigration Index–Personal Accounts, *Westmoreland*, (April 1857).

13 . Mormon Immigration Index–Personal Accounts, *Antarctic* May 1863 of *Autobiography of Thomas Henry White, Autobiography of Thomas Wright Kirby* and *Journal of Carl Dorius*.

14. Russell M. Nelson, in *From Heart to Heart: An Autobiography*, Chapter 2, "From Europe to Ephraim," p. 7 tells how his Jensen great-grandparents and family came west by handcart.

15. Richard L. Jensen and Richard G. Oman, *C. C. A. Christensen, Mormon Immigrant Artist...*, pp. 14-15.

16. Andrew Jenson, *Church Chronology, Historical Record 1890*, p. 55.

17. D&C 112:33.

18. Andrew Jenson, *Church Chronology, Historical Record 1890*, p. 55.

19. From an article in the *St. Louis Republican* as reported in the Saturday December 5, 1857 *Millennial Star*, No. 49 Vol. XIX:780.

20. Andrew Jenson, *Church Chronology, Historical Record 1890*, p. 55.

21. *St. Louis Republican* article as quoted in the Millennial Star No. 49, XIX:779-780.

22. The excerpts from the *Commercial Buffalo Advertiser* and the *St. Louis Democrat* are found in the *Millennial Star* No. 49, XIX:780.

23. Arthur L. Crawford, *Jacob Bastian...*, p. 3.

24. Arthur L. Crawford, *Jacob Bastian...*, p. 4.

25. *History of Niels Otto Mortensen*, p.3.

Chapter 17

A SEASON OF UNCERTAINTY

Early fall 1857 to mid-year 1858 could be called a season of political uncertainty. Though faced by a sizeable U.S. Army, the Latter-day Saints were nonetheless determined to stand whatever test the coming months might bring. Faithful members had unwavering confidence in the leadership of the Church. On September 30, four days after the arrival of the season's last pioneer company, Lieutenant General Daniel H. Wells and 1,250 men were ordered to Echo Canyon where they were engaged in digging trenches across the canyon's floor, in throwing up breastworks, and loosening the rocks along the canyon's rim, which could then be released as bouncing boulders, a type of nature's cannon shot, on any advancing army.[1] In a few weeks, Echo Canyon's ridges would become the Utah Militia's fortress line through all those cold winter months. Johnston and his shivering men might be more reasonable after a winter out in the cold. The death dates on some of the markers at the Camp Floyd Cemetery indicate a number of the troopers died in present-day Wyoming that winter and the following spring.[2]

Little did 13-year-old Niels Christensen realize, as he and his stepfather pulled their handcart in 1857, that in the near future the army's horses and mules would create an important market for the hay they grew. He became fascinated with the soldiers' accounts of the 1857 plains crossing for that was a fresh, significant period in his life. As a teenage boy during the 1859-61 period in Utah Territory, Niels Christensen hauled grass hay to sell to the army at Camp Floyd. He had heard the stories of the Utah Militia and their engagements with Johnston's men. (Niels would serve as a cavalry trooper in the

Utah Militia's First Company during the 1866 Black Hawk War.) During the 1857 conflict, Governor Brigham Young ordered the militia to avoid taking human life. Rather, Lot Smith and his men were to harass, annoy, delay and where possible, burn the supply trains. One stratagem employed by Smith's men was to wait until the army had bedded down for the night. Suddenly the sleeping soldiers would hear the militia's bugler blowing charge. The Mormon cavalry troopers would ride hard at the camp, fire some shots in the air, and then beat a hasty retreat to their secluded encampment a safe distance away, where they then retired for a full-night's sleep. Meanwhile, the men of the army, many of them teenagers, would remain on high alert all through the long night, awaiting the attack which never came. Such tactics compromised the army's energy and no doubt led their officers to conclude that the Mormon militia had taken the field with a force of considerable size. On one such raid, some of Johnston's men grabbed their rifles and got off a few shots at the retreating militia cavalrymen. As one ball whistled near the head of one fellow, he ducked quickly and low over the neck of his horse. The rapid movement resulted in his hat flying off of his head. During the Camp Floyd years, when telling Niels Christensen of this episode, the U.S. soldier said: "I shot the d_____d Mormon's head off, and he still kept right on riding."[3]

As the advance units of Johnston's army made their way across present-day Wyoming, they kept to the open terrain. The Utah Militia, though few in numbers, were becoming masters of illusion. Along the route west were plateau and mesa areas, the ridges of which overlooked the lower regions through which the streams flowed. These ridges presented unique opportunities for maneuver. One particular ridge line was broken by a V-shaped saddle. To the U.S. troops moving at lower elevations some distance away, the saddle appeared as a pass through the high country. A small cavalry group of the Utah Militia was moving along the backside of that ridge. As they rode single file across the V-shaped saddle, for a brief moment horse and rider were exposed to the detachment of U.S. troops. Disappearing

The marker at Simpson's Hollow. It was in this vicinity that Major Lot Smith of the Utah Militia burned the wagon train captained by Lewis Simpson in October 1857. The pioneers of the 7th Handcart Company would have passed through this area in early September 1857. Photograph by the author, July 1992.

from sight rather quickly, the troopers would turn their horses down the hillside where they had stacked various items of clothing and equipment. Quickly, the men swapped horses, coats, hats and gear. The dozen or so militia cavalry were, in fact, riding in a rather tight circle, something akin to a merry-go-round on a tilt, with live horses and men who were enjoying quick costume and horse changes. The militia troopers repeated the theatrical process over and over again.[4]

To concerned U.S. Army officers observing the movement of distant militia through their field glasses, it gave every appearance of a large Mormon force moving along their flank. However, these encounters occurred at some point after the handcart pioneers had moved through the area.[5] The last of the season's Mormon wagon trains would have been in the valley for eight days when Lot Smith, with a small company of men, surprised and burned three trains of government supplies near the Big Sandy and Green River.[6] Undoubtedly, the various ruses staged earlier by the militia helped give the army, and especially those freighting the quartermaster's supplies, the troubling impression that they were vastly outnumbered.

Brigham Young's intuition about the harsh weather of the upper Green River region had been correct. Another long and bitter winter was underway. Colonel Johnston rendezvoused with his frostbitten troops at the confluence of the Ham and Black's Forks on November 4. The campaign over for 1857, Johnston took his men into winter quarters at Camp Scott, near what had been Fort Bridger. In his wake lay hundreds of dead draft stock.[7] A November 6 report states that 500 animals belonging to the U.S. Army had perished from cold and starvation at Black's Fork.[8] Colonel Phillip St. George Cooke, under the date of November 10, speaks to the terrible weather in the region east of South Pass. He called the night of November 9 the worst night he had ever spent. He wrote of a blizzard driven by fierce, hurricane-like winds, of the piteous cries of their famished mules as they crowded the campfires begging for feed. They found dead and dying mules strewn about when they awoke. It was difficult to get those who were still alive to stand long enough to be harnessed. "One of the government teamsters left five mules mired in a slew with the harnesses on. At least fifty mules and horses were left in camp because it was impossible to drive them." That night, they found a somewhat sheltered place among the willows along the Sweetwater. They fed their famished mules a little corn, shoveled away the deep snow and succeeded in building a fire. Only by constant exertion were they able to avoid freezing. That night, the thermometer dropped to -20° F, and a great number of the stock died.[9] One report states that even given Cooke's remarkable leadership, the Second Dragoons lost 130 of 274 horses to starvation and 77 men to desertion.[10] This was not Colonel Cooke's first foray into this part of the American West. Prior to his assuming command of the Mormon Battalion in the 1846 Mexican War in its epic march to the Pacific, Cooke had been the first to lead a U.S. battalion of dragoons over the Oregon Trail and through South Pass.[11] Colonel Cooke's weather report seems to have been precise and written without exaggeration.

Ultimately, Cooke, by then a full colonel, succeeded Johnston as commanding officer at Camp Floyd which became Fort Crittenden with Floyd's defection to the South. Cooke, though a Virginian, had determined in the 1840s that genuine freedom lay with the northern cause. That decision embittered his family. His son, John Rogers Cooke, and son-in-law, Brigadeer General J. E. B. Stuart of Confederate cavalry fame, disowned him. Nonetheless, Cooke fought for the Union and the flag which he had served with distinction for 30 years.[12] With the outbreak of the Civil War, Colonel Cooke withdrew the Fort Crittenden garrison, disposing of some $4,000,000 worth of federal property for $100,000.[13] Regarding those cheap prices, Nick Wilson, a former Pony Express rider who served as an army scout during Johnston's desert campaign against the Gosiutes said: "I bought a yoke of oxen for eighteen dollars and a new wagon for ten."[14]

At the time of those dispersal sales, Niels Otto Mortensen walked the 200-plus miles from Parowan to Fort Crittenden and purchased a yoke of oxen. He then drove them back to

Parowan on foot. He seemed to make the trip with little difficulty until he came to a stream called Little Creek, some two to three miles north of Parowan. It was getting on toward night. The creek's banks were quite steep and the muddy banks were slick. The largest ox successfully crossed the creek, but the smaller one was unable to climb the slick south bank. After a number of attempts to get the ox out of the creek bottom, Niels determined he would have to go back to Paragonah some two miles to the north and get help. He took the large ox and returned to "Brother Prothew's" place. He put the ox in Prothew's corral and went to his house to request his help. When they returned to the corral, to their pleasant surprise, there stood the other ox. Seemingly faced with abandonment, the ox had gotten himself out of the creek bottom and had followed Niels and his teammate to Paragonah.[15]

Niels Christensen, now approaching 17, was one who observed the withdrawal. Ammunition was dumped into the large spring which had been the source of water for the camp. Muskets were stacked and burned and their barrels bent. Six large brass cannon were dumped in the Jordan River during the withdrawal. Niels was one of those who had wanted to purchase a rifle from the army. When it came to selling arms to the Mormons, the officers would not allow it. At least one trooper disobeyed those orders, for Niels saw a farmer meet a trooper in the brush away from the camp, where the farmer traded the soldier a bottle of whiskey for a musket. Some of the federal troops attempted to remain behind. The bitter quarrel between the states held no appeal for them. The memories of the terrible winter at Camp Scott and the subsequent fierce and terribly cruel battle in the Deep Creek Range with the Gosiute, Pocatello, and Shoshone, in which all the Indian women, children, and most of the warriors had been killed, had been more than enough blood for some. Two soldiers, caught in the attempt to desert as the garrison started east, were tied by their wrists to the back of a tall supply wagon, so that only their toes could barely touch the ground. As the supply wagon passed from view, the two men were still dangling from the back of the wagon.[16] Colonel Cooke had no patience for traitors. Fascinatingly, the army which had come to subjugate the Mormons, became instead a principal federal subsidy which supported the expansion of the Great Basin economy and the Mormon colonization effort.

In 1857, an especially fierce and bitter winter struck the upper Green River. Winter, rather than the Mormon militia, became the army's deadliest foe. On December 4, Captain John R. Winder of the Utah Militia was appointed to take charge of the picket guard stationed at Camp Weber at the mouth of Echo Canyon. One of their assigned duties was to watch and report the movement of the federal troops. Two weeks later, when deep snow fell in the mountains, the guard was reduced to a mere ten men. The remainder of the militia returned to their homes for the winter.[17] There were wise men in the nation's capital who recognized the folly of the Utah Expedition. In a speech of protest and warning on the floor of the United States Senate regarding Buchanan's military action against the Mormons, Senator Sam Houston of Texas warned the U.S. Army would have to fight a war like the one Napoleon fought with Russia. "Consider the facilities these people have to cut off your supplies. I say your men will never return, but their bones will whiten the valley of Salt Lake."[18]

Reinforced by the lack of rapid progress in the field, and the reports of the bitterly cold winter in the West, the logic of cooler heads prevailed in Washington, DC. Faced with the stark reality that for the immediate present, the U.S. Army's battle for survival was with the vagaries of nature, the hot passions of policy makers who wanted a shooting war with the Mormons subsided. Perhaps within their Utah mountain bulwark, congregations of Latter-day Saints from many lands gratefully sang in praise, "For the strength of the hills we bless Thee, our God, our fathers' God."[19]

The end of the trail did not end sacrifice and hardship. Anders and Sophie Marie's son, Peter Christian Christensen, was among the young men called by Brigham Young to go to the Green River and Fort Bridger country and prevent the U. S.

Army from entering the valley of the Great Salt Lake. Peter helped burn the grass on which the army had planned to winter their horses, cattle, and mules. He was a part of the militia force which stampeded the army's livestock and drove them to the Salt Lake Valley and burned the supply trains.[20]

Circumstances were such that individuals were assigned to live with others for the winter. Niels Christensen stayed with a family in the Cottonwood area of Salt Lake Valley. This family lived in a two-room dugout. There were three women, two girls and a little boy of six, in addition to Niels, who had turned 13 on August 4, probably in the neighborhood of Scott's Bluff, Nebraska. It was from that little boy that Niels learned to speak English. The father of this family was at Echo Canyon as a part of the militia's effort to hold back the army. Niels chopped wood, and herded and milked cows. Potatoes and pumpkin butter were the chief foods. He had been promised a pair of boots as soon as the shoemaker could secure the leather. After weeks of waiting, he went to see if the boots were ready. The shoemaker's wife handed him a stout pair. The happy lad turned and hurried away, only to be stopped by the shoemaker who came running after him. The shoemaker said he was the wrong boy—these boots were for another. Niels handed them back and with tears in his eyes, walked away. It would be another three weeks before his boots were ready.[21]

In the spring of 1858, Hans, Ellen, Paul, and Niels Christensen moved to Lehi. They lived in a dugout near the place where the Lehi sugar factory would later stand. It was a difficult summer with little to eat. Sheep had been pastured in and about the area where the family lived. Tufts of wool had been caught on the greasewood, a shrub common to the Great Basin. Ellen painstakingly gathered the tiny bits of wool and spun it into yarn. From that yarn, she knitted stockings for Hans and the boys.[22] An Indian taught Niels how to peel and eat thistles. Hunger can make a bitter food taste tolerable.

After hardship and sacrifice came the quiet miracle. The comforting answer to Mads Christensen's boyhood prayer in the woods of Denmark had gradually faded from his memory.

Then on March 15, 1858, when Mads was ordained a Seventy by A. M. Musser, the largely forgotten incident was suddenly and vividly brought to his remembrance for the Spirit whispered, "Your prayers are now answered, and the Holy Priesthood with all its gifts and powers are sealed upon your head."[23] In 1875 Mads returned to Denmark as a missionary. The miracle of technological progress in transportation enabled him to return to Copenhagen in a sixth of the time required for the 1857 journey.[24]

In Mormon history, 1858 is called the year of the move, although by midyear the threat of war was essentially over. With the exception of Lot Smith's burning of the supply trains along the Big Sandy in October 1857, and a rattled Private McCarty who mistakenly fired on Thomas L. Kane on April 17, 1858, at Fort Bridger,[25] the hottest battles were the blistering attacks of New York and London editorial writers regarding Buchanan's handling of all the affairs of state. If savage criticism sells newspapers, then sales were brisk indeed, for there was no shortage of editorial targets. The *Millennial Star* made Utah's case in Liverpool, England, simply by quoting from the "Gentile press" the caustic editorial wrath directed at the Buchanan administration.

The Saturday July 24, 1858 edition of the *Millennial Star* quotes the May 8 edition of the *New York Tribune* as stating: "The driving of the Mormons from their homes by military terror, will hardly contribute much to the honour of the country, or the posthumous reputation of Mr. Buchanan's presidency." The *Tribune*'s June 12 edition noted: "Whatever may thus far have been done toward establishing the authority of the United States in Utah, it is pretty certain that nothing which has yet transpired can have much tendency to shake the confidence of Mormons in Brigham as a Prophet."

Those were mild shots compared to the heavy salvos fired in the June 17 edition of the *New York Times*. Had the editorial heat arising from the fierce castigation of the President in that lengthy piece been transferrable to the printing press, it would have warped the type set. *The Times* wrote:

No dispassionate person, whatever his political partialities, can fail to see that the various enterprises undertaken by Mr. Buchanan do not seem to prosper in his hands. He has meddled in nothing, suggested nothing, entered upon nothing, since he entered the White House, which has not ended in confusion worse confounded. His rosiest apples have proved Dead Sea fruit and "turned to ashes on his lips;" his "dear gazelles" no sooner come to "know and love him well, than they are sure to die." The most monstrous fraud and swindle, if he only takes to back it up, ends in being a tolerably decent and fair proceeding. The prettiest quarrel, under his manipulation, turns into a humdrum, inglorious peace. He devoted the first year of his reign to trying to prevent the people of Kansas from voting on their own constitution, and he finally had to join in rejoicing over an arrangement by which it was submitted to them in full. The British cruisers seemed disposed to help him out of his predicament, and committed a score of outrages on our ships; but he no sooner set about preparing for war, and dispensing fat contracts, than the foe apologized for everything, and disavows everybody who has done wrong. The Mormon war was as promising a little quarrel as ever an enterprising statesman gloated over. It contained every element of success and popularity. Impudent imposture, murders, rapes, polygamy, treason, intrusion on the United States' Territory, defiance of the Government and public opinion—nothing was wanting to convert our venerable President into a glorious crusader on behalf of law, order, morality, and national dignity. The pudding was full of plums. It, too, has failed him. Even Brigham the Prophet has not turned out as well as expected and refuses to be a traitor; and when the Lord's anointed deserts our President in his hour of need, his case is indeed pitiable.

The latest news from Utah places the Administration in a position marked by a singular mixture of farce and tragedy, and the whole story of the war is crowded by as much ignorance, stupidity, and dishonesty as any Government ever managed to get in the annals of a single year. An army was sent to chastise the rebels before it was clearly ascertained whether or not there were any rebels to chastise. It was sent forward in the fall just when it ought to have reached its destination, and was marching through the snow over a howling wilderness when it ought to have been in winter quarters. After it had gone six months of suffering, and was fully prepared to force the strongest natural position in the world, Commissioners were sent in search of the rebel foe, and then it was discovered there was no foe at all. Governor Cumming ought to have gone to Salt Lake City in the autumn. He goes in the spring, and is received with all the honours, assumes the reins of authority without opposition, and writes home that the whole affair, like the Willet's Point business, is all a mistake, and there is no war at all. The Commander of the Forces writes, by the same mail, that Cumming is deceived and that the Mormons are still hostile. The public is in suspense, and knows not which of the two authorities to believe, when the news comes there are no Mormons left, either to fight or obey us, as they are abandoning our Territory en masse, sooner than submit to our rule. "We have made a desert and call it peace."

Whatever our opinions may be of Mormon morals or Mormon manners, there can be no question that this voluntary and even cheerful abandonment by 40,000 people of homes created by wonderful industry, in the midst of trackless wastes, after years of hardship and persecution, is something from which no one who has a particle of sympathy with pluck, fortitude, and constancy can withhold his admiration. Right or wrong, sincerity thus attested is not a thing to be sneered at. True or false, a faith to which so many men and women prove their loyalty, by such sacrifices, is a force in the world.

After this last demonstration of what fanaticism can do, we think it would be most unwise to treat Mormonism as a nuisance to be abated by a posse comitatus. It is no longer a social excrescence to be cut off by the sword; it is a power to be combatted by the most skillful, political, and moral treatment. When people abandon their homes to plunge with their women and children into a wilderness, to seek new settlements, they know not where, they give a higher proof of courage than if they had fought for them. When the Dutch submerged Holland, to save it from invaders, they had heartier plaudits showered on them than if they had fertilized its soil with their blood. We have certainly the satisfaction of knowing that we have to deal with foemen worthy of our steel.

However this singular affair may end, nothing can release us from the responsibility we have incurred in it. It may be that the sect may die out in Central America, through pestilence, famine, or the hostility of Indians. It may be that a complete isolation from the influence of public opinion and complete subjection to the will of the Prophet may bring a state of things which even Mormon zealots will find intolerable, and once foreign persecution has ceased to create a bond of cohesion, the sect will go through internal dissensions or sheer inanition. All these may be, but they may not be; and we may yet encounter our truant subjects in Mexico or elsewhere, and find them more troublesome customers than ever, and have to undertake a Mormon war, which will be a war in earnest. As long as they were at Salt Lake, we were sure, in a few years of absorbing them or surrounding them by the march of emigration, and had a chance, in the meantime, of bringing the influences of Christianity and civilization to bear on them. If the conduct of recent operations has had the effect of strengthening their fanaticism, by the appearance of persecution, without convincing them of our good faith and good intentions, and worse still, has been the means of driving away 50,000 of our fellow-citizens from their fields which their labours have reclaimed and cultivated, and round which their affections were clustered, we have something serious to answer for. Were we not guilty of a culpable oversight in confounding the insubordination of conscientious fanaticism with the insubordination of ribald license or ambition, and applying the same harsh treatment which the law intends for the latter alone? Was it right to send troops composed of the wildest and most rebellious men of the community, commanded by men like Harney and Johnston, to deal out fire and sword upon people whose faults even were the result of honest religious convictions? Was it right to allow Colonel Johnston to address letters to Brigham Young, and through him to his people, couched in the tone of an implacable conqueror towards ruthless savages? Were the errors which mistaken zeal generates ever cured by means such as these? And have bayonets and cannon ever been used against the poorest and the weakest sect that ever crouched beyond a wall to pray or weep, without rendering the faith more intense, and investing the paltriest discomforts with the dignity of sacrifice?

We with our Bibles, our churches, our single wives, our education, our sacred family life, ought to know better than to entrust the extirpation even of a creed which inculcates rebellion to such men as General Harney and Colonel Johnston; and Mr. Buchanan ought to know enough to do something at the right time in matters of such moment. His Peace Commissioners and Governor ought to have tried the effects of confidence and conciliation before our bayonets glistened in the canons of the Rocky Mountains, and his admonitory proclamation ought to have made its appearance before the General in command had addressed language to the malcontents worthy of Bajazet dealing with a rebellious Pasha. We placed ourselves all through on a level with these

Mormons, and talked to them as we would talk to European diplomatists. We stand on the vantage ground of higher knowledge, purer faith, and acknowledged strength. We can afford to be patient and merciful. At all events, the world looks to us now for such an example of political wisdom, such as few people, now-a-days, are called on to display. Posterity must not have to acknowledge with shame that our indiscretion, or ignorance, or intolerance drove the population of a whole State from house and home, to seek religious liberty and immunity from the presence of mercenary troops, in any spot of the continent to which our rule was never likely to extend.[26]

A July 3 *New York Tribune* report is particularly critical of military and civil attitudes at Camp Scott and Fort Bridger, claiming the people at these outposts "judge the Mormons a little too much by themselves." *The Tribune* stated:

Whether or not Brigham Young and his people have combined together, while seeming to acknowledge Cumming as Governor–in fact to set aside and override his the authority, at least it is very certain that such a combination exists in full force at Camp Scott with Mr. Chief-Justice Eckels at its head. Perhaps there is something in the air of Utah that stimulates treason, rebellion, and resistance to authority. Whether that be so or not, the authority of Cumming as Governor seems just now quite as much in danger from the Chief-Justice, the civil officers, and the army sent to Utah at such an expense to place him and sustain him in the Governor's chair, as from those whose anticipated opposition to his authority led to such costly preparation to uphold it. In fact, it would seem that, on the question of due respect to Cumming's gubernatorial authority, the people inside the Valley and those out of it had completely changed ground. The resistance to Gov. Cumming is not now on the part of Brigham Young and the Mormons generally, but on the part of Chief-Justice Eckels, Marshal Dotson, Gen. Johnston, the camp, and the camp-followers . . .

We have heard a great deal heretofore about the danger of personal violence and the loss of property to which the Gentiles in Utah have been exposed on the part of the Mormons. At present, the danger seems to be entirely the other way. Nothing can exceed the rancorous and even ferocious feelings against the Mormons with which the army at Camp Scott appears to be penetrated. They regard themselves as engaged not so much in a public service as in the prosecution of a private quarrel. They regard the Mormons as having subjected them to all the hard service of this campaign—as having kept them encamped all winter on short rations amid the mountains—as having derided, maligned, and insulted them; and even the very common soldiers are represented as having put on an air of offended dignity at the idea that the Peace Commissioners had arrived to snatch these hated victims from their revengeful grasp. This state of feeling on the part of the soldiers affords abundant justification for Gov. Cumming's objections to their entry into the Valley and for the dread and horror with which the Mormons regard their presence there. If it be deemed proper that or necessary to station troops in Utah, they ought to be some fresh corps, and not a body of men filled with such hatred and prejudice. Let some of the troops now on their march across the Plains be engaged in this service, and the force now accompanying Gen. Johnson [sic] be sent some other direction. That officer, however, would seem bent upon entering the Valley, in spite of remonstrances of Gov. Cumming, whose authority over the troops he denies, with the very object, it would seem, of driving the Mormons to destroy their houses and to prevent them from gathering their crops, thus subjecting thousands of women and children to the danger of starvation.[27]

The thoughts of the bugler sounding charge, of battlefield glory to be won, of booty to be taken by those who would be spoilers, were in the process of vanishing, tone and tint. While reports of news from the American West lagged considerably behind the pace of events, people in Britain were curious about the unfolding story of the conflict in the Great Basin. Under a New York dateline of June 23, the July 5 *London Times* wrote:

> The intelligence from Utah is confirmatory of the news that went out by the last steamer. [The mail was apparently transported by steamship and the dates suggest the west-to-east crossing must have been made in ten days.] This strange people were again in motion for a new home, and all the efforts of Governor Cumming to induce them to remain and limit themselves to the ordinary quota of wives have been fruitless. We are told they have left a deserted town and deserted fields behind them, and have embarked for a voyage over 500 miles of untracked desert, to a home, the locality of which is unknown to any but their chiefs. [The speculation in the press continued to be that the Latter-day Saints were headed for Sonora, Mexico.] Does it not seem incredible that, at the very moment when the marine of Great Britain and the United States are jointly engaged in the grandest scientific experiment that the world has yet seen, 30,000 to 40,000 natives of these countries, many of them men of industrious and temperate habits, should become the victims of such arrant imposition? Does it not seem impossible that men and women brought up under the influence of British and American civilization can abandon it for a wilderness and Mormonism? There is much that is noble in their devotion to their delusions. They step into the waves of the desert of the Great Basin with as much reliance on their leaders as the descendants of Jacob felt when they stepped between the walls of water in the Red Sea. The ancient world had individual Curiatii, Horatii, and other examples of heroism and devotion. But these western peasants seem to be a nation of heroes, ready to sacrifice everything rather than surrender one of their wives or a letter from Joe Smith's golden plates.[28]

On June 12, 1858, Buchanan's Peace Commissioners, L. W. Powell and Benjamin McCulloch, sent official dispatches to Secretary of War John B. Floyd and General Albert Sidney Johnston, notifying them they had successfully concluded a peace with the Mormons. The people and chief men of the Territory had cheerfully yielded obedience to the Constitution and laws of the United States. They confirmed the Latter-day Saints had abandoned Salt Lake City and had gone south 50 miles to Provo and beyond.[29]

On June 9, President Buchanan received from Governor Cumming a report dated May 2, which indicated that in Cumming's considered judgment, the difficulties in Utah were over. In a June 10 message addressed to the Senate and House of Representatives, the President congratulated the Congress on the satisfactory conclusion of "this auspicious event." The President expressed gratitude that the happy conclusion would "afford some relief to the treasury at a time demanding from us the strictest economy; and when the question which now arises upon every appropriation is, whether it be of a character so important as to brook no delay, and to justify and require a loan, and most probably a tax upon the people to raise the money necessary for its payment."

Obviously, the cost of putting down a rebellion which did not really exist had not been cheap. Mr. Buchanan declared it would not be necessary to call into service the two regiments of volunteers authorized by the April 7 Act of Congress to quell the disturbance in Utah, to protect the supply trains, and suppress the Indian hostilities on the frontier. The mention of Indian difficulties which no longer needed attention in connection with the Utah Expedition tends to confirm that Washington officialdom had genuine, and, in their minds, substantiated fears that the Mormons had indeed been in league with Native Americans of the mountain west, because the President now requested that he be allowed to redirect these regiments to the defense of Texas against Indian hostilities which were occurring there.[30]

Better times came shortly. The initially uncertain days of occupation by Johnston's Army became a blessing in disguise.

Rather than the army becoming the agent for subduing and scattering the Latter-day Saints, Camp Floyd became the site of a thriving market for hay, grain, flour, beef, eggs, butter, and vegetables, all of which brought very good prices; Brigham Young had seen to that. He requested that Latter-day Saints not undercut each other in pricing their commodities to the army. The Latter-day Saints were obedient to his counsel. Those top-dollar sales to Johnston's quartermaster provided a much-needed infusion of hard cash and had been an invaluable contributor of capital to the Great Basin's developing economy. Though scheming conspirators had designed a contrary outcome, neither the army nor the unhallowed hands of its lawless camp followers had stopped the latter-day work from progressing. The faithful paid their tithing and labored diligently to build settlements, farms and industry in the wilderness. The gathering of Israel from the four corners of the earth gained new momentum. All of this must have found special meaning when they read the words of the ancient Psalmist who declared: *God is our refuge and strength, a very present help in trouble...He maketh wars to cease unto the end of the earth: he breaketh the bow, and cutteth the spear in sunder; he burneth the chariot in the fire. Be still, and know that I am God: I will be exalted among the heathen, I will be exalted in the earth. The Lord of hosts is with us; the God of Jacob is our refuge.*[31]

NOTES

1. Andrew Jenson, *Church Chronology, Historical Record 1890*, p.55.

2. There are 72 grave markers at the Camp Floyd Cemetery. Fifteen of those markers have death dates between 25 September 1857 and 21 May 1858. The army broke its winter encampment on 13 June 1858. There were additional deaths in June which are, at least in part, attributable to a cold winter on short rations followed by the stress of a hard march by out-of-condition men.

3. Personal Communication. Niels Christensen told these events to his grandson, Clare Bernard Christensen, during the years he worked by his grandfather's side on the Christensen farm. Clare, in turn, repeated them to his son, Bernard Niel Christensen.

4. Personal Communication, Clare B. Christensen family.

5. Niels Christensen shared these stories with his grandson, Clare B. Christensen. Clare shared them with his sons as he worked with them in the same farm fields where, as a young fellow, he had heard them from his grandfather. See *Journal of Allen C. Christensen* XXIII:84-85.

6. William F. Cody describes the burning of the Simpson wagon train in "Robbed by Danites." He mistakenly remembers the Mormon militia leader as Joe Smith. He wrote they were about 18 miles from the Green River when they camped at noon. From this campsite they had to drive their cattle a mile-and-a-half to a creek to water them. Lewis Simpson, his assistant, George Woods, and Cody and a number of guards took the cattle to water at the creek. On the drive back they noticed a party of some 20 mounted men rapidly approaching them. They were still not in view of their wagon train. They were unsuspecting of any difficulty and had no idea they were about to be trapped, for the approaching horsemen were white. The leader rode in front and said: "How are you Mr. Simpson?"

    "You got the best of me, sir," said Simpson who did not know Lot Smith.

    "Well, I rather think I have," coolly replied the stranger, whose words conveyed a double meaning.

    Cody wrote they had all come to a halt at this point. These mounted men quietly and quickly surrounded them. They were all armed with double-barreled shotguns, rifles, and revolvers. Taken completely by surprise, they were at the mercy of Smith and his troopers. Cody's account recorded the exchange between the militia leader and Simpson:

    "I'll trouble you for your six shooters, gentlemen," said Smith.

    "I'll give them to you in a way you don't want," replied Simpson.

    In a split second three guns were leveled at Simpson. He was informed that if he made a move he'd be a dead man. Simpson recognized his situation was hopeless and surrendered. Lot Smith and his men escorted their prisoners back to the train, where much to Simpson and Cody's surprise they realized all of their fellow bull-whackers had been taken and disarmed. At the noon break, all of the teamsters except for the cooks had been napping under the wagon beds. Lot Smith's timing had been superb. No shots had been fired. No one had been hurt. Recognizing he was powerless to stop Smith, Simpson turned his attention to survival. He first requested one wagon and six yoke of cattle to carry their personal provisions, and then asked for their weapons. After conferring with his troops, Smith granted their requests. Simpson and his men had gone about two miles when they saw columns of smoke arising from what had been their heavily laden supply train. When the fires hit the wagons loaded with ammunition, there were loud explosions. Arriving at Fort Bridger they learned they were the third train which had fallen victim to Lot Smith and his cavalry troop. Cody wrote: "This made 75 wagon loads, or 450,000 pounds of supplies, mostly provisions, which never reached General Johnston's command."

Major Lot Smith wrote an account of the event. His description of the burning of Simpson's train is recorded in B. H. Roberts' *A Comprehensive History of the Church* Volume 4:283-285. This report states that when Major Smith came up to the train and asked for the wagon master, the bull-whackers informed him the captain was out after cattle. The teamsters were disarmed. Smith and some of his men rode out to meet Captain Simpson who was about a half mile from the train. Smith told Simpson that he had come on business. Simpson inquired the nature of it when Smith demanded his pistols. Simpson said that no man had ever taken them yet, and "that if you think you can without killing me, try it." According to Smith, they were all heading toward the train, "with our noses together about as close as Scotch terriers would have held theirs–his eyes were flashing with fire; I couldn't see mine–I told him that I admired a brave man, but that I did not like blood–you insist on my killing you, which will only take a minute, but I don't want to do it. We had by this time reached the train. He, seeing that his men were under guard, surrendered, saying: 'I see you have me at a disadvantage, my men being disarmed.' I replied that I didn't need the advantage and asked him what he would do if we should give them their arms. 'I'll fight you!' "Then,' said I, 'We know something about that too–take up your arms!' His men exclaimed, 'Not by a damn sight! We came out here to whack bulls, not to fight.' 'What do you say to that, Simpson?' I asked. 'Damnation,'he replied, grinding his teeth in a most violent manner. 'If I'd been here before and they had refused to fight, I would have killed every man of them.'"

This was the third train burned by Lot Smith and his command of 40 men. Smith's report indicates that Simpson was a son-in-law of Mr. Majors, that Smith considered Simpson the bravest man he met during the campaign, and that Smith actually allowed Simpson and company to keep two wagons. The point on the Big Sandy where this train was burned has since been known as Simpson's Hollow. The Simpson train was burned October 5, 1857. The first two trains had been burned on the evening of October 4 following an all-night ride from Fort Bridger which had begun October 3.

7. Durwood Ball, *Army Regulars...*, p. 162.

8. Andrew Jenson, *Church Chronology*, Op cit., p. 55.

9. *The Cooke Journal* is quoted in Howard R. Driggs' *Westward America...*, pp. 111-12.

10. Durwood Ball, *Army Regulars...*, p. 163.

11. Howard R. Driggs, *Westward America...*, p. 40.

12. Durwood Ball, *Army Regulars...*, p. 84.

13. Durwood Ball, *Army Regulars...*, p. 170.

14. Howard R. Driggs, *The White Indian Boy...*, p. 166.

15. *History of Niels Otto Mortensen*, p. 3.

16. Clare B. Christensen, *History of Niels Christensen...*, pp. 3-4.

17. Andrew Jenson, *Church Chronology, Historical Record 1890*, p. 55.

18. *Congressional Globe*, 35th Congress, 1st Session, February 25, 1858, p. 874. Quoted by B. H. Roberts, Op cit., IV:295-295. According to Leonard J. Arrington's *Great Basin Kingdom: An Economic History of the Latter-day Saints*, University of Nebraska Press, Lincoln, 1958, p. 175, Governor Brigham Young, in a martial law proclamation declared: "Citizens of Utah—we are invaded by a hostile force." If the army were to advance into the territory, the Mormons would "make a Moscow out of every settlement, a Potter's Field of every cañon." Sam Houston had led Texas in its war for independence from Mexico. Through the eyes of personal experience, he knew what Brigham Young and the Mormons could do. His opinion must have carried considerable weight with many of his Senate colleagues. After all, he had been there and done that himself. Arrington's source for the proclamation is House Exec. Document, No. 71, 35th Congress, 1st Session, X, pp.34-35. The source for the Moscow and Potter's Field analogy is Edward J. Tullidge, "The Reformation of Utah," *Harper's New Monthly Magazine*, XLIII (1871), p. 603.

19. Hymn #35, "For the Strength of the Hills," *Hymns of The Church of Jesus Christ of Latter-day Saints*, Deseret Book Company, Salt Lake City, Utah, 1985.

20. *A Sketch of the Lives of Anders Christian Christensen and his Wife, Sophie Marie Christensen*, p.4-5. The writer of this sketch said that during his lifetime Peter would tell of these exploits with a twinkle in his eye. It is indicative of the tremendous sense of adventure and courage which seems to have characterized the handcart pioneers.

21. Clare B. Christensen, *History of Niels Christensen*, Op cit., p. 2.

22. Clare B. Christensen, *History of Ellen Christensen*, Op cit., p. 2.

23. Phyllis Christensen, Mads Christensen..., p. 4.

24. Phyllis Christensen, Mads Christensen..., pp. 8-9.

25. Durwood Ball, *Army Regulars...*p. 164.

26. Taken from the *New York Times*, June 17, 1857 as quoted in the Saturday, July 24, 1857 edition of the *Millennial Star* No. 30 Bol. XX:470-472.

27. Taken from the July 3 *New York Tribune* as quoted in the Saturday July 31, 1858 *Millennial Star*, No. 31, Vol. XX: 493-494.

28. Quoted from the July 5 *London Times* by the Saturday, July 24, 1858, edition of the *Millennial Star*, No. 30, Vol. XX:472.

29. Copies of the official dispatches are recorded in the Saturday August 21, 1858, *Millennial Star*, No. 34, Vol. XX: 531-532.

30. Taken from the June 12 *New York Tribune* as quoted in the Saturday July 10, 1858 *Millennial Star*, No. 28, Vol. XX:445-446.

31. Psalm 46:1, 9-11.

EPILOGUE

The question considered early on as to where and how to begin this account must now be superseded by another, "How does one end?" Great faith had been required to undertake such a demanding journey. Only leaders of equally great faith would have had courage sufficient to ask new disciples to place their all on the altar of sacrifice. It was an Abrahamic-type request which had been asked. In the face of tremendous adversity, the overwhelming majority of the Scandinavian saints did not flinch. In the fires of such trials are forged men and women of celestial character. Simply put, they became extraordinary people, although given the hardship, the hunger, the dust and disease which had resulted in deaths that tithed their ranks during the long pull west, they probably did not consider themselves as extraordinary.

In 1868 Niels Christensen, Martin Hansen and Peter Niels Garff all went back east as teamsters to bring oncoming immigrants west in wagon companies from the railroad's end. The handcart days had become a thing of the past, and, in 1869, the pioneer wagon trains would cease to be. Among the pioneers in the Rawlins Company, of which Peter Garff had been a teamster, was a 12-year-old boy named Evan Stephens who would one day compose significant Latter-day Saint music and serve as director of the Mormon Tabernacle Choir. Years later, Stephens composed the words and music of the "Teamsters' Chorus." In a dedicatory note, Stephens wrote: "To the Teamster, Peter Garff, who drove the 'Welsh Ox Team' in Captain Rawlins' train, 1868, with which the author walked one thousand miles across the plains."[1] (As an aside, when a person of complete integrity and significant leadership ability was needed to address worrisome concerns arising from some questionable practices associated with the initial organization of the Salt Lake City 2002 Winter Olympic games, the city officials turned to a former speaker of the Utah House of Representatives and highly respected Utah businessman, Robert Garff. A great grandson of Peter Niels Garff, Robert Garff has followed the tradition of his faithful kinsmen and has given distinguished service as president of the England Coventry Mission and in 2003 was called as an Area Authority Seventy.)

Niels Christensen and Martin Hansen were a part of the John Doddle Company which went to Omaha. The eastbound trip involved crossing of treacherous rivers swollen by the spring rains. Two teamsters were drowned in one river crossing. They waited seven weeks for immigrants who had been delayed by a cholera outbreak on the Atlantic voyage. That ship was probably the *Emerald Isle*. One of the *Emerald Isle* passengers struck with the dreaded disease was Peter Anton Mortensen. Peter survived, spent time in a New York hospital, and probably came west with the John Doddle Company in which his first cousin, Niels Christensen, was a teamster.

Mads Christensen also served as a teamster. On April 25, 1864, Mads was called to go east to with an ox-team to assist other oncoming emigrants. It must have been a rigorous test of faith, for on March 4, 1864 Maren Johanne had given birth to a daughter, Annie Sophia. Peter, now six-and-a-half, was his mother's chief help. Mads returned to the Salt Lake Valley on 3 October 1864. The tremendous sacrifice requested by the leadership was again matched in service rendered by these faithful Scandinavian Latter-day Saints. The zeal for Zion was real; it was a manifestation of their deepening discipleship, of their love of the Lord Jesus and all who would follow Him.

What became of the descendants of the many unsung heroes among the 7th Handcart Company? Perhaps typical of others is the experience of the family of Niels Christensen. Niels would have but one month of schooling in America. He taught himself to read English by studying the Doctrine and Covenants night after night. Fifteen grandchildren came into his life. Two

An actual surviving handcart, although this one was pulled along side an ox-team company rather than one from the original handcart companies. The Church Museum of History and Art.

of his seven grandsons earned doctorates. Another grandson would have earned a Ph.D. had not the government taken him away from his doctoral studies at Cal Tech to do electronic systems research on the east coast during the bitter war with Nazi Germany. That grandson's research reached its zenith with Mariner's photographic mission to Mars. There are, within his complement of great grandchildren, two Ph.D.s, two M.D.s, one D. Sc., three Juris Doctorates, a former member of the Mormon Tabernacle Choir, one stake president, two mission presidents, one great-granddaughter who is the wife of a stake president and another who has been the wife of mission president, five bishops, and several whose husbands have been bishops. On June 10, 2001, the Iowa City Iowa Stake was created under the direction of Elder Donald L. Stahlei of the Seventy. It had been exactly 144 years since the Scandinavian Company had camped on Clear Creek just west of the city. A great granddaughter of Niels Christensen was called as Relief Society president of the new stake. Yet, these examples are but a superficial indication of their contributions as Church and community members.

Undoubtedly, many other families have similar stories regarding the accomplishments and service given by their descendants. For example, the writer knows that two of Karen Marie Olsen's descendants, Horace D. Ensign and Dale Ensign, have served as mission presidents. Her second great-grand-daughter, Elaine Wright Christensen, has served with her husband, Roger Paul Christensen, Niels Christensen's great-grand-son, since his 2001 call to preside over the California Long Beach Mission. Hans Christensen's great-grandson, David Christensen Harvey, has served as a mission president. Hans' second great-granddaughter, Joan Christensen Baugh, has served with her husband, Gary Baugh, who in 2002 was called to preside over the Sweden Stockholm Mission. Samuel Lublin's descendant, Kenneth L. Zabriskie, has served as a mission and temple president. Martin Hansen's grandson, Cecil Ray Hansen, is the patriarch of the American Fork West Stake.

Essentially all Latter-day Saints who carry the Bastain name are descendants of Jacob. Their contributions have been many and varied. His great-grandson, Morris Bastain, served as president of the South Dakota Rapid City Mission. Another descendant, Larry Bastain, has made a significant contribution to the music of the Church. Dr. Eric Bastain is a prominent food scientist. Jacob's daughter, Serena Amanda Bastain, married Lewis Edwin Farnsworth. Their oldest son, Philo Taylor Farnsworth, is recognized in America as the inventor of television.

Anders Christian Christensen and his wife, Sophie Marie, ultimately settled in Hooper, Utah. Their last child, a son whom they named Anton Christopher, was born 5 November 1859 in Riverdale, Utah. He was twenty years younger than their next youngest child. Thus the remarkable blessing pronounced two-and-a-half years earlier in Denmark was fulfilled. There was another wonderful blessing for Anders and Sophie that season. Christiania came west with the 8th Handcart Company, which was captained by George Rowley. It arrived in the Salt Lake Valley in early September. On 13 October 1859 in the Endowment House, Christiania Sophie married Lars Christian Christensen. Lars had come west in the 7th Company. Ultimately, their marriage was blessed with seven children. The faith so evident in the lives of Anders and Sophie Christensen continues to be manifest in the lives of their descendants. Anton's grandson, Val R. Christensen, serves as a member of the Seventy of the Church.

These visible assignments are only anecdotal samples. Significantly, there are many who have served with devotion as missionaries, teachers, workers in the Sunday School, Relief Society, Primary, Young Women and Young Men's organizations, in the elders quorums and high priest groups, ward organists and choir members, counselors in bishoprics and as members of stake high councils and stake presidencies, wonderful men and women and youth who have gone about privately, quietly doing much good. They are those who have served in the temples and the family history centers, those who have taken orphans and foster children into their homes, committed Latter-day Saints who in the pattern of their devoted ancestors, have paid their tithing and contributed to the care of the poor and needy with no thought of notoriety. They are those who have taken the reverential shepherds at Bethlehem's manger as a model, whose witness of the divinity of the latter-day work has caused many to ponder the meaning of the significant and sacred things of life. They have been among the salt of the earth. They are the seeds spoken of so long ago which fell among the good deep soil, which seeds became rooted deeply and, being nourished by faith in God and the sustenance of their own Christian service, did not wither away and die in the heat of the summer, but valiantly and nobly have withstood the tares sown by an unrelenting adversary. Of them, like their distinguished ancestors, we can sing "blessed, honored pioneer."

And the end is not yet, for this seems to be that time foretold by Joseph Smith when the Scandinavians would play a significant role in the Church. Around the hearthsides of their posterity other fascinating things are known, which should be told, for history is not history until it is written. However, in a very real sense, the history of 7th Handcart Company is ongoing and will not end as long as their descendants are striving for Zion in their own lives. Would those who have given so much to so great a cause expect anything less?

NOTES

1.   Peter Niels Garff, *A Biographical Account...*, pp. 27-29.

APPENDIX I: *Westmoreland* PASSENGER COMPLEMENT

The passenger summary from the *Journal History of the Church* provides the following: "Adults, 8 years and upwards, 404; Children, under 8 years and over one year, 105; Infants under one year, 30." However, names are given only for 319 people, although the Journal History does seem to list husband and wife together. There are a few other family groupings. That roster may have been written by an English clerk as passengers boarded the *Westmoreland,* for the listing is not alphabetical. Furthermore, there is considerable spelling inconsistency between the two passenger lists. The Mormon Immigration Index gives the names for 517, but they are not arranged by family groups. It does give the approximate year of birth. This listing is an attempt to merge the information from both registries and other genealogical information into family units. Heads of families and or single passengers apparently traveling alone are shown in bold type. There is no known roster for the 7th Handcart Company. Therefore, known and probable 7th Handcart Company members are identified in bold type.

Origin:

Ticket#

AHLGREN, Amalia

<1835>

BMR, p. 62

ANDERSEN, Karen [This may be Karen Marie Hansen Anderson, the mother of Mads Christensen. Pages 5-6 of the Mads Christensen history indicate she joined the Church and went to Utah with her son in the 7th Company. However, Mads mother was born/ christened September

29, 1798 at Stokkemarke, Maribo, Denmark so there are possibly two in the company named Karen Andersen.]
<1795> Jutland (SMR)

ANDERSEN, Jens Christian

<1822> born May 4, 1821 (Vesterhedegaard). He and his wife, Margreta, and children, Lauritz Peter, Andrea Cathrine, Boletta Kirstine and Josephine Brighamina were members of the 7th Handcart Company.

Jutland (SMR)

Shoemaker

ANDERSEN, Margreta Christiansen Nielsen

<1831> born June 29, 1830

BMR, p. 70 Sealand (SMR)

ANDERSEN, Lauritz Peter

<1850> born July 23, 1849

ANDERSEN, Andrea Cathrine J.

<1852> born November 14, 1851

BMR, p. 55 Lolland Conf. (SMR)

ANDERSEN, Boletta Kirstine

<1854> born February 18, 1855

ANDERSEN, Josephine B.

<1856> March 4, 1856

Infant" (BMR) "Age: 1/2" (SMR)

ANDERSEN, Ole [Ole is spelled Ota in the *Journal History*]

<1822>

BMR, p. 67 Jutland (SMR)

Farmer

ANDERSEN, Anna

<1831>

BMR, p. 68

ANDERSEN, Karen Marie

<1800>

ANDERSON, Gustav [Mulder, Op cit., p.218 identifies Gustav Anderson as a master stonemason. Gustav, wife Maren, and son Carl August as members of the **7th Handcart Company**.]

<1821>

Stonemason
ANDERSON, Maren
<1823>
ANDERSON, Carl August
<1846>
ANDERSON, Anders
<1824>
Tailor
ANDERSEN, Anna Chr.
<1827>
BMR, p. 60
ANDERSEN, Karen Marie
<1838>
BMR, p. 64 Falster (SMR)
ANDERSEN, Anna Nelsine
<1841>
BMR, p. 58 Jutland (SMR)
ANDERSEN, Anne
<1841>
BMR, p. 66 Jutland (SMR)
ANDERSON, Anna Catrine
<1836>
ANDERSON, Anna
<1837>
ANDERSON, Karen
<1837>
ARVIDSON, Anna [Anna Arvidson is given in the *Journal History*]
AXELSEN, Johanne
<1812>
BMR, p. 59 Sealand (SMR)
BASTIAN, Jacob Married **Gertrude Petersen** April 24, 1857 on board the *Westmoreland* at Liverpool, England. <1836> born 14 March 1835. After Gertrude's death September 16, 1857 in Salt Lake City, Utah Jacob married Johanna Marie Sander (Sanderson, October 25, 1857. Members of the **7th Handcart Company**.

BMR, p. 62 Sealand (SMR)
Carpenter
BENTSON, Jorgen
<1807>
BMR, p. 55 Lolland Conference (SMR)
Mechanic
BENTSON, Bertha
<1818>
BENTSON, Anna Kirstine
<1842>
BENTSON, Caroline Frederikka
<1850>
BENTSON, Nils Peter
<1852>
BENTSON, Anna Thora
<1855>
BERTHELSEN, Karen
<1831>
BMR, p. 58 Jutland (SMR)
BERTHELSEN, Anne Maria [Anne Maria and Johannes were apparently a sister and a brother.]
<1837>
BMR, p. 58 Jutland (SMR)
BERTHELSEN, Johannes
<1843>
BLOMDAL, Anders [his name is also given as Anders Hakenson or Blomdahl or Blumdoll. Given as Blomdallia in the *Journal History*.] <1850> born 1829 at Malmo, Sweden
BMR, p. 67
Carpenter
BLOMDAL, Mary [Marie Pehrson and Mary Nelson (?)]
<1821>
BLOMDAL, Anna
<1850>
BLOMDAL, Kirsti
<1856> born January 21, 1855
BLOMDAL, Peter

<1857> born January 4, 1857 at Ostra, Skravlinge, Sweden Infant" (BMR)

infant

BOHNE, Helsina [A widow with five children, Jens Carl J., Henrik Morten, Sophus Morten, Anna Sophie and Joseph Smith Bohne. Her husband, Carl Frederick Bohne, died in the Baltic Sea in the 1854-55 period. Helsina remarried Svend Larsen sometime after her arrival in Utah. Bohne is also spelled Bohna in some documents.]

<1819> born: April 11, 1819; died: June 11, 1890, Mt Pleasant, Utah.

BMR, p. 57 Jutland (SMR)

BOHNE, Jens Carl J.

<1844> died in 1888.

BOHNE, Henrik Morten, born: October 29, 1845; died May 15, 1920, Cardston, Alberta, Canada.

<1846>

BOHNE, Sophus Morten, born: March 29, 1848; died: March 23, 1933, Mt. Pleasant, Utah.

<1849>

BOHNE, Anna Sophia, born: August 8, 1851; died: October 23, 1895, Mt. Pleasant, Utah

<1852>

BMR, p. 57

BOHNE, Joseph Smith, born March 8, 1855; died February 12, 1917.

<1855>

BRODERSON, Christian [First wife, Ane Mortensen, died May 2, 1851]

<1812>

BMR,p.56 Falster,Lolland,SMR

Farmer

BRODERSON, Elsa Mortensen [Second wife of Christian Broderson or Brothersen, married March 19, 1852]

<1827>

BRODERSON, Dorthea [Diantha]

<1847> born December 18, 1847 at Maribo, Denmark to

Christian Broderson and Ane Mortensen

BRODERSON, Hans

<1850> born February 15, 1850 at Maribo, Denmark to Christian Broderson and Ane Mortensen

BRODERSON, Bohn or Bohne

<1852> born April 4, 1851 to Christian Broderson and Ane Mortensen at Maribo, Denmark

BRODERSON, Morten

<1854> born May 30, 1853 to Christian Broderson and Elsa Mortensen at Falster, Walser, Denmark

BRODERSON, Anna

<1856> born January 6, 1856 to Christian Broderson and Elsa Mortensen

CARLSEN, Lars [Karlsen or Karolson] Lars, his wife, Brita Andersen and son Claus Herman were 7th Handcart Company members. Lars died September 6, 1857 at Fort Bridger.

<1813>

BMR,p.63 Copenhagen Conf.SMR

Farmer

CARLSEN, Brita Andersen

<1823>

CARLSEN, Claus Herman

<1850>

CARLSEN, Rasmus [Listed in the *Journal History.* However, a Rasmus Clausen is given in the MII.]

CHRISTENSEN, Stephen

<1801>

BMR, p. 66 Jutland (SMR)

CHRISTENSEN, Anna Maria

<1799>

CHRISTENSEN, Karen Margreta

<1843>

CHRISTENSEN, Anders Christian [Anders Christian Christensen, his wife and children were **7th Handcart Company** members according to Val R. Christensen, a great-grandson. Christiania Sophie, the oldest daughter, did not emigrate until 1859. Christiania married Lars C. Christensen of the **7th Handcart Company** October 13, 1859 in the Endowment House.]

<1809> born: September 4, 1808, Mijgdale, Denmark

BMR, p. 66 Jutland (SMR)

Farmer

CHRISTENSEN, Sophia Maria

<1815> born: March 13, 1814 Snells, Triested, Denmark

CHRISTENSEN, Anna Margreta

<1838> born: January 20, 1837

CHRISTENSEN, Peter Christian

<1841> born: February 5, 1839

CHRISTENSEN, Hans [Hans, his wife, Ellen Poulsdatter Christensen Christensen, and her sons, Poul Pedersen (Paul Christensen) and Niels Pedersen (Niels Christensen), were 7th Handcart Company members.]

<1820> born: September 12, 1819 in Denmark

BMR, p. 61 Sealand (SMR)

Farmer

CHRISTENSEN, Ellen Poulsdatter Christensen [Hans Christensen was her second husband]

<1811> born: December 5, 1810 at Nykobell, Sorø, Denmark

CHRISTENSEN or CHRISTENSON or CHRISTIAN-SON, Jacob. [This may have been the family who bought a wagon while crossing Iowa with the 7th Company, and went west from Florence with Captain Cowley s wagon company. Frederick Hansen reports this incident and gives the spelling as Christenson. The children of Jacob and Dorthea are Hans, Anna, Niels, Anton Peter, Inger Maria, and Franklin.]

<1807>

CHRISTENSEN, Dorthea Chr.

<1818>

CHRISTENSEN, Hans [Apparently the son of Jacob and Dorthea Christensen]

<1841>

Farmer

CHRISTENSEN, Anna
  <1843>
CHRISTENSON, Niels
  <1847>
CHRISTENSEN, Anton Peter
  <1852>
CHRISTENSEN, Inger Maria
  <1855>
CHRISTENSEN, Franklin **[Apparently died in June 1857.]**
  <1857>
Christensen, Jacob and I. C. Christensen [listed only in
the *Journal History.*]
CHRISTENSEN, Jacob
  <1828>
CHRISTENSEN, Magdalena
  <1829>
  Jutland (SMR)
CHRISTENSEN, Thomas
  <1856>
CHRISTENSEN, Hans
  <1831>born 1831. [A sub-captain of 10 handcarts who rescued Christina Olsen during a handcart crossing of the
Platte. Member of the **7th Handcart Company.**]
  BMR, p.55 Lolland Conf.(SMR)
  Farmer
CHRISTENSEN, Carl Chr. A. [Was a full-time missionary
serving as president of the Brevig Norway Conference composed of eight branches when he was released and allowed
to emigrate in 1857. Married Elise Haarby of Norway on
board the *Westmoreland* April 24, 1857 at Liverpool. He
and his wife were members of the 7th Handcart Company of
which he was a sub-captain of 16 handcarts after the reorganization at Florence, Nebraska.]
  <1832> BMR, p. 68 Copenhagen (SMR)
  Painter
CHRISTENSEN, Jens Chr. [Son of Stephen and Anna Maria
Christensen]

<1833>
Jutland (SMR)
Laborer
CHRISTENSEN, Lars Christian [Member of **7th Handcart Company.**]
<1833>
Jutland (SMR)
Laborer
CHRISTENSEN, Karen
<1837>
BMR, p. 65 Jutland (SMR)
CHRISTENSEN, Nils
<1833>
BMR, p. 58 Jutland (SMR)
Farmer
CHRISTENSEN, Christiana
<1834>
CHRISTENSEN, Carolina C.
<1854>
CHRISTENSEN, Andrea
<1856>
CHRISTENSEN, Christina
<1857>
Infant" (BMR)
infant
CHRISTENSEN, Maren Cathrine
<1839>
BMR, p. 63 Lolland (SMR)
CHRISTENSEN, Karen K.
<1840>
BMR, p. 60
CHRISTENSEN, Maren Sophia
<1841>
Lolland Conference (SMR)
CHRISTENSEN, Mads [Mads, wife, Maren Johanna and son, Peter were members of the 7th Handcart Company along with his mother, Karen Marie Hansen Andersen.

Members of the C. C. A. Christensen sub-company according to Mads Christensen history, p.7]
<1824> born March 24, 1825
Lolland Conference (SMR)
Farmer
CHRISTENSEN, Maren Johanna
<1827>
CHRISTENSEN, Peter [Born December 9, 1856, Peter survived the handcart journey and grew to maturity.]
<1857>
Infant" (BMR) "Age: 5/12" (SMR)
infant
CHRISTENSEN, Christiane
<1835>
CHRISTENSEN, Sohie or Sohie CHRISTOPHERSON
[Either the nurse or midwife to Marie Jacobsen Garff. Given as a Sophia Christopherson in the *Journal History*.]
<1837> Sealand (SMR)
CHRISTENSEN, Karen
<1837>
CHRISTENSON, Madselina
<1851>
CHRISTENSEN, Christian S.
<1854>
CHRISTENSON, Sarah K.
<1856>
Christianson, Hans and M. S. Christianson [are listed in the *Journal History*.]
CLAUSEN, Rasmus
<1844>
BMR,p.55Falster,
Lolland Conf. SMR
CLOUSON, Niels
<1841> BMR, p. 56 Lolland Conf (SMR)
Laborer
Cowley, Matthias [President of the Latter-day Saint Company on board the *Westmoreland*.]

DORIUS, Carl Chr. N. [Released as a missionary to Norway and allowed to emigrate in 1857. Married Ellen Rolfson of Norway on board the *Westmoreland* at Liverpool April 24, 1857. Was a sub-captain of 16 handcarts after the reorganization at Florence. Carl and Johan were brothers. Member of the 7th Handcart Company.]
<1831> BMR, p. 68 Copenhagen (SMR)
Carpenter (*History of Scandinavian Mission* p.86 identifies his trade.)

DORIUS, Johan Fr. F. [Released as a missionary and allowed to emigrate in 1857. Married Karen Frantzen of Norway on board the *Westmoreland* at Liverpool April 24, 1857. Was a sub-captain of 16 handcarts after the reorganization at Florence. Member of the **7th Handcart Company**.] As a priest, he and John E. Forsgren were the first missionaries to the island of Falster. <1833>
BMR, p. 68 Copenhagen (SMR)
Shoemaker

EGGERTSEN, Simon Petersen [Member of the **7th Handcart Company**. Served as a missionary from 1854-57. Performed military service in Echo Canyon following his arrival in Utah. Married Johanne Andreason, February 7, 1858.] <1826> BMR, p. 68 See "Petersen, Simon" (EECI). Given as Simon Petersen in the *Journal History*.
Farmer

ERIKSEN, Marcus [Marcus, his wife, Kirsten, daughter, Kirstina, and mother-in-law Metta Nielsen (Nilson) crossed Iowa with the **7th Handcart Company**, at which point, due to the health of others, Kirstina went on alone to join a sister who had emigrated earlier. The others came west in either 1858 or 1859 for Metta died at Lehi, Utah, 1859.]
<1809>
BMR, p. 57 Jutland (SMR)
ERIKSEN, Kirsten Christensen
<1808>

ERIKSEN, Kirstina [Daughter of Marcus and Kirsten. 7th Handcart Company.]

<1838>
Spinster
ERIKSEN, Erik G. [Single, according to the *Journal History*. Erik Gustaf Eriksen was a missionary in Sweden according to Andrew Jenson, History of the Scandinavian Mission, pp.77, 101.] <1826>
ESBJORNSEN, Anna
<1825>
BMR, p. 63 Copenhagen Conf.(SMR)
ESKILDSEN, Jens [Jens Weaver Eskelson. Name is given as Fakjldsen on the *Journal History* list. Jens and his family were among those who stayed for a time in Nebraska. Probable **7th Handcart Company** members from Iowa City to Florence. Two children were born 10 miles west of Nemaha, Nebraska: Oscar in 1858 and Elnora Ellen in 1860. Three additional children were born in Utah: Ephraim in 1863, James in 1865 and David in 1867.]
<1826>
BMR, p. 62 Copenhagen Conf. (SMR)
Weaver
ESKILDSEN, Sophia Cathrine
<1831>
Slesvig (SMR)
ESKILDSEN, Emina E.
<1851>
Copenhagen (SMR)
ESKILDSEN, Rosa Fransisca [Twins Rosanna Francisca and Rosa Frances. Rosa apparently did not survive.]
<1853>
Copenhagen (SMR)
ESKILDSEN, Malvina Josephine
<1854>
ESKILDSEN, Joseph E.
<1856>
FOLKMAN, Jorgen Chr. [Member of the **7th Handcart Company**.]
<1793>

BMR, p. 68 Bornholm Conf.SMR

FOLKMAN, Jens Peter [Son of Jorgen C. Folkman. Member of the **7th Handcart Company.** Served as cook on board the *Westmoreland* according to the *Journal History*.]
<1829>
Tailor

FRANTZEN, Lars [Lars' wife, Martha Marie, his daughter, Karen, who married Johan Dorius, and son, Johannes, came west with the **7th Handcart Company.**]
<1812>
BMR, p. 68
Farmer

FRANTZEN, Martha Maria
<1812>

FRANTZEN, Karen
<1836>

FRANTZEN, Johannes
<1838>
Printer

FREDRICKSEN, Dorthea
<1844>
Listed on the *Westmoreland* [1857]; p. 56. "Shall not emigrate" (SMR)

FUNCH, Kirstine Mathilde [Christine Funck]. Born May 2, 1840, Aakirkeby, Bornholm, Denmark; baptized June 30, 1858; married Peder Jensen March 12, 1865; died February 11, 1900.
<1837>
BMR, p. 57 Bornholm Conf SMR

GARFF, Niels [Niels and his family came west with the **Cowley Wagon Train.** After his death on the plains near Fort Laramie, when the co-owner of his wagon turned back, his oldest son **Peter Niels** came west with the **7th Handcart Company.**]
<1811>
BMR, p. 61 Sealand (SMR)
Farmer-freeholder

GARFF, Maria
<1821>

GARFF, Peter Niels [Member of the **7th Handcart Company**.]
<1844>

GARFF, Christian
<1847>

GARFF, Lauritz
<1852>

GARFF, Trine [Died two or three days after her father in the vicinity of Fort Laramie.]
<1855>

Garff, Decan "Dicken" *Westmoreland*, born on the Atlantic on board the *Westmoreland*, May 3, 1857.]

GUDMUNDSEN, Gudmund [Married Marie Jacobsen Garff some months after arriving in Utah. Came west with either the Cowley Wagon Company or the **7th Handcart Company**. Served as cook on board the *Westmoreland* according to the *Journal History*.] <1828>
BMR, p. 70 Sealand (SMR)
Goldsmith

Hagerup, Jorgen [is listed as a member of the *Westmoreland* Company in the *Journal History*, but is not listed in the *Mormon Immigration Index*.]

HAHNBERG, Johanna M. [Johanna Christine Hahnberg or Handberg, daughter of John Hahnberg and Christine Tratne of Denmark. Member **7th Handcart Company**.]
<1839> BMR, p. 63 Fuen (SMR)

HNSON, Elsa [Member of **7th Handcart Company**. On the *Journal History* list the spelling is given as Havkunsen.]
<1836>
BMR, p. 64
Spinster

HNSON, Anna [Member of **7th Handcart Company**. On the *Journal History* list the spelling is given as Havkunsen.]
<1840>
Spinster

Halner, Hans [Given in the *Journal History.*]
HALVORSEN, Olaus
<1847>
BMR, p. 68
HAMMER, Hans [Bornholm, Denmark. Died during the rail journey from Philadelphia to Iowa City.]
<1793>
HANSEN, Anna Cathrina [This may be **Johanne Cathrine Hansen**, the mother of Johanna Marie Sanderson or Sander. If so, this individual came in the 7th Handcart Company.]
<1819>
HANSEN, Gottlob Andreas [Father of Peter HANSEN
<1824>]
<1804>
BMR, p. 60 Sealand (SMR)
Farmer
HANSEN, Jorgen [Husband of Anna HANSEN.]
<1819>
BMR, p. 69 Fuen (SMR)
Farmer
HANSEN, Anna
<1821>
HANSEN, Karen
<1849>
HANSEN, Hans
<1852>
HANSEN, Hans
Musician
HANSEN, Christian [Members of the **7th Handcart Company** from Iowa City to the Loup Fork crossing at which point the strength of both Christian and his wife, Inger, failed. Stayed at Genoa for a time, then returned to Council Bluffs. Came on to Utah by wagon in 1861 and settled in American Fork. Children are Morten who changed his name to Martin, Karen, Anna, Hans and Maren.]
<1820>

BMR, p. 64 Copenhagen (SMR)

Shoemaker

HANSEN, Inger

<1826>

HANSEN, Morten [Martin Hansen]

<1847>

HANSEN, Karen

<1849>

HANSEN, Anna

<1851>

HANSEN, Hans

<1853>

HANSEN, Maren

<1856> [Died: June 6, 1857 during the rail journey from Philadelphia to Iowa City.]

HANSEN, Anna

<1821>

HANSEN, Hans [Hans and Bertha Maria and their six children were members of the **7th Handcart Company** from Iowa City to Florence at which point the health of the mother, Bertha Maria, required them to remain at Florence. Apparently this family never came west. Ultimately their son, Frederik, and perhaps others became affiliated with the Reorganized Church of Jesus Christ of Latter Day Saints, a denomination which changed its name to the Community of Christ on April 6, 2001.

HANSEN, Bertha Maria

<1823>

BMR, p. 63 Sealand (SMR)

HANSEN, Frederik

<1845>

BMR, p. 64

HANSEN, Hans

<1848>

BMR, p. 64

Farmer

HANSEN, Maria

<1850>
BMR, p. 63
HANSEN, Ola
<1852>
BMR, p. 64
HANSEN, Erastamine [Erastusina]
HANSEN, Haightina
<1856>
BMR, p. 64 "Inf." "Age: 1/2" (SMR)
HANSEN, Peter
<1824>
37 or 35?
Tailor
HANSEN, Jens Peter
<1827>
BMR, p. 60 Copenhagen (SMR)
Tailor
HANSEN, Bengte Kristine [Also given as Gengia Ch. Hanson.
Listed as Bengt Hansen in the *Journal History*.]
HANSEN, Anders
<1828>
BMR, p. 69 Fuen (SMR)
Stonecutter
HANSEN, Maren Kirstine
<1828>
HANSEN, Peter
<1828>
BMR, p. 70 Sealand (SMR)
Laborer
HANSEN, Karen
<1849>
HANSEN, Hans
<1852>
HANSEN, Mads
<1854>
HANSEN, Hannah M.
<1857>

Infant" (BMR)

infant

HANSEN, Sarah

<1857>

Infant" (BMR) "Age: 1/4" (SMR)

infant

HANSEN, Christian

<1838>

Joiner

HANSEN, Embret [Embreth, his wife Hannah, and her daughter by a prior marriage, Maren Christina, were members of the **7th Handcart Company.** Embreth died at Devil s Gate, August 22, 1857.]

<1826>

Joiner

HANSEN, Hannah M. [Margrette Ohlsen Englestead Jacobsen Hansen]

<1820>

HANSEN, Maren Christina [Mary Jacobsen]

<1852>

Hanson, Jorgen and Anna [Listed in the *Journal History.*]

HARBYE, Elise Rosalie Sternhjem Scheel [Haarbye which was her step-father's name] married C. C. A. Christensen on board **the** *Westmoreland* at Liverpool April 24, 1857. Member **7th Handcart Company.** Scheel is the name given on the *Westmoreland* roster in the *Journal History.*   <1835>

BMR, p. 68

HJETTING, Mette Maria. Born November 28, 1830, the younger sister of Helsina Jensen Hjetting Bohne.

<1832>

BMR, p. 57 (Kietting) Jutland (SMR)

HOLM, Jens N. Born: March 23, 1818, Dyndegaard, Bornholm, Denmark; died: April 22, 1908, Lehi, Utah.

<1818>

BMR, p.57Bornholm Conf SMR

Shoemaker

HOLM, Margreta Chr. Born: August 14, 1817; married April 30, 1842, Arnager, Nylarsker, Bornholm; died January 28, 1890, Lehi, Utah.

<1818>

BMR, p. 57

HOLM, Margreta Christina. Born: September 5, 1843, Nylarsker, Bornholm, Denmark; married David J. Evans May 4, 1861, Endowment House, Salt Lake City, Utah; died June 17, 1898, Lehi, Utah.

<1844>

BMR, p. 57

HOSTGAARD, Mariana

<1815>

BMR, p. 57 Jutland (SMR)

HULTBERG, Christopher [Christopher, his wife, Karna and children Anna Catrina and Anders were from Sweden. They were members of the **7th Handcart Company**.]

<1822>

BMR, p. 67

Farmer

HULTBERG, Karna

<1821>

BMR, p. 67

HULTBERG, Anna Catrina

<1850>

BMR, p. 67

HULTBERG, Anders

<1854>

BMR, p. 67

IVERSON, Malena

<1779>

JACOBSEN, Ingeborg [Spelled Jacobson in the *Journal History*.]

<1806>

BMR, p. 68

JACOBSEN, Olaus

<1847>

JACOBSEN, Karen
<1827>
BMR, p.61 Sealand (SMR)

JACOBSEN, Soren
<1832>
BMR, p. 65 Jutland (SMR)
Weaver

JACOBSEN, Lars [7th Handcart Company, husband of **Inger Andrea THOMSEN.]**
<1834>
BMR, p. 54 Jutland (SMR)
Laborer

JACOBSEN, Camilla Dorthea
<1841>

JENSEN, Peter
<1804>
Laborer

JENSEN, Jacob <1806> [Married to **Maria JENSEN** <1812> (?) according to the *Journal History* record.]

JENSEN, Anders [Anders Jensen and wife, Anna Rasmussen, were members of the **7th Handcart Company.** They had buried four of five children in Denmark.]
<1806> BMR, p.8 Jut., Lolland Conf SMR)
Farmer

JENSEN, Anna Rasmussen
<1811>
Lolland Conference (SMR)

JENSEN, Christiane [7th Handcart Company, daughter of Anders and Anna Jensen. Married Anders Thomsen or Thomson, a pioneer of the 1853 Forsgren company on November 21, 1857. (Christiana Jensen Thomsen by Ethel S. Lowe. Mulder Op cit., 189-190.)] <1838> Born August 6, 1837, Lolland, Denmark.
Lolland Conference (SMR)
Spinster

JENSEN, Mariane [7th Handcart Company, daughter of

Anders and Anna Jensen. Mariane Mary Ann was born a twin, but her twin sister had not survived.] <1843>
Lolland Conference (SMR)
Denmark

JENSEN, Jens [Jens and his family were members of the **7th Handcart Company**. Given as Jens and K. K. Jenson in the *Journal History*.]
<1809>
BMR, p. 59 Sealand (SMR)
Tailor

JENSEN, Karen Kirstine
<1819>
BMR, p. 59

JENSEN, Karen Sophia
<1843>
BMR, p. 59

JENSEN, Hans Peter
<1845>
BMR, p. 59

JENSEN, Christiana Maria
<1851>
BMR, p. 59

JENSEN, Josephina Jacobine
<1856>
BMR, p. 59 "Inf"BMR "1/2" SMR

JENSEN, Karen [Karen and Ludvig Jensen are listed in succession in the *Journal History*. Perhaps Karen is a widow, and Ludvig is her son.]
<1811>
BMR, p. 58 Jutland (SMR)

JENSEN, Ludvig D.
<1841>

JENSEN, Hans [Hans and wife, Sissie Marie, and children were members of the **7th Handcart Company.**]
<1817>
BMR, p. 61 Sealand (SMR)
Farmer

JENSEN, Marie [Sissie Marie]
<1815>
JENSEN, Jens [James Jenson wrote an account of the journey.] James is the name given in Hafen and Hafen s account, but not on ship's listing.
JENSEN, Karen
<1844>
JENSEN, Jacob
<1846>
JENSEN, Soren Peter
<1851>
JENSEN, Maria Sophia [Died on the plains, probably in July 1857.]
<1856> Infant" (BMR) "Age: 1/2" (SMR)
JENSEN, Jorgen [Spelled Jenson in the *Journal History*.]
<1818>
BMR, p. 68 Fuen (SMR)
Miller
JENSEN, Birthe Maria [Given as Bertha M. Jenson in the *Journal History*.]
<1842>
BMR, p. 68 Fuen (SMR)
JENSEN, Jens
<1823>
BMR, p. 70 Jutland (SMR)
Weaver
JENSEN, Anna Marie
<1824>
Jutland (SMR)
JENSEN, Jens Christian
<1843>
JENSEN, Soren Peter
<1847>
JENSEN, Anna
<1850>
JENSEN, Andreas
<1852>

JENSEN, Mads
    <1823>
    BMR, p. 65 Jutland (SMR)
    Farmer
JENSEN, Maren
    <1824>
JENSEN, Ane
    <1849>
JENSEN, Peter
    <1851>
JENSEN, Jacob J. H.
    <1854>
JENSEN, Jens Martin
    <1857>
    Inf "BMR"Age: 2 mo. (SMR)
    infant
JENSEN, Jens
    <1824>
    BMR, p. 60
    Farmer
JENSEN, Ida Louise
    <1821>
    BMR, p. 60
JENSEN, Anders
    <1827>
    BMR, p. 60 Cop. Conf.(SMR)
    Laborer
JENSEN, Ingeline
    <1824>
    BMR, p. 50
JENSEN, Ephraim Gottfred [Son of Anders and Ingerline Jensen, died on the Atlantic May 17, 1857.]
    <1856>
    BMR, p. 60 "Inf" BMR "1/2" SMR
JENSEN, Adolphia
    <1857>
    BMR, p. 60

infant

JENSEN, Anna Sorene [Given as Anna S. Jenson in the *Journal History.*]

    <1827>

    BMR, p. 71

JENSEN, Jens [Jens and wife Maria were members of the **7th Handcart Company**. Jens had been serving as a missionary and as president of the Lolland Conference composed of eight branches when he was released and allowed to emigrate.] <1831>

    Jutland, Lolland Conf.(SMR)

    Carpenter

JENSEN, Maria

    <1831>

    BMR, p. 61 Sealand (SMR)

JENSEN, Ellen Catrina [Ellen C and Karen Jenson are listed together in the *Journal History.*]

    <1822>

    P. 67 Jutland (SMR)

JENSEN, Karen

    <1836>

    Jutland (SMR)

JENSEN, Stine [Given as Stina in the *Journal History.*]

    <1839>

    Sealand (SMR)

JENSON, Jens and Johanna [Are listed together in the *Journal History,* but do not seem to be given in the *Mormon Immigration Index.*]

JENSEN, Anna

    <1821> [Given as Anna Jenson in the *Journal History.*]

JENSEN, Anna Marie [**7th Handcart Company.** Given as Anne M. Jenson in the *Journal History.* Born September 23, 1833, Rybjorg, Denmark; baptized July 20, 1854 .]

JENSEN, Anna <1833> [Given as Anna Jenson in the *Journal History.*]

Jepperson, Nils P. [Shipped as a seaman, according to the *Journal History.*]

Jepperson, Susanna [Listed in the *Journal History*.]
JEPPESEN, Soren
  Farmer
JEPPESEN, Anne Katrine
JEPPESEN, Niels S.
  Farmer
JEPPESEN, Peter S.
  Farmer
JEPPESEN, Anne Kirstine
JEPPESEN, Johanna S.
JEPPESEN, Karen S.
JOHANSEN, Maren Kirstine
  <1824>
  BMR, p. 58 Jutland (SMR)
JOANSON, Frederikka
  <1841>
JOHANESEN, Jens
  <1837>
JOHANSEN, Anna Maria
  <1785>
JOHANSEN, Anna Else [Given as Anna F. Johanson in the
  Journal History]
  <1816>
JOHANSEN, Maren Kirstine
  <1824>
JOHANSON, Christiana
  <1829>
JOHNSEN, Maria Elisabet [Given a Maria E. Johnson in
  the *Journal History*]
  <1803>
  BMR, p. 68
JOHNSEN, Eric [The Johnsens were all part of a family unit.
  Relationships are not known. Maria is possibly an older sis-
  ter of Eric who may be married to Johanna, with the possibility that Caroline Cecilia is their daughter. Spelled
  Johnson in the *Journal History*]
  <1805>

Joiner

JOHNSEN, Johanna [A Johanna Johanson is given in the *Journal History*]

<1811>

BMR, p. 68

JOHNSEN, Caroline Cecilia [Given as Johnson in the *Journal History*]

<1835>

BMR, p. 68

JORANSON, Frederick

<1838>

JORGENSEN, Jacob [Jacob and Elina Cathrine Jorgensen are listed together in the *Journal History*.]

<1819>

BMR, p. 59 Jutland (SMR)

51&826?

JORGENSEN, Elina Cathrine

<1818>

JORGENSEN, Thorwald Herman G.

<1850>

Copenhagen Conference (SMR)

JORGENSEN, Jens [Had been serving as a missionary and as president of the Frederica Conference which was composed of eight branches when he was released and allowed to emigrate.]

<1824>

BMR, p. 71 Jutland (SMR)

Farmer

JORGENSEN, Christiana

<1829>

JORGENSEN, John Smith

<1856>

Jorgensen, Niels Otto [Given as Nils Otts Jorgeson in the *Journal History* and Jorgansen in the Sorensen Family papers. He was a wheelwright apprentice in Nicholai Sorensen s shop in Haverup, Sorø, DK. <1838>]

JULANDER, Jacob Andreas [Died June 5, 1898 Monroe,

Sevier, Utah.]

<1813> BMR, p. 57 Copenhagen (SMR)

Iron Founder

JULANDER, Johanna Kirstina [Maiden name: Johanna Kirstina Voight or Vacht]

<1821>

Jutland (SMR)

JULANDER, Johan Wilhelm [Son of Jacob Andreas Julander and Henrietta Kyhnall.]

<1842>

JULANDER, Anna Carolina [Daughter of Jacob Andreas and Johanna Kirstina Julander.]

<1847>

JULANDER, Brigham Nephi [Son of Jacob Andreas and Johanna Kirstina Julander.]

<1854>

JULANDER, Juliana Cecilia [Son of Jacob Andreas and Johanna Kirstina Julander.]

<1856>

JUST, Peter Andersen [Of the 5 JUST children, apparently only Nils Andersen Just survived. That statistic would suggest they were probably members of the **7th Handcart Company**.]

<1817>

BMR, p. 65 Jutland (SMR)

Brickmaker

JUST, Karen Marie Christensen

<1824>

JUST, Christen

<1846>

JUST, Nils Andersen [born: April 17, 1847]

<1848>

JUST, Jens

<1850>

JUST, Joseph

<1856>

JUST, Hyrum

<1857>

Infant" (BMR) "Age: 1/4" (SMR)

infant

KAGERUP, Jorgen N.

<1828>

BMR, p. 70 Sealand (SMR)

Coachman

KNUDSON, Christen [Christen and Karen are listed together in the *Journal History*.]

<1805>

BMR, p. 60 Sealand (SMR)

Farmer

KNUDSON, Karen

<1789>

KOFOED, Margreta Cathrine [Sina Dorthea and Thora Maria are apparently her daughters.]

<1820>

BMR, p. 57 Bornholm Conf SMR

Spinster

KOFOED, Sina Dorthea

<1848>

KOFOED, Thora Maria

<1852>

KOFOED, Else Kirstina [Mother of Hans Anker Kofoed. **Apparently died at Omaha prior to 1860 census.**]

<1785>. She was one of two women in the 7th Company were known to have been blind.

KOFOED, Hans Anker or Ancher [Probably members of the 7th Handcart Company from Iowa City to Florence. In 2001, the Kofoed family is uncertain about whether they came by wagon or handcart, but they were dealing with a difficult health situation. Several of the children were ill as was Hans mother, Else Kirstina Kofoed. That would tend indicate they were among those whom the leadership thought best to remain in Nebraska and get their strength before coming on to Utah. The Jimmy Parker account p. 52 indicates that Hans had told the story of their walking barefoot across Iowa, because their shoes were worn out. The Kofoed family remained at Florence. They went west with the **John P. Taylor Wagon Train** which departed Florence July 3, 1860.]

<1812>

KOFOED, Cecelia

<1816>

KOFOED, Mesella Christena [Daughter of Hans and Cecelia KOFOED. Married George Stevens and remained in Nebraska.]

<1840>

KOFOED, Christian Anthon

<1841>

KOFOED, Anna Elisina (Ane Elisine)

<1842>

KOFOED, Hans Peter [Not in the 1860 Nebraska census. May have died.]

<1844>

KOFOED, Johanna Margrethe

<1846>

KOFOED, Ancher August

<1848>

KOFOED, Jens Hansen

<1849>

KOFOED, Wilhelmina Frederickke (Amelia F.)

<1851>

KOFOED, Josephina Brighamine

<1855>

KRAGSCHOU or Kragskov, Soren Jensen [Soren Jensen Kragschou, his wife, Maren and their children Christina Maria, Peter Christian and Joseph Severin all went west with the Matthias Cowley Wagon Train. Soren Jensen Kragschou died June 29, 1857 and was buried in Iowa.]

<1778>

KRASCHOU or Kragskov, Maren

<1802>

KRAGSCHOU or Kragskov, Christina Maria

<1830>
KRAGSCHOU or Kragskov, Peter Christian
    <1831>
KRAGSCHOU or Kragskov, Joseph Severin
    <1855>
LARSEN, Johanna Maria
    <1803>
    Jutland (SMR)
LARSEN, Petronella
    <1822>
LARSEN, Ole
    <1823>
LARSEN, Christen Greis. Born December 17, 1828, bap-
    tized March 15, 1851, married Karen Maria Sorensen,
    daughter of Peter H. Sorensen April 1, 1857 at Copenhagen.
    Christen had been serving as a missionary and as president
    of the Bornholm Conference composed of four branches.
    Christian and Karen would have 11 children. <1829>
LARSEN, Mads
    <1831>
    BMR, p. 61 Sealand (SMR)
    Farmer
LARSEN, Lauritz [Lauritz had been serving as a missionary
    and as president of the Vendsyssel Conference composed of
    12 branches, when he was released and allowed to emigrate.
    Married **Anna Marie THOMSEN** on board the
    Westmoreland, April 24, 1857.]
    <1834> Jutland (SMR)
    Laborer
LARSEN, Marina
    <1837>
    BMR, p. 54 Jutland (SMR)
    Spinster
LARSEN, Kirstine Marie [Came with the Kragschou family
    to Iowa City but went west in the **7th Handcart
    Company**.]
    <1842>

BMR, p. 66 Jultand (SMR)

LARSEN, Niels Christian
<1848>
BMR, p. 63 Sealand (SMR)

LARSEN, Karen [Infant daughter of Lars and Anna Pedersen, died May 12, 1857 on the Atlantic.]
<1856>
Infant" (BMR) "Age: 1/2" (SMR)

LEDET, Mads Thomsen [Mad and Inger listed as husband and wife in the *Journal History* where name is spelled Leedat.]   <1809>
LEDET, Inger Marie
<1814>

LILJENQUIST, Oluff N (Ola N.). [Ola N. was serving as a missionary and as president of the Copenhagen Conference composed of 19 Branches when he was released and allowed to emigrate. Ola N. crossed Iowa with the **7th Handcart Company**, his family with the Cowley Wagon Train. From Florence all of the Liljenquist family went with Matthias Cowley.]
<1826> BMR, p. 64
Tailor and a burgher of Copenhagen
LILJENQUIST, Kirstina
<1822>
LILJENQUIST, Nicolai Theodor
<1850>
LILJENQUIST, Clara J. Josephina
<1854>
LILJENQUIST, Olaf Oscar
<1856>
LILJENQUIST, Harlad Frithiof
<1857>

LORENTSEN, Maria [Spelled Laurenson in *Journal History*]
<1832>
BMR, p. 58 Jutland (SMR)
LORENTZEN, Elizabeth

<1823>
BMR, p. 62 Copenhagen (SMR)

LOVENDAHL, Olaf

<1827>
BMR, p. 69
Cabinet Maker

LOVENDAHL, Olina

<1832>

LOVENDAHL, Enoch H. P. [Apparently died en route west.]

<1857>
Infant" (BMR)
infant

LUND, Maren [Mother of Rasmus R Lund]

<1803>

LUND, Rasmus R [Married to Maren Catherine Lund according to *Journal History*. A family history of Niels Otto Mortensen indicates they came west by covered wagon with the family of John Lund. However, there is no John given in the ship's company roster, although John could well be an assumed name. If that is the case, the Lund and Mortensen families were part of the **Matthias Cowley Wagon Company.**]

<1831>

LUND, Maren Catherine [Clemensen]

<1835>

LUND, Rasmus. Born May 16, 1854, Tjennmarke, Maribo, Denmark; married Elizabeth Hughes January 6, 1887, Farmington, Utah where he died September 12, 1935.

<1855>

LUND, Anna. Born July 1855; married Calvin Columbus Johnston in 1879 by whom she had 9 children. Died September 21, 1922, Salt Lake City, Utah.

<1856>

LUND, Maren Maria [There does not seem to be any report of Maren Maria in Utah. She may have been an infant who died en route.]

<1857>

LUNDBY, Kristine P.

LUNT, Henry [Born July 20, 1824 in England. His first child, Martha Henrietta, was born November 15, 1858 in Old Fort, Cedar City, Utah. Moved to Arizona and ultimately became part of the Mormon colonies of Mexico. Served as a counselor to **Matthias Cowley** on board the *Westmoreland.* Went west as chaplain in the **William G. Young Wagon Company** which departed Florence July 19, 1857.]

MADSEN, Adolph. [Page 6 of the Mads Christensen account indicates the Adolph Madsen family went west with **7th Handcart Company**. However, an Adolph Madsen is not given in either the *Journal History* or the Mormon Immigration Index as they presently exist. (Possibly one of the missing families)]

MADSEN, Peter
    <1804> BMR, p. 55
    Farmer

MADSEN, Berthe
    <1785> Lolland Conference (SMR)

MADSEN, Johana
    <1820> BMR, p. 62 Sealand (SMR)

MADSEN, Pouline Auguste
    <1850> Copenhagen (SMR)

MATHIESEN, Christiane Johanne [*History of the Scandinavian Mission*, p.50 identifies a Miss Mathiesen as a teacher of languages who assisted in translating the Book of Mormon and Doctrine and Covenants into Danish. Erastus Snow's correspondence indicates Miss Mattisen (Mathiesen) joined the Church. There was a Miss Mathiesen who sailed on the *Forest Monarch* in 1853, so it would appear that Christiane Johanne Mathiesen is not the translator. There was an Ane Catherine Mathiesen listed on the 1851 records of the Copenhagen Branch. However, neither Erastus Snow nor Peter O. Hansen gave her first name.]
    <1828> BMR, p. 59 Copenhagen (SMR)

MIKKELSEN, Hans W.

<1819> BMR, p. 59 Sealand (SMR)
Tailor
MIKKELSEN, Karen S.
   <1824>
MIKKELSEN, Wilhelmina M.
   <1850>
MIKKELSEN, Jensine K.
   <1853>
MIKKELSEN, Jens Peter
   <1856>
   Infant" (BMR) "Age: 1/2" (SMR)
Mink, Augusta [Listed in the *Journal History*, but not the Mormon Immigration Index]
MORTENSEN, Niels Otto [Niels and his wife, Maren Kristine, son Hans Peter, and daughter, Maren, were members of the 7th Handcart Company according to some sources. However, a Mortensen history of Niels Otto said his family had come west in a "prairie schooner with four oxen" purchased by a friend, John Lund. That would indicate they had come west with **Matthias Cowely**. Their daughter, Bodil, died in 1856 while going west with the Willie Handcart Company and was buried in a common grave of 13 pioneers at Rock Creek Hollow.]
   <1818> [Born: July 20, 1817] BMR, p. 55 Falster, Lolland Conference SMR
   In Denmark, Niels Otto was a Weaver and Well Digger. He became a Farmer and Sheepman in Parowan, Utah.
MORTENSEN, Maren Kristine
   <1812> [Born: October 3, 1812]
   Falster, Lolland Conference (SMR)
MORTENSEN, Hans Peter
   <1845> [Born: June 14, 1846]
   Falster, Lolland Conf. (SMR)
MORTENSEN, Maren
   <1850> [Born: August 8, 1849]
   Falster, Lolland Conf. (SMR)
MURAITSEN, Anna

<1819>
BMR, p. 59 Sealand (SMR)
Tailor
NIELSEN, Inger [Apparently a widow. Spelled Nelson in the *Journal History*.]
<1805>
BMR, p. 60
NIELSEN, Kristine
<1831>
NIELSEN, Peter
<1832>
NIELSEN, Anna
<1837>
NIELSEN, Inger
<1847>
NIELSEN, Ola
<1817>
BMR, p. 56 Lolland Conf. (SMR)
Farmer
NIELSEN, Carolina
<1821>
NIELSEN, Hans Jorgen
<1842>
NIELSEN, Wilhelmine Kirstine
<1847>
NIELSEN, Frederik Ferdinand
<1849>
NIELSEN, Dorthea Olivea
<1851>
Falster (SMR)
NIELSEN, Bernhard
<1855>
NIELSEN, Peter
<1819>
BMR, p. 60 Sealand (SMR)
Farmer
NIELSEN, Elsa

<1813>
NIELSEN, Hans Christian [Died en route to Utah, September 1857. Given as Hans C. Nilson in the *Journal History*.]
<1823> [Born: July 2, 1816]
BMR, p. 69 Fuen (SMR)
Carpenter
NIELSEN, Kirsten Marqvardsen
<1817>
Fuen (SMR)
NIELSEN, Nils Christian
<1849>
NIELSEN, Jorgen Christian
<1852>
NIELSEN, Peter
<1853>
NIELSEN, Christiana
<1840>
Jutland (SMR)
NIELSEN, Lars
<1823>
Jutland (SMR)
NILSEN, Christian [Given as Nilson in the *Journal History*.]
<1819>
BMR, p. 68
Farmer
NILSEN, Anna Margreta
<1805>
NILSEN, Karen Marie
<1843>
NIELSEN, Christen
<1829>
BMR, p. 58 Jutland (SMR)
Farmer
NIELSEN, Kristine Amalia
<1819>
NIELSEN, Kristine

<1854>
NIELSEN, Peter Christian
    <1856>
NIELSEN, Metta [Mother of Kerstenn Christensen Ericksen. Came with the **7th Handcart Company** to Florence where her health required that she remain for a time.]
    <1785>
    BMR, p. 57
NIELSEN, Ingeborg
    <1832>
    BMR, p. 64
NIIM, Johanna Augusta
    <1834>
    BMR, p. 66 Jutland (SMR)
NIELSON, Anders
    <1815> and **Bodil Kristine NIELSON** <1818> were husband and wife according to the *Journal History.*
NYBOLLE, Rasmus
    <1805>
    BMR, p. 71 Fuen (SMR)
    Brazier
NYBOLLE, Hedvig Lucia
    <1809>
NYBOLLE, Hansine Jacobine
    <1837>
NYBOLLE, Karen
    <1840>
NYBOLLE, Jens Christian
    <1847>
NYSTROM, Johanne Petronelle
    <1811>
    BMR, p. 59 Cop. Conf.(SMR)
OLSEN, Peter [Peter and Anna Olsen were members of the **7th Handcart Company.**]
    <1822>
    Jutland (SMR)
    Farmer

OLSEN, Anna
<1824>
OLSEN, Frederik [Frederik and Maren and their three sons, Ole, Anders and Ludvig Just or Levi were members of the **7th Handcart Company.**]
<1825>
BMR, p. 64 Sealand (SMR)
Farmer
OLSEN, Maren
<1822>
Falster (SMR)
OLSEN, Ole
<1851>
OLSEN, Anders
<1845>
OLSEN, Ludvig Just [Levi]
<1857>
Inf "BMR"Age: 1Mo." (SMR)
infant

OLSEN, Ole Christopher [Ole Christopher Olsen, wife, Karen Margrete, and daughter, Caroline Oliva were members of the **7th Handcart Company** of which Ole was one of the 4 sub-captains after the reorganization at Florence. Elder Ole C. Olsen served as president of the Copenhagen Branch. Ola N. Liljenquist said that Ole was "a most faithful shepherd of the flock entrusted to his care." (*History of the Scandinavian Mission*, p. 99)]
<1826>
Bornholm (SMR)
Tailor
OLSEN, Karen Margrete
<1824>
Bronholm (SMR)
OLSEN, Caroline Olivia
<1855>
Copenhagen (SMR)
OLSEN, Helge [Given as Helga in the *Journal History*.]

<1832>

OLSEN, Karen Maria [Karen Maria or Marie changed her name in Utah to Caroline and married Judge Wright. She and her sisters, Kirstina or Christina and Nicolina came with the 7th Handcart Company. Their parents and other siblings had gone to Utah in prior years.]

<1833> [Born: May 27, 1832, Aalborg, Denmark]

BMR, p. 58 Jutland (SMR)

OLSEN, Kirstina

<1835>

OLSEN, Nicolina

<1837>

OTTESEN, Jens

<1814>

OTTESEN, Anna

<1829>

OTTESEN, Niels Christian

<1856> [September 3, 1855, Denmark; died September 9, 1861]

PEHRSEN, Poulana

<1804>

PEHRSON, Ola

<1811> [Born: September 29, 1810 in Sweden; died: October 1, 1857 Cottonwood, Utah.]

PEHRSON, Bengta Andersson

<1815> [Born: March 23, 1814 in Sweden; died July 4, 1881 Ephraim, Utah. Second spouse: Ole Hague.]

PEHRSON, Nils or Nils OLSSON

<1839> [Born: January 9, 1838 in Sweden; married February 22, 1862 in Salt Lake City, Utah; died September 28, 1920. Nils and his siblings used the patronymic name OLSSON.]

PEHRSON, Berta or Berta OLSSON

<1842> [Born: June 14, 1841; married January 31, 1859; died June 26, 1898]

PEHRSON, Jons or Jons OLSSON

<1851>

PEHRSON, Kristi or Kjerstina OLSSON
<1855> [Born: October 5, 1854; died April 6, 1858]
Another child, Bengta OLSSON or PERHSON was born
October 17, 1846 in Sweden and died there April 1, 1848.

PETERSEN, Karen Maria [Either a nurse of midwife to the
Niels Garff family. Apparently went west with them.]
<1837>

PETERSEN, Karen Maria
<1832>

PETERSEN, Ingeborg
<1804>
BMR, p. 62 Jutland (SMR)

PETERSEN, Simon
<1826>
(See Eggertsen, Simon Peter) (EECI) p. 68

PETERSEN, Anna [Mother of Karen Larsen who died on the
Atlantic.]
<1827>

PETERSEN, Gjertrud [Married Jacob Bastain on board the
Westmoreland April 24, 1857 at Liverpool. Went west with
the **7th Handcart Company**. Died September 16, 1857 in
Salt Lake City.]
<1835>
BMR, p. 62

PETERSEN, Mika Martina [Given as Michael M. Petersen
in the *Journal History*.]
<1835>
Jutland (SMR)

PETERSEN, Johanna Jorgina
<1855>

PETERSEN, Julia Sophia
<1844>
BMR, p. 66

PETERSEN, Karen Maria
<1837>
Sealand (SMR)

PETERSEN, Kristen

<1835>
BMR, p. 56 Lol.Conf. (SMR)

PETERSEN, Jorgen

<1840>

Laborer

PETERSEN, Dorthea

<1843>

PETERSEN, Poul

<1844> [Born August 22, 1843 as Poul Pedersen at Nykobell, Sorø, Denmark to Peder Christensen and Ellen Poulsdatter Christensen, stepson of Hans Christensen. Member of the **7th Handcart Company**. Changed name to **Paul Christensen**.]

BMR, p. 61

PETERSEN, Nils

<1845> [Born August 4, 1844 as Niels Pedersen at Nykobell, Sorø, Denmark to Peder Christensen and Ellen Poulsdatter Christensen, stepson of Hans Christensen. Member of the **7th Handcart Company**. Changed name to **Niels Christensen**.]

PETERSEN, Jens

<1850>

PETERSEN, Niels

<1811>

Sealand, Lol.Conf.(SMR)

Farmer

PETERSEN, Sophia

<1824>

PETERSEN, Rasmus

<1848>

Sealand, Lol.Conf. (SMR)

PETERSEN, Sina

<1851>

PETERSEN, Ola [Ole Petersen. Traveled with wife Maren, and children, Peter, Soren and Anna Christine to the Omaha/Council Bluffs area with the **7th Handcart Company** where they remained until 1861 when they came

to Utah with the John P. Taylor Wagon Train.]
<1816>
BMR, p. 63 Sealand (SMR)
Farmer
PETERSEN, Maren
<1824>
PETERSEN, Peter
<1848>
PETERSEN, Soren
<1853>
PETERSEN, Anna Christine
<1856>
Infant" (BMR) "Age: 1/2" (SMR)
PETERSEN, Niels Christian
<1832>
Jutland (SMR)
Laborer
PETERSEN, Metta Cathrina
<1840>
BMR, p. 66 Jutland (SMR)
PETERSEN, Rasmus
<1844>
BMR, p. 56
PETERSEN, Peter Wilhelm
<1849>
Copenhagen (SMR)
POULSEN, Anna Maria
<1816>
BMR, p. 63 Sealand (SMR)
POULSEN, Jens
<1820>
BMR, p. 62 Copenhagen (SMR)
Laborer
RASMUSSEN, Niels
Farmer
RASMUSSEN, Mads Peter. Born: November 1, 1809, Copenhagen, Denmark; died: November 18, 1899, Salt Lake

City, Utah.
<1810>
BMR, p. 62 Sealand (SMR)
Tailor

RASMUSSEN, Berthe Maria
<1824>

RASMUSSEN, Bodil [Isabel (?)]. Born: November 8, 1845, Copenhagen, Denmark; married April 16, to Henry James Leyland, Ogden, Utah; died: February 1, 1907, Salt Lake City, Utah.
<1845>

RASMUSSEN, Lars Peter
<1848> Baptized 1857

RASMUSSEN, Nils [Niels]. Born: November 15, 1846; married twice, (1) Stella Neilson; (2) Marry Ann Morris.
<1850>

RASMUSSEN, Kristine [Christine]. Born: March 3, 1854, Dk.; married: Charles Julius Bassett, March 1, 1876, Salt Lake City, Utah; died: September 10, 1927, Boise, Idaho.
<1855>

RASMUSSEN, Joseph. There is no record. Apparently died en route.
<1856>

RASMUSSEN, Rasmus
<1813>
BMR, p. 55; "Cancelled" (BMR)
Tailor

RASMUSSEN, Hans Christian
<1817>
BMR, p. 59 Fuen,Cop.Conf.SMR
Laborer

RASMUSSEN, Caroline Henr.
<1825>

RASMUSSEN, Peter Fred. Christ.
<1847>

RASMUSSEN, George Thorvald
<1849>

RASMUSSEN, John Willard
<1855>
RASMUSSEN, Hector Jacob
<1856>
Inf "BMR"Age: 10/12ths" (SMR)
RASMUSSEN, Elizabeth
<1818>
RASMUSSEN, Anders
<1819>
BMR, p. 56 Falster, Lol.Conf. (SMR)
Laborer
RASMUSSEN, Anders
<1826>
Joiner
RASMUSSEN, Marie Augusta
<1823>
RASMUSSEN, Agnes Kathinka
<1849>
RASMUSSEN, Julia Randine
<1852>
ROLFSEN, Gjertrud Maria [Mother of Ellen and Gjertrud
Rolfson. All three came in the 7th Handcart Company.]
<1801>
ROLFSEN, Gjertrud M.
<1831>
ROLFSEN, Elen Gurena [Married C. C. N. Dorius, April 24,
1857 on board the *Westmoreland* at Liverpool.
<1838>
RUDD, Lorenzo D. [Returning missionary, member of the
7th Handcart Company of which he was a sub-captain of
200 from Iowa City to Florence.]
<1830> BMR, p. 69
Farmer
RYBECK, Maria [Given as Maria Rybey in the *Journal
History*.]
<1837>
BMR, p. 62 Cop. Conf.(SMR)

SAHLBERG, Aake [This may be the O. K. Salisbury as given by Hafen and Hafen or Oke Salisbury of Sonasslof, Sweden of the **7th Handcart Company.** The O. K. Salisbury name is not part of the *Mormon Immigration Index,* whereas **Aake SAHLBERG** is listed in both the *MII* and the *Journal History.*]

<1837>

SANDERSON, Johanna Maria [Sander. Member of the **7th Handcart Company.** Married Jacob Bastain afer the death of his first wife, Gjertrud Petersen. Johanna Maria s mother, Johanne Catrine Hansen of Liedfrost, Veile, Denmark was apparently a member of the **7th Handcart Company.**]

<1836>

BMR, p. 66 Jutland (SMR)

SCHOU, Soren Jeppesen

<1797>

BMR, p. 65 Jutland (SMR)

Farmer

SCHOU, Anna Cathrina

<1808>

SCHOU, Nils S.

<1837>

SCHOU, Peter S.

<1843>

Farmer

SCHOU, Anna Kirtina

<1845>

SCHOU, Johannes S.

<1847>

SCHOU, Karen S.

<1852>

SCHOU, Hans Sorensen [An Elder H. Sorensen Schou was listed as president of the Kolding Branch January 4, 1857. Kolding is on Jutland.]   <1826>

BMR, p. 65 Jutland (SMR)

Farmer

SCHOU, Maren
<1827>
Farmer
SCHOU, Anna Marie H.
<1855>
SCHOU, Hyrum Smith
<1856>
Infant" (BMR) "Age: Ω" (SMR)

SCHRAM, Jorgen Jensen of Vendsyssel, Denmark [Died May 30, 1857 between 6 and 7 P.M. on board the *Westmoreland* as they were coming up the Delaware River. Buried in Philadelphia. The Company Journal indicates the Jorgen Schram had made the voyage without any relatives accompanying him] <1776>

SCHRODER, Solenoe
<1812>
BMR, p. 62 Slesvig (SMR)

SORENSEN, Abelone
<1809>
BMR, p. 66 Jutland (SMR)

SORENSEN, Jorgen
<1817>
BMR, p. 60 Sealand (SMR)
Laborer
SORENSEN, Johanna
<1806>

SORENSEN, Jens [John Jens]. Born: July 12, 1847(?); baptized 1857; married Jacobine Gjettrup, July 25, 1878, Endowment House, Salt Lake City; died: September 28, 1925, Salt Lake City, Utah.
<1847>

SORENSEN, Nils [Spelled Sorenson in the *Journal History*.]
<1824>
BMR, p. 61 Sealand (SMR)
Tailor
SORENSEN, Kristen
<1819>

SORENSEN, Anders

<1849>

SORENSEN, Anne Marie

<1854>

SORENSEN, Morten [Spelled Sorenson in the *Journal History*.]

<1830>

Sealand (SMR)

Tailor

SORENSEN, Anna

<1827>

SORENSEN, Nils [Nils and his wife, Anna Marie, and their daughter, Julia Marie, born at the Wood River about July 21 or 22, 1857 were members of the **7th Handcart Company**.]

Potter

<1824>

SORENSEN, Anna Marie

<1825>

BMR, p. 65

SORENSEN, Nicholai [Nicholai and his family went west with the Matthias Cowley ox-team company.]

<1800>

Farmer and Wheelwright

SORENSEN, Line [Magdelena]

<1808>

SORENSEN, Ole Peter. Born: October 10, 1832, Sorø; Denmark; baptized May 12, 1856; married Rikke Anderson, December 10, 1857; died October 19, 1874 at Mendon, Utah. **Rikke or Rikka Anderson** appears to be the same individual who had come to America on the James J. Boyd. Given the fact that she and Ole Peter Sorensen married within three months after his arrival, may indicate she joined the 1857 company in which Nicolai s family went west.

Carpenter

SORENSEN, Kirsten [Christena]. Born: January 18, 1836, Sorø,

Denmark; baptized May 12, 1856; married James Hood Hill, January 7, 1860; died April 7, 1896 Mendon, Utah.

SORENSEN, Frederik Abraham. Born November 18, 1837, Sorø, Denmark; baptized June 18, 1855; married Mary Jensen, November 1857; died June 1928, Mendon, Utah. **Wheelwright**

SORENSEN, Frederik Isaac. Born: February 24, 1840, Sorø, Denmark; baptized June 18, 1855; married Mary Jacobsen November 15, 1869; died November 7, 1922, Mendon, Utah. **Wheelwright**

SORENSEN, Karen Maria [Mary Caroline]. Born: June 25, 1843, Sorø, Denmark; baptized September 6, 1855; married William Hood Hill, January 1, 1860; died January 20, 1928, Millcreek, Salt Lake, Utah.

SORENSEN, Frederik Jacob [Jacob Frederik]. Born September 29, 1844, Sorø, Denmark; baptized December 14, 1856; married Susan Hancock, December 1, 1873; died February 5, 1934, Mendon, Utah.

SORENSEN, Soren Christian. Born: December 7, 1846, Sorø, Denmark; baptized December 14, 1856; married Caroline Wilhelmina Halverson, November 16, 1874.

SORENSEN, Henrik Carl Christian. Born: May 21, 1851, Sorø, Denmark; baptized July 1, 1861; married Mary Anderson, June 26, 1876; died November 26, 1884.

SORENSEN, Ingeborg Kirstine. Born: March 2, 1854, Sorø, Denmark; married Alexander Willard Hill Richards, April 10, 1976; died November 28, 1916, Mendon, Utah.

SORENSEN, Peter H. Born: August 14, 1807, Arnager, Bornholm, Denmark. Baptized: June 20, 1854. Had been serving as a missionary in Arnager, Bornholm. Was released at a March 2, 1857 conference and allowed to emigrate. (Jimmy B. Parker, Op cit., p.18.) Wife: Annika Marie Olsdatter, born: March 8, 1808; married: December 27, 1837, Arnager, Bornholm; baptized: June 20, 1854; sealed, Endowment House October 18, 1865; died: August 27, 1886, Castle Dale, Utah.

SORENSEN, Annika Marie

<1808>

SORENSEN, Karen Maria. Born: October 27, 1838; baptized June 21, 1854; married Christian Geis Larsen, April 1, 1857, Copenhagen, Denmark; died January 21, 1895, Castle Dale, Utah.

STECK, Wilhelmina (Peck)

<1826>

Jutland (SMR)

SUNDBYE, Christiana P. (Lundby)

<1826>

BMR, p. 63 Copenhagen (SMR)

SVAF, Han

<1797>

BMR, p. 67

Farmer

SVAF, Hanna

<1795>

SVAF, Anna

<1818>

SVAF, Nils

<1824>

TAYLOR, Rebecca [Apparently joined the company at Liverpool.]

<1833>

THOMSEN, Johanna [Born: May 18, 1825 at Pesenstifh, Denmark; married Thomas Christian Pedersen; died in 1912 at Ovid, Bear Lake, Idaho.]

<1826>

BMR, p. 57 "Simon P. Eggertsen"

THOMSEN, Inger Andrea [Wife of Lars Jacobsen. Member of the **7th Handcart Company**.]

<1829>

Jutland (SMR)

THOMSEN, Anne Maria [Married **Lauritz Larsen** April 24, 1857 on board the *Westmoreland* at Liverpool. **Sister to Inger Andrea Thomsen**.]

<1830>

BMR, p. 67 Jutland (SMR)

THOMSEN, Nils Peter [Brother of Inger Andrea and Anne Maria Thomsen. The three Thomsen siblings were probably **7th Handcart Company members.**]

<1838>

Jutland (SMR)

Laborer

THORBJORNSEN, Nils [This is possibly **Niels Torbjørsen**, the **district magistrate of Kil, [near Kragen] Norway**, who not only refused to jail the missionaries, but assisted in C. C. A. Christensen s emigration to Utah. Spelled Thorbiorson in the *Journal History*.]

<1798> BMR, p. 68

Farmer

THUESEN, Niels [Niels and Englika had lost four children to death prior to leaving Denmark.]

<1813>

BMR, p. 59 Jutland (SMR)

Carpenter

THUESEN, Englika Christine Lund

<1809>

Bornholm (SMR)

THUESEN, Johannes Niels [John Nicolas]

<1844>

Copenhagen (SMR)

THUESEN, Julia Marianne [Julie Margreta died June 1857 in Iowa.]

<1847>

Copenhagen (SMR)

THUESEN, Laura Hansine

<1847>

Copenhagen (SMR)

Thurston, George W. [Given in the *Journal History*.]

VINBERG, Maria Lovisa

<1839>

BMR, p. 63

ZACHARIUSEN, Frederik Chr. Thorvald
  <1844>

APPENDIX II: 7th Handcart Company Members Not on *Westmoreland*

Individual	Ship	Year
PARK, James P. captain from Iowa City to Florence	*George Washington*	1857
CHRISTIANSEN, Christian, captain from Florence west	*Forest Monarch*	1853
GREEN, William	*George Washington*	1857
SALISBURY, O. K. [may be Aake SAHLBERG of the *Westmoreland*]	Unknown	
Dillie, David B., a sub-captain of 200 from Iowa City to Florence	*George Washington*	1857
GOTTFREDSON or GODTFRESEN, Jens	*John J. Boyd*	1855
GOTTFREDSON, Karen		
GOTTFREDSON, Jens Peter		
GOTTFREDSON, Hans		
GOTTFREDSON, Metta Kirstine		
GOTTFREDSON, Joseph Smith		
GOTTFREDSON, Platine (Born/died at Loup Fork July 1857)		
LARSEN, Anders		
LARSEN, Caroline or Karna		
LARSEN, Louis or Lorents		
LARSEN, Anne Hannah or Anna Joanna		
LARSEN, Christine		
PAULSEN or POULSEN, Ingeborg		
SORENSEN, Christian		
SORENSEN, Mette		
SORENSEN, Bodil		
SORENSEN, Else		

Individual	Ship	Year
SORENSEN, Anders	*John J. Boyd*	1855
SORENSEN, Bodil Marie		
SORENSEN, Soren Peter		
SORENSEN, Niels		
LUBLIN, Samuel	*Charles Buck*	1855
LUBLIN, Johanne Christine		
LUBLIN, Johanne Sophie B.		
LUBLIN, Herman or Heimann Magnus		
LUBLIN, Hyrum (born Alton, Illinois 31 December 1856)		
[Five-year old Anna Kristine Lublin was left to come later by wagon. There is no mention of daughter Josephine.]		
MORTENSEN, Didrick James	*Nesmith*	1855
MORTENSEN, Maren		
MORTENSEN, Anne Christine		
MORTENSEN, Morten		
MORTENSEN, Inger		
MORTENSEN, Johanne		
MORTENSEN, Jens		
MORTENSEN, Elisa K.		
JENSEN, Peder or Peter (farmer)	*Thornton*	1856
JENSEN, Kjersten or Kirsten		
JENSEN, Jorgen or Jens Carl		
JENSEN, Dorthea		
JENSEN, Hans		

INDEX

DR. ALLEN C. CHRISTENSEN is the Director of the Benson Agriculture and Food Institute at Brigham Young University. He has also been a professor and administrator at Cal Poly Pomona. And he served as mission president in the Philippines, San Fernando mission.

Dr. Christensen is a descendent of Mormon pioneers, some of whom were members of the Seventh Handcart Company. And he is a lifelong student of LDS history. He and his wife Kathleen are the parents of five children and five foster children.